Play and Playwork

101 Stories of Children Playing

Play and Playwork

101 STORIES OF CHILDREN PLAYING

Fraser Brown

Open University Press

Open University Press
McGraw-Hill Education
McGraw-Hill House
Shoppenhangers Road
Maidenhead
Berkshire
England
SL6 2QL

email: enquiries@openup.co.uk
world wide web: www.openup.co.uk

and Two Penn Plaza, New York, NY 10121–2289, USA

First published 2014

A catalogue record of this book is available from the British Library

ISBN-13: 978-0-33-524465-2 (pb)
ISBN-10: 0-33-524465-3 (pb)
eISBN: 978-0-33-524466-9

Library of Congress Cataloging-in-Publication Data
CIP data applied for

Typesetting and e-book compilations by
RefineCatch Limited, Bungay, Suffolk

Praise for this book

"Play and Playwork *starts as a rich compendium of vignettes of everyday playfulness. But it goes well beyond this. Brown takes readers on a personal reflective journey that questions some well-rehearsed maxims of play and playwork. His aim is to show – not state – the depth and complexity both of children's play and of the influence of adults (for good or ill). In this, he succeeds admirably.*"

Tim Gill, author of No Fear: Growing Up in a Risk Averse Society.

Dedication

In memory of Gill Evans, Play Wales Communications Manager, 1967–2011

All royalties from this book go to:
Aid for Romanian Children
www.arccharity.org

Contents

About the author

Dr Fraser Brown is the first person from a playwork background to be appointed as a university professor. He leads the Playwork Team at Leeds Beckett University, where he contributes to the BA (Hons) Playwork degree and the postgraduate courses in Play Therapy offered by the Academy of Play and Child Psychotherapy (APAC). For ten years he was Director of the playwork training agency, *Children First*, and previously held advisory posts with Playboard and the NPFA. He spent three years on an adventure playground in Runcorn, and managed a range of projects for the North West Play Association. For two years he was District Leisure Officer in Middlesbrough. His publications include *Rethinking Children's Play* (2013); *Foundations of Playwork* (2008); *The Venture: A Case Study of an Adventure Playground* (2007); *Children Without Play* (2005); *Playwork: Theory and Practice* (2003); *School Playgrounds* (1990); and *Working With Children: A Playwork Training Pack* (1989). He has spoken throughout the UK and around the world about his research into the impact of therapeutic playwork on a group of abandoned children in Romania.

Acknowledgements

I am very grateful for the cooperation of all those who have contributed stories to this book. Without their goodwill, it would not have been possible to complete the task. In addition, I would like to acknowledge the contributions to specific chapters of the following: Sage Publications for permission to quote extensively from an article that first appeared in the *Encyclopedia of Play in Today's Society* (edited by R Carlisle), under the title 'Idealization of play' (Brown 2009); Play Wales for permission to reprint an extract from the book *The Venture: A Case Study of an Adventure Playground* (Brown 2007), also Joe Rowley's reflection on the Welsh Assembly's Play Policy Implementation Plan, which originally appeared in its spring 2006 magazine and Maria Rowley's article in the autumn 2008 magazine; the National Children's Bureau for permission to reprint brief extracts from its *Highlight no. 223, Play Theories and the Value of Play* (Brown 2006); *iP-D!P* magazine for permission to reproduce 'Fat bastard's first days at work'; Pearson Publications for permission to reproduce extracts from chapters that first appeared in Brock *et al.* (2008) *Perspectives on Play: Learning for Life*; Sutcliffe Play for permission to reprint extracts from the consultancy report *Reflections on the Impact of Snug at Two Schools in Yorkshire*; Sophie Webb for permission to reproduce extensive extracts from her initial research diary; BADth – the early part of Chapter 11 was originally produced as part of a presentation at a Festschrift for the dramatherapist Sue Jennings, and subsequently reproduced in the British Association of Dramatherapist's journal, *The Prompt* (Brown 2013); White Rose Initiative – first, for its permission to conduct the research project referred to in several chapters and, second, for its permission to report on its remarkable achievements; Dr Cornel Puscas, who at the time of the research was Director of the Sighisoara Paediatric Hospital, gave permission to refer to the hospital records, and so allowed us to report honestly on the lives of the children in his hospital – without his support the Therapeutic Playwork Project would not have existed. I would also like to place on record the fact that the hospital has subsequently made giant strides towards changing things.

I would like to express my thanks to Jim Henderson for the generous offer not to charge for the index for this book, so that more money can go to Aid for Romanian Children, which the royalties for this book are supporting. Every penny raised for the

Aid for Romanian Children charitable trust goes into working with some of the most needy children in Europe. The charity provides food, shelter, education, medicines, summer play activities and more.

I should also like to thank colleagues and students at Leeds Beckett University for their dedication and commitment to the Playwork course, and for the inspiration they provide on a daily basis.

Finally, I want to thank my family and friends for their patience and support. It's never easy when I'm working on this sort of thing. So, thank you to mum, Anne, Louisa, Marie, James, Lucy and Emily.

Photographic acknowledgements

Cover photographs

© Stenhills Adventure Playground – The Bonfire
© The Old Quarry Adventure Playground, Wakefield – Walking in the Snow; Hula Hoops
© Wakefield & District Play Forum – Woodworking; Paint Table; Go Karting; Crafts on the Grass

1

Introduction: play and playwork

It is never really possible for an outsider to understand the subtle nuances of meaning that a specific piece of play may have for any particular child. That is one of the recurring themes of this book, namely the often paradoxical nature of play, and the way in which children's play is so often misinterpreted by adults. Put very simply, the concept of this book is to use 101 stories of children playing to examine a range of play and playwork theories. Where this approach has been used previously it has often been contrived, with the stories being made to fit the theory. The intention here is to let the stories speak for themselves, while at the same time triggering theoretical explorations that will be interwoven within the stories in each chapter.

The dramatherapist Sue Jennings, in her thought-provoking book *Healthy Attachments and Neuro-dramatic Play*, talks of a 'play to play therapy continuum, where playing can be considered a "preventative" activity and play therapy a "curative" activity'. She says, 'there is a large gap in the middle where children are able to generate their own play to help themselves; this often does not need the intervention of play therapists' (2011: 64). If only that were the case!

Jennings provides a fascinating insight, but she is making a very specific point about play therapy, and the therapeutic nature of play. Of course play is much more than just a preventative activity. It is also developmental in every sense of the word. Returning to Jennings' continuum, contrary to her optimistic view, there is an increasingly 'large gap in the middle' where children are *not* able to generate their own play. This is due to a combination of socio-cultural circumstances – for example, increase in traffic, suspicion of strangers, excessive emphasis on academic attainment, and so on (Gill 2007). That is where playwork comes in. Put simply, the more socio-cultural changes restrict children's freedom to play, the more will be the need for playworkers. In its most straightforward expression, playwork is about creating environments that enable children to generate their own play. Thus it is possible to construct a play to playwork continuum, where playing can be considered a 'developmental and evolutionary' activity and playwork a 'compensatory' activity.

This statement highlights both developmental and evolutionary aspects of playing. The playwork theorist Bob Hughes, in his ground-breaking book *Evolutionary Playwork*, focuses on the latter. He says playwork should be considered to be:

a comprehensive support for deep biological processes – expressed through mechanisms like adaptation, flexibility, calibration and the different play types – that enable the human organism to withstand the pressures of extinction.

(2012: 44)

Those who emphasize this evolutionary perspective suggest that playwork has the potential to help keep children sane in an increasingly unpredictable and non-child-friendly world, because it creates the conditions where (in the words of Sue Jennings, previously quoted) 'children are able to generate their own play to help themselves'. In other words, good-quality evolutionary playwork means children are less likely to need the intervention of a play therapist. This also suggests that play, freely chosen, intrinsically motivated and personally directed, by its very nature, offers new and challenging alternatives in an increasingly rigid stagnating world. In other words, play is the catalyst for human evolution. Thus, playworkers have a very substantial responsibility not just to the individual children, but to society as a whole.

I do not disagree with this viewpoint, but feel it has been thoroughly explored by Hughes (2012), and so for now that whole approach will be set to one side, and the focus of this book will instead be on the developmental aspects of children's play – not in the sense that the role of a playworker is one of teacher or social worker, but rather that playworkers need to be aware of the developmental benefits of play, if their compensatory approach is to have the most value.

It was this concern for the significance of children's play that led to it being included in Article 31 of the original United Nations Convention on the Rights of the Child (UNCRC), where we find the following statement:

States parties recognise the right of the child to rest and leisure, to engage in play and recreational activities appropriate to the age of the child and to participate freely in cultural life and the arts.

(UNICEF 1991)

Only one UN member nation has actively chosen not to ratify the Convention.[1] However, on the basis that actions speak louder than words, there is little evidence that many of the signatories take Article 31 seriously, and children remain the sector of society whose rights are most frequently ignored – especially the right to play. Consequently, on 1 February 2013, the United Nations Committee on the Rights of the Child adopted a General Comment that clarifies for governments worldwide the meaning and importance of Article 31. The General Comment provides the following statements about children's play:

Play and recreation are essential to the health and well-being of children and promote the development of creativity, imagination, self-confidence, self-efficacy, as well as physical, social, cognitive and emotional strength and skills. They contribute to all aspects of learning:[2] they are a form of participation in everyday

---

[1] As of June 2014 the United States has still not ratified the UNCRC.
[2] UNESCO, *Education for the Twenty-first Century: Issues and Prospects* (Paris, 1998).

life and are of intrinsic value to the child, purely in terms of the enjoyment and pleasure they afford. Research evidence highlights that playing is also central to children's spontaneous drive for development, and that it performs a significant role in the development of the brain, particularly in the early years. Play and recreation facilitate children's capacities to negotiate, regain emotional balance, resolve conflicts and make decisions. Through their involvement in play and recreation, children learn by doing; they explore and experience the world around them; experiment with new ideas, roles and experiences and in so doing, learn to understand and construct their social position within the world.

All of these factors will be explored via the stories that appear in the coming chapters. The General Statement goes on to offer a definition of children's play:

> Children's play is any behaviour, activity or process initiated, controlled and structured by children themselves; it takes place whenever and wherever opportunities arise. Caregivers may contribute to the creation of environments in which play takes place, but play itself is non-compulsory, driven by intrinsic motivation and undertaken for its own sake, rather than as a means to an end. Play involves the exercise of autonomy, physical, mental or emotional activity, and has the potential to take infinite forms, either in groups or alone. These forms will change and be adapted throughout the course of childhood. The key characteristics of play are fun, uncertainty, challenge, flexibility and non-productivity. Together, these factors contribute to the enjoyment it produces and the consequent incentive to continue to play. While play is often considered non-essential, the Committee reaffirms that it is a fundamental and vital dimension of the pleasure of childhood, as well as an essential component of physical, social, cognitive, emotional and spiritual development.

There are clear shortcomings with this definition (see Brown 2008 for a discussion of some of these concepts) but nevertheless it provides a working definition around which most of the playwork profession would be happy to gather. Finally, the General Statement provides a summary of the sort of things children engage in, while they are playing:

> In addition, children reproduce, transform, create and transmit culture through their own imaginative play, songs, dance, animation, stories, painting, games, street theatre, puppetry, festivals, and so on. As they gain understanding of the cultural and artistic life around them from adult and peer relationships, they translate and adapt its meaning through their own generational experience. Through engagement with their peers, children create and transmit their own language, games, secret worlds, fantasies and other cultural knowledge. Children's play generates a 'culture of childhood,' from games in school and in the playground to urban activities such as playing marbles, free running, street art and so on. Children are also at the forefront in using digital platforms and virtual worlds to establish new means of communication and social networks, through which different cultural environments and artistic forms are being forged. Participation

in cultural and artistic activities are necessary for building children's under-standing, not only of their own culture, but other cultures, as it provides opportu-nities to broaden their horizons and learn from other cultural and artistic traditions, thus contributing towards mutual understanding and appreciation of diversity.

Taking these three extracts from the General Statement together, we have a very useful summary of the themes contained within the following chapters. Let's start with an apparently straightforward story of a child at play.

The footballer

Author's observation

Stamford Bridge (home of Chelsea FC), Sunday 18 May 2013

At the end of the final game of the season both teams leave the pitch; the crowd remains behind. About ten minutes later the Chelsea players and coaching staff emerge with their wives, girlfriends and children – around 50 people in all. They all make their way to the centre circle, where they begin to make speeches, cele-brating their achievements during the preceding year, and thanking the fans for their support. While all this is happening, one of the children, a 2-year-old boy (maybe still in nappies) starts to kick a football out of the centre circle towards one of the goals, apparently unnoticed by anyone (except most of the crowd). Gradually, one determined step at a time, he wobbles and tumbles his way towards one of the goals. The nearer he gets, the more the crowd noise rises. By the time he enters the penalty area the whole ground is cheering him, and as he kicks the ball into the goal, the crowd roars as if Frank Lampard had just scored the winner in the FA Cup Final. At this point the little boy stares up at the crowd behind the goal, apparently noticing them for the first time. He then turns back towards the centre circle and throws his arms straight up in a classic celebratory gesture. The crowd starts singing 'Sign Him Up, Sign Him Up . . .!'

(See www.youtube.com/watch?v=alFjnWX_1is)

This incident took nearly five minutes from beginning to end, and illustrates a number of things about play. The toddler was clearly exhibiting learned behaviour as part of his play. It is inconceivable that he was not to some extent copying the behaviours of his father and his team-mates. This is the sort of play behaviour described by Piaget as 'a happy display of known actions' (1951: 93). In fact Piaget thought play was largely a matter of 'repetition, reproduction and generalization' (p. 162) – a trivializing view that I do not share. In this small example it is clear the child is developing his motor skills (Sheridan, Sharma and Cockerill 2007); and it is arguable that he is starting to explore his sense of self (Henricks 2013). It is also worth noting that he is totally focused on his task. This is a state of mind that Csikszentmihalyi (1980) calls 'flow', and which he says typifies play. Thus, in one apparently simple example of a child playing, we can already see how complex this type of behaviour really is.

The element of this story that might easily pass us by is the playful behaviour of the crowd. Contrary to Piaget's (1951) view, we don't stop playing once we reach adulthood. In fact, in words that are generally attributed to George Bernard Shaw, 'we don't stop playing because we grow old; we grow old because we stop playing'. In this case the crowd was playing its own game, exhibiting what Durkheim (1893) refers to as its 'collective consciousness'. The crowd's game was full of social interaction, community of purpose and a considerable element of playfulness. Meyer (2010: 36) explains this succinctly: 'As individuals co-create playspace through engaged participation, they experience increasing awareness, acceptance and appreciation in action'. Here she is talking about:

- awareness of the experience
- acceptance of themselves
- appreciation of their own and others' perspectives.

For Meyer, action is part of that dynamic process. It is not separate from thinking and being.

In the DCMS (2004) report 'Getting Serious About Play', play is defined as:

> what children and young people do when they follow their own ideas and interests, in their own way and for their own reasons.

This is a useful working definition, but clearly doesn't do justice to the subtlety and complexity of the subject. Taken as a whole the stories contained in this book will do just that. The stories are amusing, amazing, touching, scary, shocking, even awe inspiring. They make you think, and make you wonder, in both senses of the word (see Guilbaud 2011 for a detailed examination of that particular duality). There are numerous lessons to be learned from each story, and indeed from any reflection on children playing. For example, children building a den are not only engaged in a creative act, but almost certainly enjoying fruitful social interaction as well; they are developing their motor skills, their vocabulary, etc.

The multi-layered nature of play is right at the heart of the title of the seminal work by the play theorist Brian Sutton-Smith. In researching for *The Ambiguity of Play*, Sutton-Smith (1997) set out to find all the different interpretations of what is going on when we play. He identified 308 different play types, and then categorized them within seven headings, which he spoke about in a recent interview (Brown and Patte 2012):

> I came up with what I call the seven rhetorics of play, which are basically the major forms that people argue in favour of. In the *Ambiguity* book I included plays about progress, fate, power, identity, the imaginary, the self, and finally frivolity.

Clearly then play is complex, and Garvey (1991) suggests the most effective way to explain it is to identify common threads within the leading theories. However, that is not simple since some of those theories are directly contradictory. For example, play has been seen as both the consumer of surplus energy (Spencer 1873) and the re-creator of lost energy (Lazarus 1883). Theories also cover a wide range of disciplines: behaviourism (Berlyne 1960), cognitive development (Piaget 1951), psychoanalysis (Axline 1969), etc. Caillois (2001: 9–10) suggests there are six essential characteristics of play. It is 'free, separate, uncertain, unproductive, governed by rules, and has make believe'. Given this range of debate, it is not surprising to find Huizinga (1949: 7) concluding that play 'is not susceptible of exact definition either logically, biologically, or aesthetically'.

Thus, a meaningful definition is illusive. For that reason the chapter headings of this book should be taken as an indication of the aspects that I regard as most important for playwork, rather than as an analytical framework. The original intention was for the book to be structured around the 11 play value headings listed previously in *Playwork Theory and Practice* (Brown 2003a). However, it soon became apparent that the stories could not be interpreted in such a way, and so the following chapters only loosely reflect that approach. In fact it would be true to say the chapter headings seemed to grow out of the first 50 stories, and by the time I had received 100 stories the structure became clear.

In a comment about playwork that is especially pertinent to this text Guilbaud says:

> A sense of wonder towards what is being created in children's play with things and spaces, as well as an attempt to vocalize it, is apparent in the contemporary playwork field.
>
> (2011: 358)

In other words, playworkers are increasingly aware that the strongest, most influential arguments for their profession lie in the powerful reality of their own reflections on their observations of children playing (Palmer 2008).

In a previous text (Brown 2003b), I suggested that playwork is essentially concerned with the following:

- creating play opportunities that enable children to pursue their own play agendas
- enriching the child's world by providing opportunities for experimentation and exploration
- creating environments that address the negative effects of play deprivation and play bias
- developing appropriate responses for individual children's play cues
- facilitating opportunities for children to develop a sense of self
- introducing flexibility and adaptability into play environments in order to enhance the prospects of children achieving their full potential.

These aspects and more are all illustrated in the stories in this book.

Although adults, especially politicians, seem to have difficulty recognizing the significance of play, no such problem exists in the mind of the child. For most children playing is the most fulfilling activity possible.

Once there was this little man

Penny Wilson – community play development worker

An experienced team of urban playworkers were engaged in an estate's community day in a space that, until recently, had been neglected and made unusable for play by dog fouling and adult complaints about children's behaviour. They had come along to run a play session as usual, and to do a bit of ambassadorial work with parents and estates workers as well. They had brought with them not only the usual loose parts (fabric, rope, chalks, bubbles), but also some publicity materials: flags and button badges with the word 'play' in white letters on a black background.

The children were by now, comfortable and familiar with the playworkers and they settled down to play as usual.

One girl started drawing, illustrating a story that she told as she drew.

'Once there was this little man . . .'

She drew a Pokémon-type mushroom-shaped creature, which she coloured in, leaving a round space where one of its spots should be.

'The little man was not happy. He knew something was missing. He went on adventure and went to fight in a war. When he had done that he still felt something was missing. So he came back home. But still there was something missing . . .'

She took one of the 'play' button badges and put it where the empty spot was.

'There. That's what was missing. Now he's better.'

This story prompted an interesting exchange between Penny Wilson and me, which raised the issue of whether it is ever really possible to second-guess what is going on in children's minds when they are playing. In this case Penny had been told the story second-hand, and wondered whether she might be reading too much into it. Possibly the button was just something that filled the space on the picture – nothing more. However, for the purposes of this book the story provides a good example of what I had in mind. The meaning of the story (and of most of the stories in the book) is highly ambiguous; it is full of paradox and mystery, which has to be accepted and talked about. It would obviously be possible to analyse this in terms of the S.P.I.C.E. model (Brown 2003b) or play types (Hughes 2002), but that would be to undervalue the true significance for the child of what's going on.

First, there is the way in which the girl's story develops as she draws. We don't know for certain that she didn't think the whole thing up before she started, but we have the strong impression that she is allowing the story to develop from out of her drawing. This is almost an archetype of one form of play – namely free-flow play (Bruce 1991).

Second, all sorts of interpretations could be made of the girl's choice of where to place the marketing button. Of course, it may be entirely random – maybe it just happened to fit the last space. More likely the placement of the button has been well thought out. Maybe it is representing the significance of either play or the play project in this child's life, i.e. you're not complete unless you have play in your heart. Or perhaps she wants to say, 'wherever you go in the world you have to have play'. On the other hand, maybe she especially liked the look of the white writing on a black background, and thought it would look good as a badge for her man.

The point is, we can't be sure, and that's one of the joys of play. So long as the child is not asked to explain her picture, she remains in total control of its meaning and its destiny. The temptation for the playworker to say, 'tell me about your picture' is immense, but has to be resisted until the child invites the exchange. To do otherwise is for the adult to take control, and at that point the activity ceases to be playful.

For some children playing is all they ever want to do.

I'm gonna play 'til I die!

Susan Caruso – Sunflower creative arts director and teacher

Miranda and Josh, both 5, had been climbing, swinging and creating tricks on the tall monkey bars for days. They had become best friends and chattered away as they challenged their bodies. I happened to be standing close by when, with great passion and intensity, Miranda said, 'I'm gonna play 'til I die! That's what I'm gonna do. I never want to stop playing! I'm gonna play until I die!' Josh said, 'Yeah, me too! I'm gonna play 'til I die! We're gonna play 'til we're dead.'

This is not an emotion that is entirely confined to childhood. Piaget (1951) suggests we grow out of play once we reach the post-operational stage of development. According to him, once we develop the ability to use logic to reason things out we no longer need to play. Experience shows him to be wrong. Although this book is essentially about children's play, it is worth noting in passing that we do not stop playing as we get older; our play merely morphs into another form. In the following story the leading childhood specialist Tim Gill recalls the thrill of playing hide-and-seek from an adult perspective.

Hide-and-seek

Tim Gill – author and childhood specialist

One Saturday my partner and I were staying with some long-time friends whose child is the same age as ours. After dinner, in an effort to engage our respective teenage daughters, we agreed that they could choose what game we played. The girls chose hide-and-seek.

It has to be said the grown-ups were not wild about this idea. But we stuck to the deal. So, for the next hour or so, two children and four adults played hide-and-seek in a modest four-bed semi. Indoors only.

We played for over an hour. My abiding memory is of the tingly thrill throughout my body when I was hiding. My breath quickened. My limbs were taut. My muscles strained with the effort of keeping still.

It seems to me now that what I was feeling was quite close to what children feel when they are truly immersed in the emotions that arise when playing games – especially physical games. I felt myself to be in the grip of the same fears, the same joys, the same thrill of victory and the same pang of disappointment from defeat. In my determination not to be found, all other concerns faded into the background.

For us grown-ups, it can be an effort to play such games, as I acknowledged above. But, for children, actively seeking out thrills and emotional uncertainty is their experiential food and drink. My teenage daughter and her friend were very keen to keep playing ('just one more round, *please*?').

Some of those at the forefront of research on play argue that emotional intensity is not simply a consequence of playing. It is, in a sense, what defines the process of playing. For the academic Brian Sutton-Smith – whose book *The Ambiguity of Play* is at the apex of modern play scholarship – all play ultimately revolves around 'affect expression and regulation'. The suggestion is that, when children are playing, whatever the surface appearance of their games, at a deeper level it is their own emotional life that is being explored.

Hide-and-seek is one case study of this process. But there are plenty more. Play-fighting, rough-and-tumble play, horseplay, dizzy play, dare games and the sharing of ghost stories are all obvious examples.

Sutton-Smith also argues that this impulse for emotional stimulation is instinctive. The young of our species are drawn to create states of heightened emotion for themselves as a result of evolution, he thinks, because of its adaptive benefits. In a striking phrase, he declares – on the very last page of *The Ambiguity of Play* – 'I define play as a facsimilization of the struggle for survival as this is broadly rendered by Darwin.' Playwork academics Stuart Lester and Wendy Russell make a parallel claim when they state that risk taking in play is centrally to do with 'being in control of being out of control' (see their publication for Play England, *Play for a Change*, 2008: 26).

These arguments about the intimate connections between play and the emotions were familiar to me. I must confess I am still wondering whether *all* play involves the emotions in quite such a fundamental way. In any case, playing hide-and-seek brought this home to me: many children's games only begin to make any kind of sense when their emotional aspects are properly appreciated.

PS: I remained unfound at the end of the last round, hidden behind a coat rack, within touching distance of my seeker. Is it wrong to take pride in that achievement?

A version of this material was originally posted on Tim's website (http://rethinkingchildhood.com).

Piaget (1951) described play as the 'happy display of known actions', which is a very simplistic view of the value and benefits of play. In fact, he suggests the value of play lies largely in the way children practise and explore things they have already learned, in order to reinforce and expand that learning. Clearly Piaget's somewhat limiting view of play leaves much to be desired. However, that does not mean we should dismiss all his ideas. The following story is a good example of Piaget's concept in action. The boy in this story has seen something that intrigues him, and he uses play to cement his understanding of the concepts involved.

Small child with big ideas

Diana Cornell – teacher and museum volunteer

Last summer, the Museum of the Broads had activity days for visiting children. There were pirate activities and wind powered activities. On a pirate activity day, an extended family – parents, grandparents and two young children – showed interest in joining in. The smallest, a girl of about 2, spent some time with her mum colouring, but the boy, who was 5, decided to become involved in making something. His first idea was to make a pirate ship, which wasn't one of the activities, but as we had a number of cardboard boxes this did not seem unreasonable. His mum, however, explained to him that it wasn't one of the options. I said that he could make a boat if he wanted to and gave him a box, which of course he climbed into. Mum, however, was still not too keen. After a while he climbed out of the box and spent some time on our 'model' boat, which has a working steering wheel attached to pulleys and chains so that it moves a rudder at the back of the model. This is a popular object with children, who like to pretend they are 'steering the boat'.

After some time, he joined his grandpa and said he wanted to make a steering wheel. Again mum said that it was not an activity available. However, he was not to be dissuaded and I said that it was fine; he could do what he wanted. I gave him some flat cardboard and a pencil so that he could draw the wheel he wanted to make. His granddad joined him at the table. The rest of the family moved off around the museum. Alex (let's call him that) became deeply engrossed in drawing his wheel, with references back to the wheel he had been playing with. I cut it out for him using a craft knife. He then said that he wanted to make it turn; again he observed the model boat he had been playing with. He then wanted to put the wheel on a board so it could 'turn'. After much looking and discussion, I asked him what he needed to make the wheel turn. He looked through our materials and came up with a piece of dowel to push through the wheel to make an axle, then a cotton reel to space the wheel from the back board of cardboard. With reference again to our model steering wheel he talked through the problem, with minor help and questions from his grandpa and from me. After he had produced a spinning wheel, free from the backboard, he was still not satisfied with his 'toy'. He could see the pulley system for driving the rudder and wanted to make that, he choose some string for the chain. His grandpa helped him to make a pulley, but with Alex choosing the materials and saying what he needed his grandpa to do. In the end he had made a turning steering wheel, a pulley system that turned another pulley that a cardboard rudder was attached to. He was extremely pleased with the result, showing it to the rest of the family. Mum said it would go in his bedroom with his other 'inventions'. She was actually quite delighted and encouraging to him when he showed her his completed design.

Throughout the activity Alex showed a great deal of perseverance and aptitude for design. He was not going to be diverted by other suggestions or his mum's apparent lack of enthusiasm or the fact that it was not something being made by other children. Although he didn't possess the language skills to describe what he needed for the design, he knew emphatically what he wanted to do. He stuck to his task, which probably took him about 30 minutes or more. Alex's grandpa, when asked what his profession was, replied that he was an architect. His son, Alex's dad, was employed on the London Underground, designing computerized systems to make sure the trains ran safely.

Does the designing and engineering gene run in families?

Clearly, play is multi-faceted, illusive and elusive. It means different things to different people. Moyles (2010: 5) suggests that trying to define play is like 'trying to seize bubbles, for every time there appears to be something to hold on to, its ephemeral nature disallows it being grasped!' In the words of Brian Sutton-Smith, 'Play is like language: a system of communication and expression, not in itself either good or bad' (1997: 219). Taking account of the breadth of respected literature about the subject, any definition of play would have to be inclusive of, and apply to:

- children and adults
- animals and humans
- both process and product
- positive and negative forms
- structured and unstructured forms
- immediate and future benefits
- passivity and performance
- fleeting moments and long-lasting periods.

No definition can address all these things, and so it is probably best to adopt the approach espoused by Catherine Garvey (1991) and Tina Bruce (2005), both of whom rely on generalized descriptions, rather than specific definitions. For me, the popular notion that play is about process not product is wrong. In fact play invariably contains elements of both, as shown in Table 1.1.

Table 1.1 The benefits of play

Key factors Contributing to development while playing	Process During play we learn, enact and develop a range of essential life skills, i.e. how to:	Product In the longer term, playing helps to produce:
Fun	– be playful – be funny – use humour – tease effectively – get and give enjoyment – reduce boredom	continuation of brain plasticity happiness
Freedom	– assess risk – test boundaries – exercise control – be assertive – use power effectively – make the best use of freedom of choice	a sense of independence an understanding of the parameters of risk, challenge and danger
Flexibility	– investigate effectively – explore the unknown – experiment with possibilities – cope with uncertainty – adapt behaviour to get the most out of the environment – develop combinatorial thinking – test unusual combinations of behaviour and thought	broader horizons an understanding of the world, and an open-mindedness about its true potential
Social interaction	– make friends – cooperate to achieve an agreed goal – chat informally with friends – understand and appreciate socio-cultural diversity – enjoy solitude – negotiate and resolve conflicts without resorting to violence – develop and use play cues – interpret mimetic actions – use a personal theory of mind	friendship groups an understanding of social networks transmission of children's cultures
Socialisation	– practise social roles – learn cultural rules – interact with children's culture – prepare for adulthood – challenge social norms – establish social hierarchies	self-acceptance respect for others

Table 1.1 (*continued*)

Key factors	Process	Product
Physical activity	– run, jump, climb, crawl, balance, swing, slide, spin, hang, etc. – develop and utilize gross motor skills – develop and utilize fine motor skills – develop hand–eye coordination – use the body effectively – develop mimetic behaviour – improve physical strength	muscular-skeletal development physical health
Environmental cognitive stimulation	– acquire information and knowledge – explore the unknown – understand cause and effect – play games with rules – understand shape, size, texture, weight, etc. – understand scaling, calibration, sharing, etc. – make good use of thinking time – analyse and evaluate – inspect and contextualize – develop and use technical prowess and competence	knowledge and understanding a sense of wonder about the potential for expanding our horizons
Creativity and problem solving	– how to use objects to represent other things – use the imagination – make-believe – adapt the environment – develop an understanding of complexity – explore combinatorial possibilities – appreciate beauty	abstract thinking aesthetic appreciation problem-solving skills combinatorial flexibility
Emotional equilibrium, sickness and health	– use symbolic play to express innermost feelings – come to terms with traumatic events (reconciliation) – reduce objective anxiety (fear of the outside world) – relieve tension and neutralize the stress of everyday life – use transitional objects as a security mechanism – master subconscious conflicts and feelings – satisfy libidinous desires – explore aspirations – construct a preferred reality – create a secure and controllable world	homeostasis and stress reduction speedy recovery from illness

(*continued*)

Table 1.1 (continued)

Key factors	Process	Product
Self-discovery	– make use of the safe practice elements of play – explore a range of different selves – mix fantasy and reality – exercise autonomy of the play experience – develop and utilize survival skills – step up the pace and range of exploratory activities – control a personal microcosm of the world	a unique individual personality – self-awareness and self-confidence

The following chapters will explore these themes in much greater depth. However, given the difficulty adults have in interpreting what is going on when children are playing, it would be interesting to conclude this chapter by exploring what a child thinks is important about play. The following reflections were produced by a child who attended the launch of the Welsh Assembly Government's Play Policy Implementation Plan (2006).

Play policies[3]

Joe Rowley – 11 years old

When I was invited to attend the launch of the Play Policy Implementation Plan at the Museum of Welsh Life I was really excited because I was pretty sure I would have a good time there and it meant a morning off school! If I knew Play Wales was going to ask me to write something about this, I might have paid more attention to the talking that day, but I was too busy climbing a tree!

I started to look at the Plan, but I had a bit of trouble reading all of it so I decided to pay attention to the things I understood. I think the bit about encouraging more play provision is really important. For my friends and me, playing is probably the most important thing we do. Sometimes we get into trouble because we end up playing when we should be doing something else, like wet play in school. It's kind of like we can't help it, and it seems that whatever we enjoy is wrong.

Anyway I think the bit about having after school clubs is good; it's good to have clubs so that mums and dads can work, but not if kids are stuck in or doing stuff organized by adults. It's good to have adults to help you with something or treat you if you are hurt, but not to tell you what to do because out of school is our own spare time.

---

[3] This reflection first appeared in the spring 2006 edition of the *Play for Wales* magazine.

The bit about schools will be really important. Right now I don't think all the adults at school understand it. There are places we could play at my school, like on the grass and in a garden, but we are not allowed to. My school is building on the grass but they still don't let us in the garden at all. That would be a really simple thing to change. I have talked about this in student council meetings but our head always talks about 'health and safety'! He says it so much even us kids say it! We have a community school near our village and the caretaker there has told us we can go and play football there when it is closed, even though all of us go to a different school, and I think it is kind because our head and caretaker would say 'NO!'

When I was reading about play in the community, I thought about where I play. I play in a lane that is good for riding bikes and making dens. We can use the cricket field and the man in charge of the field lets us play there. One of the most important things about where I live that helps us to play is that we do not live on a fast road, so I am glad that the Assembly is going to try to do something to make it easier for kids who do live on busy roads.

One of the best things we ever did down the lane was to build a leaf pile at the bottom of a tree. We got a ladder from one of the bigger boy's houses and used it to climb because there were no low branches. Then we jumped into the huge pile. A lady walking past told us it was dangerous. It probably looked like it was, but my brother and me were careful at first because we didn't know what would happen. We followed the older boys and once we did it a few times, we got used to it, and it was fantastic fun.

I don't have a playworker but I do think it's good to have them around. When we were at the Museum of Welsh Life at the launch, there were some playworkers there who watched us and played with us when we asked them. They gave us the tubes and net. My sister fell out the wheelbarrow there, but she was okay. In my school, teachers and dinner ladies make such a big deal out of a tiny scratch. It's unbelievable! I don't think we should rely on playworkers to do everything for us and to get everything all the time, but it's good to have them around because they can carry heavy things for us and understand how we feel, and if we're upset they would try and help us.

I have written about the things in the Plan that mean something to me. Some of it is stuff for adults to do and I think that most kids would like to be involved when it is something they understand and can get involved in.

2

Fun, freedom and flexibility: anything goes!

The butterfly

Kitty Press – playworker

. . . so I had one child on my lap reading a *Diggers* book, one child next to me reading *The Gingerbread Man,* and one boy facing me reading *Old Macdonald had a Farm.* They were all reading to themselves, but each had some kind of contact with me, which seemed to be important to them. The little boy who was reading *The Little Gingerbread Man* changed his book and picked *The Hungry Caterpillar.* He asked me to read it to him. The other two children put their books down and pointed to the book.

I started to read the story. On the last page I pointed to the 'beautiful butterfly' and talked about the colours. The little boy who was on my lap put the book away and reached for *Spot's Birthday Party.* But I then noticed something really magical . . . One little boy who was listening to the *Hungry Caterpillar* story was sitting very still, cupping his right hand and looking at it. I asked him what he was holding. He replied 'a beautiful butterfly'. I asked if I could see it. He then told me that I had one in my hand too. I followed his cue and cupped my hand in the same way. 'Oh yes, it's beautiful,' I said. I asked him what we should do with the butterflies and he told me that he was going to let his fly away outside.

He ran off and came back about one minute later, wearing his coat and hat. He whispered in my ear: 'It's in my pocket'. I followed him outside. He reached into his pocket and slowly brought out his closed fist. He opened his hand, threw his hand upwards into the air, and laughed. I imitated his actions and our butterflies flew away together – it was Magic!!!

This is a 'magical' example of a child's imagination being stimulated by the content of a story. Eventually that culminates in the playful outcome of releasing the butterflies with his playworker. There is no question that the story is enchanting. This might lead us to conclude that children's play is something precious, something to be protected at all costs. But, that would be to do it a disservice.

As we have seen in the previous chapter, attempts to define play are many and varied, and have proved largely fruitless, because of the complexity of the subject. The folly of trying to reach a definition was emphasized by Sutton-Smith (1997), who made the point that no definition would be worthy of the name unless it covered all aspects of play, no matter how unattractive they might be. In an earlier piece with Kelly Byrne (1984) he highlighted an unfortunate tendency among most commentators to focus solely on the positive aspects of play. For example, Garvey (1991) identifies five commonly accepted characteristics of play in most leading theories: positive effect, intrinsic motivation, free choice, active engagement, and non-literality. Garvey's summary will be familiar to many in today's playwork profession, because of its similarity to the definition developed by Hughes (1996), and subsequently appearing in the second Playwork Principle, which defines play thus:

> Play is a process that is freely chosen, personally directed and intrinsically motivated. That is, children and young people determine and control the content and intent of their play, by following their own instincts, ideas and interests, in their own way for their own reasons.
>
> (PPSG 2005)

In the last 30 years this approach to the definition of play has become increasingly common. However, such an idealized view does not really stand up to scrutiny. Much of the following critique of that approach is taken from a chapter in the playwork textbook *Foundations of Playwork* (Brown and Taylor 2008).

First, is it always true to say that play is freely chosen, personally directed and intrinsically motivated? In reality play takes many forms, not all of which manifest themselves in that way. Such a description is not just idealizing play; it actually understates the value of play – and that is something we should never do. Time spent in a school playground during break-time immediately confronts us with the complexity of play, and the fact that many forms of play are:

- 'chosen', but not 'freely'
- 'directed', but not 'personally'
- 'motivated', but not 'intrinsically'.

The crucial point that is missed by such a restrictive definition is that play has developmental value, even when it is not freely chosen, personally directed and intrinsically motivated. For example, children who join in with the large game of football that often dominates school playgrounds are clearly playing, but some are playing only because they have been bullied into it. Obviously the quality of their play is substantially different from those children who have freely chosen to join in, but they still gain all sorts of developmental benefit from the experience. For example, being confronted with the stark realities of social interaction probably helps children develop their understanding of how to cope with differing levels of social status.

Lots of children take part in group activities that they are not personally directing – some children freely choose to be part of the crowd, even if that means being directed by someone else. In role play, the child who is directed to act the part of the baby when they would rather be the mum or dad is clearly not personally directing their play, but they may be gaining enormous social benefits as a result of their compliant behaviour, in terms of group membership and possibly even negotiation skills.

The play behaviour of teasing, which is often quite cruel, has clear developmental benefits for both parties involved. However, the person on the receiving end cannot be said to be intrinsically motivated to take part. One of the most important benefits of play is the way in which it teaches us about hierarchies and helps us find ways of coping with the injustices of everyday life. These are often harsh lessons, but nonetheless valuable.

In fact, we are seriously underselling the value of play in terms of both individual and species development, if we continue to espouse such definitions. The idealistic view of play provided by the 'freely chosen, personally directed, intrinsically motivated' approach is not really tenable as a definition. Nevertheless, when working with children it is not necessary to abandon the idea altogether. In fact I would want to argue that the most valuable form of playwork is that which seeks to encourage the sort of play that is 'freely chosen, personally directed and intrinsically motivated'.

The second major way in which play has come to be idealized is in the idea that children determine and control the content and intent of their play. It is probably true that play is the only experience in a child's life where they may be in control of events. However, rather like the 'freely chosen . . .' definition, this is too often stated as if it were an all-encompassing fact. Clearly, it is often true, but in reality there are many instances where children do not determine the content of their play and yet still gain great benefit from the experience. For example, I used to play 'house' with my sister and her friends. She is four years older than me, so I pretty much had to do as I was told. The 'content' of my play was largely dictated to me, but the excitement and satisfaction I got from being able to play with my older sister and her friends was immeasurable. As for children controlling the 'intent' of their play, in many cases there is no 'intent', except in the broadest emotional sense. Sometimes, children are just playing for the thrill it gives them.

There are many reasons why children play. From the adult point of view, some characteristics of play may appear to be somewhat negative. Play behaviours such as teasing, hazing and profanity do not sit comfortably with concepts of free choice and personal direction, especially for those on the receiving end. However, excluding such behaviours from our definitions of play is neither accurate nor helpful. In fact there may be benefits to be gained from even the most negative forms of play. Sutton-Smith (2008: 142) suggests that 'play has to do with the mammal need for protection and for stimulation'. If so, then behaviours such as teasing and hazing probably have the function of preparing us to cope with social hierarchies, and the complexity of social status later in life. Whatever the function (and there may even be none at all), it is not helpful to exclude such behaviours from our understanding of the subject.

The third way in which play is idealized is in the categorization of certain behaviours as not just shocking or disgusting, but completely intolerable, anti-social, etc. For example, it is generally considered wrong to be cruel to animals, and so children who chop up worms and pull the legs of crane flies, are chastised and told to 'play properly'. This social construction of acceptable and unacceptable behaviour means that some forms of playful behaviour are being excluded from the adult view of what constitutes children's play. In effect, play is being defined as something that should have only a positive outcome for society.

The following juxtaposed examples illustrate why that position is untenable.

Two frogs

Joan Beattie – international playworker

June 2011

Three children, aged 4, 6 and 9, found a tiny frog in their garden in the Scottish highlands. It must have hopped in from the field next door. The frog fitted into the palm of the 4 year old. It was then cupped between the hands of the 9 year old and shown round all the members of the children's family. The parents oohed and aahed as they peeped through the child's fingers and asked them to be careful not to hurt it. The children spent all that afternoon making play areas for the frog. Pools were designed in old metal pans and buckets; cardboard boxes filled with earth, stones and moss; and any container they could find adjoined the next. Other loose parts were added – plastic tubes for it to walk through so that the children could see it; a boulder for it to sit on; a grass surround in a plastic plant pot for a bed so as to make a home for their new pet. All the time one of the children was in charge of making sure the frog did not escape as it was passed from small hand to smaller hand to keep it safe until it was time for tea. The frog was not allowed in the house. The teatime conversation was all about the welfare of the tiny frog.

This recent observation of children with a frog reminded me of a previous encounter.

June 2004

My first camp with a group of Roma children from a village in Transylvania. The campsite is by a lake – a home for thousands of frogs and toads. One of my 8-year-old charges played alone most of the time, and appeared very sullen and sad for the first couple of days. I found him very difficult to relate to until one day he showed me his pet frog. Due to the language barrier most communication was done by body language, facial expressions and made-up sign language, sprinkled with tone of voice and, when necessary, translation into English from the Romanian playworkers. The child had found an empty water bottle and filled it with water and squeezed the large frog into it and was shaking it a bit trying to get the frog to the top so it could breathe. He was showing it to me and he had a huge smile on his face. To me, the frog had broken down all barriers and I was thrilled with the child's compassion for his new pet. One of the Romanian play-workers walked past and shouted at the child then explained to me that the child was being bad to the frog and he should return it to the lake. I said that I thought the child was pleased with his new pet and explained to the playworker that I thought it may be best for the child to keep the frog as a pet for a while as it seemed to be making him happy. The playworker continued telling me that the child was being bad. As we were having this conversation the child removed the frog from its bottle, grabbed a tennis racquet and using the frog as a ball, served it over the high wire fence into a field of sweetcorn!

Background info

The Scottish frog – I got a text the next day from the children's mother: the tiny pet frog had been released from captivity into the field next door and only had one broken leg.

    The Romanian frog – This child was away from home for the first time, his younger brother was very ill, his mother was in hospital with complications in pregnancy and his father was an alcoholic. I don't want to think what happened to that pet frog . . .

These two examples are illustrative of two extremes of children's play behaviour. The Scottish story, with its idyllic charm and obvious positive outcomes, contrasts quite starkly with the apparently impulsive, brutal nature of the play exhibited in the Romanian example. As such they bring to mind Nietzsche's (1999) Apollonian vs Dionysian dialectic (broadly speaking, the rational vs the emotional). Unfortunately in both those paradigms the child is seen as a problem. In the Apollonian view, the child is immature and not yet fully rational, and is therefore seen as a 'problematic innocent' (in need of protection). In the Dionysian view, the child is seen by some as the 'devil incarnate'. At best s/he is seen as a mischievous rascal having fun (and in need of control). Spariosu (1989) suggests this sort of apparently irrational behaviour may actually be a complex expression of power. Either way the adult inclination is to intervene in the child's play, ostensibly for the good of the child, but more accurately in defence of a view of what is good for society. Nowadays, this is often absorbed into childhood policy, where modern politics tends to focus on the concept of protection – protection of children from adults, and vice versa (Roche 2004).

    Returning to the two examples provided by Joan Beattie, although we may be shocked, and even appalled, by the play behaviour of the Romanian child, it is nevertheless possible to argue that the outcomes for the child in both stories are equally significant. In both cases the children have learned something, not only about frogs, but also about themselves.

    Speaking of playful behaviour that adults often find unacceptable, the source book *Children's Folklore* (Sutton-Smith *et al.* 1999) provides hundreds of examples of children's jokes and rhymes that would not be acceptable to a lot of adults, including several I remember from my own childhood. For example:

I see London
I see France
I see _____'s
Underpants

More recently, in an interview for the *International Journal of Play* (Brown and Patte 2012), Sutton-Smith referred to his research into children's jokes and stories. He quoted numerous examples to illustrate the fact that the imagination of children is often crude and earthy. It is not unusual for adults to find the play behaviour of children unpleasant, at times even disgusting. In the following example, Sutton-Smith's mother was clearly not happy.

Cow pot wars

Brian Sutton-Smith – Professor Emeritus University of Pennsylvania

When I was growing up in New Zealand in the 1930s we had a wonderful game involving cow pots. Now a cow pot is a big round cow poop and it dries on the surface and underneath is still soft and sloppy. And we had fights and you put your hand on top and you had to scoop it out on the dry part and then you'd throw it at each other's faces. It was sort of difficult as it would break and get on your clothes and your mother would go nuts and things like that. That was combined with horse dung grenades – use your imagination.

Sutton-Smith himself would argue that the benefits of this form of play were wide ranging and not insignificant. For example, the activity clearly promotes the development of motor skills (gross and fine), and the children are happily engaging in complex social interactions. The point is, it's what children get up to when left to their own devices, and as playworkers we have to ask ourselves what are the implications for our professional practice. After all some would argue that playwork is essentially a compensatory profession – attempting to fill the gaps left where children's play opportunities have been restricted by modern life (Wilson 2009). Does this mean we should be providing opportunities for children to throw cow dung at each other?

Here is a more recent example of play that many adults would say is completely unacceptable.

Pooh and wee pie

Ben Greenaway – playworker

In the village playscheme, which was run in the school, two boys, aged 5 and 7, had disappeared for quite some time. The playworkers found them in the boys' toilets with a bowl and mixing spoons. When asked what they were up to, their reply was, 'We're making pooh and wee pies.' The ingredients were real.

The most obvious point about these examples is that, in both cases, the children were playing, perhaps not in a way that adults would have found comfortable, but undeniably they were enjoying the experience.

A less obvious point is that it is often the case during play that anything goes. Children's imaginations are not necessarily limited by rational parameters. In fact, as Ken Robinson (2006) tells us, 'kids will take a chance – if they don't know, they'll have a go ... they're not frightened of being wrong'. That is one of the wonderful things about play. As Bruner (1972) says, play gives children the freedom to fail, which means their imagination sometimes knows no bounds, even when their play is a reflection of events in the wider world.

The Falklands War

Mick Conway – playworker

It was the annual box-cart derby event and we were talking about what ours should be. A child said, 'a Harrier Jump-Jet', and everyone cheered. We looked at the rules and decided we could do it. There had to be four wheels – one at the front, one at the tail and one at each wing tip. The finishing touch was plastic pipes stuffed with fire crackers slung under the wings.

On the day, as we pushed off for the race, we lit the fuses; the fire-crackers exploded and all the other box carts crashed. We won, but were disqualified for aggressive driving!

Sometimes the play is a reflection of the interest of one child, which then gets taken up enthusiastically by other children. In those circumstances it often ceases to matter what the activity is, just so long as it's possible to join in. The pull of joint activity is strong. When I worked on an adventure playground (see Chapter 10) I often started to dig a hole, in the certain knowledge that before the night was out at least half a dozen children would have joined in. There was no need to say, 'Let's dig a hole' or 'We need to dig a hole', it just happened. Hughes (2012) might argue that there is a recapitulative significance in the digging action, but I would also want to emphasize the significance of social interaction in this process. In the following example it is difficult to tell what the pull was, but it is clear that the ambitious (perhaps unrealistic nature) of the venture was not enough to put off the participants, with the result that one child's dream was eventually achieved.

The withy whale

Mick Conway – Play England development officer

For years we had been using withies (willow stems, also called osiers) and plastic bin bags with the children to create all sorts of things – igloos, geodesic giant balls you could get into and 'walk' around the park, angel or bee wings to wear, giant dreamcatchers, and so on. But we were completely gobsmacked by an idea that a small boy came up with – and which was actually made at a Playday in Hackney.

He was obsessed with whales and said he wanted to make one. No problem, we thought, until he explained it had to be at least 5 metres long 'to be a proper whale'. We thought 'OK, let's give this a go' and started to work with him making hoops as the armature for the whale. Other children came over, asked what we were doing, and when it was explained most of them enthusiastically joined in. Over the next few hours, more than 100 children – directed by our 8-year-old whale expert – helped to make hoops of various shapes and sizes, and join them with lateral plaited withies to make a realistic whale shape.

Next thing was to cover it with opened-out bin bags – black on the top, blue on the sides and white towards the bottom. A large dorsal fin was added – our whale expert wasn't so sure about this, but eventually agreed it made it a shark whale – though insisted that the tail flukes remained horizontal and not vertical as some other children thought they should be.

The bottom was left open and a dozen or so children lifted it up, got underneath and paraded it around the park – with other children screaming and laughing as they ran away from the shark whale. At the end of the Playday, the inventor and his mates walked it back across Hackney to their playscheme base, and to their immense pride caused a traffic jam that featured on the front page of the local newspaper.

Another aspect of play that adults find difficult is the fact that some children like to be scared. When my granddaughter was about 5 years old she would regularly complain because my stories were 'not scary enough'. The truth is that most children are easily able to differentiate between reality and fantasy – even the scariest fantasy – as shown in the following story.

Dr Death

Philip Waters – play project coordinator, the Eden Project

'Oh, go on, Phil. Wear it,' she said, thrusting the laboratory coat in my direction. I looked at their faces, filled with anticipation and excitement, yet I detected a hint of trepidation. Sophie, the oldest, had already started to wrestle my arm into one of the sleeves, while Frankie prepared my other with a yank and a tug. Tom was much smarter and had already made it to the door before the words had left my mouth. 'Okay then,' I began, 'I'll be Dr Death!'

Sophie and Frankie beamed, and were instantly out the door running towards the bushes shouting at the tops of their voices, 'Dr Death is coming, hide!' Like a rapidly spreading infection, screams sounded all around as children came spilling out of doorways. Some headed for salvation in the toilets, others dived under pool tables, while a handful foolishly hid behind couches in the TV room – did they really think cushions would keep me away?

I buttoned up the white laboratory coat and caught a glimpse of my reflection in the window, the blood that splattered down one of my sleeves had faded, it was time to add some more. We'd played this game for over five weeks, the coat having been decorated with just about every red felt-tip pen we could find. I smiled.

I loved playing Dr Death. Chasing the children, catching a few, kidnapping them and threatening to do horrible things somewhere back in my lair. And while I knew that I ought to have capped my enthusiasm, just in case I played more than the children, in the moment, in my heart, in the magic of the play narrative, I was as much lost in the play as they were. Would I have played as meaningfully any other way?

I threw open the doors, stepped out on to the grass and bellowed at the top of my voice: 'Death is coming!'

On the other hand, we sometimes get this wrong, and the scary image is just too real.

Bandage Man

Jess Milne – play consultant, lecturer, builder and trainer

The adventure playground attracted all manner of children and young people, mostly from the local area but some from up to two miles away. One young person was Albert, who came strolling on to the playground one day, all six foot and with big shoulders and a Canadian accent. He lived some way from the playground, was not interested in pubs and had to wait for work, as he was only 15. He had heard about the playground and thought he might 'check it out'.

As with all older young people it was explained that because there was only one playworker the older ones had to help out and become deputies. Albert readily agreed and was a tower of strength, literally, as in a former career while at school in Canada he had helped out of school as a lumberjack and was seriously strong.

Winter was coming and preparations were being made for Halloween when Albert asked me if he could 'scare the kids a little', but he would need some help from me as he wished to resurrect Bandage Man. This seemed to be some character loosely based on 'Return of the Mummy'. I agreed and Albert explained that, during the later part of the evening, around seven when it was dark, I would somehow draw attention to the bottom end of the site, which was a fair way from the building, and Bandage Man would appear.

There were many excited children, mostly under 12 years old, at our Halloween do; the older ones had drifted off to a party locally. During a lull in the noise, I said 'What was that?' looking out of the door. Some of the children heard me and ran to the windows, at which point all of them became aware something was going on. I repeated, 'What was that?' pointing down towards the structures. What I finally caught a glimpse of actually frightened me for a second, as Albert had dressed in a long pale coat buttoned up with a hat on. His face and hands were completely covered in bandages. He flitted through the structures with just enough light from a distant street bulb for us to see the dark shape wrapped in white bandages appearing and disappearing. One of the kids finally saw him and let out a scream you could hear miles away. More and more kids started to scream – what is it? – it's a ghost – it's horrible – it's gonna kill us – and finally one boy said, 'It's Bandage Man', and ran into the office to hide. The children, already hyped up by the Halloween thing, ran around yelling and screaming. A few were even brave enough to go just outside the door and yell insults at Bandage Man.

Complete chaos! After a brief period of absolute mayhem, Bandage Man disappeared. The braver ones assured me he had gone, as they had 'had a look'. Some 20 minutes later Albert walked in, dressed in his normal jacket and jeans. The children surrounded him and told him of the terrible thing that had happened. In their imagination Bandage Man had been there and grew in to this terrifying, really scary thing. I finally managed to pack all the children off home, some telling the story over and over again. A good night I said, thanking Albert, and locked up.

The next day, as I approached the playground, I was greeted by a score of angry mothers who took me to task for scaring their kids so much that they could not sleep, had locked themselves away and had been genuinely terrified. In the end Albert and I had to explain what had happened, and Albert had to dress up again and then take the bandages off so the children could see it was him. Some children still were not convinced. Bandage Man was just too real for them.

He lived on for quite a while . . .

Most children like to be teased a little, so long as they know they're being teased and trust the person doing the teasing. Lots of children (not all) like 'scary' things, but in general they prefer to have some choice in the matter, such as when they watch a scary film or read a scary story. By way of contrast, there are several issues with the whole concept of Bandage Man. First, in the half-light the bandaged figure would present an exceptionally frightening image for children of any age; a Jungian (1956) archetype that even some adults might find challenging. Perhaps more fundamental, though, was the fact that the children had no warning of the event, and so for some of them the initial reaction was pure shock, and genuine terror. Even the more rational children probably didn't have a convincing explanation, so there would be no check on the version of the experience being retold by those who were most scared. Consequently a mild form of mass hysteria seems to have set in. Once that happens an event can take on a life of its own, in this case allowing the mythology associated with Bandage Man to spiral out of control.

From the playwork perspective, we often learn more from things that go wrong than when everything goes smoothly. On this occasion, we can see an example of Schechner's (1988) 'dark play' taking place – a form of play characterized by the player suspending the normal frame that everyone recognizes as play, with the result that only the player actually knows she is playing. The other participants experience something that is not play – usually something quite disturbing. Sometimes, though not in this case, the player engages in dark play with deliberately malicious intent. For many developmental psychologists, this form of activity is simply the product of a disturbed mind and cannot be described as play. Whatever your interpretation, it is nevertheless clear that the player thinks she is playing.

Quite often the content of the play makes no sense if we take it too literally. However, it is best not to over-analyse such a fundamental behaviour. In fact Garvey (1991) suggests that non-literality is one of the salient features of children's play. For example, a fight is literally a fight (and we might attempt to break it up) – a play-fight is not literally a fight (and there are very good reasons for *not* breaking it up). We all recognize, and accept, the sort of behaviour described in the following story, and yet if we were to take the children's actions literally, we might see them as quite shocking. Tinbergen (1975), when talking about social development through play, suggests that children's play often has recognizable elements of adult behaviour, but he says these are:

- clumsily executed
- often chaotically arranged
- generally performed with abandon.

The following story is a good example.

The party

Rachel Kelly – playwork student

A group of five Year 1 children, four girls and a boy, decide to play families. The girls choose to wear long dresses and two have aprons. The boy chooses a base-ball shirt and a cap. There is much discussion about who should play what role. The group finally finishes up as mum, dad (the boy), two sisters and a baby. They also add a soft doll as another baby. They decide that they are going to cook a meal for a birthday.

Linda starts to give orders about the setting of the table, but mostly she seems to be talking to herself because no one takes any notice, but she doesn't seem to mind. Jane and James set the table, talking together excitedly. Lottie crawls around the floor making baby noises. Jane is nursing the doll. Lottie says 'I hate babies.'

Linda telephones her mummy and asks for party lights. Jane leaves the group and goes to the computer. Mary is busy cooking, James is helping. There is much discussion as to whether the carrots are ready. Mary shakes the cooking pans furiously. She seems fascinated by the sound and the plastic food swirling round the pan. Linda announces she has put up the decorations. Mary says food is ready, but James looks at the timer and says there are ten minutes left. He then counts down from ten to zero and the others join in.

Lottie retires to bed and says, 'Let's pretend dad has cut my arm off.' James obliges and soon they are all having bits cut off by dad with a plastic knife. They are all laughing and there is no hurt done. Jane rejoins the group as a doctor, and examines Lottie's glands and listens to her chest. Suddenly the meal is remembered and they return to the table.

For Tina Bruce (2005: 261–262) there is nothing chaotic about this at all. She calls this type of activity 'free flow play', which she describes as having 12 distinctive features.

1   It is an active process without product.

2   It is intrinsically motivated.

3   It exerts no external pressure to conform to rules, pressures, goals, tasks or definite direction. It gives the player control.

4   It is about possible, alternative worlds, which lift players to their highest levels of functioning. This involves being imaginative, creative, original and innovative.

5   It is about participants wallowing in ideas, feelings and relationships. It involves reflecting on, and becoming aware of, what we know – metacognition.

6   It actively uses previous first-hand experiences, including struggle, manipulation, exploration, discovery and practice.

7   It is sustained, and when in full flow, helps us to function in advance of what we can actually do in our real lives.

8   During free-flow play, we use the technical prowess, mastery and competence we have previously developed, and so can be in control.

9   It can be initiated by a child or an adult, but if by an adult he/she must pay particular attention to 3, 5 and 11 of the features.

10   Play can be solitary.

11   It can be in partnership or groups, with adults and/or children who will be sensitive to one another.

12   It is an integrating mechanism, which brings together everything we learn, know, feel and understand.

It is interesting that Bruce includes the concept of metacognition in her description. This is the term used to describe the fact that the brain is constantly monitoring its own thinking processes. The best evidence of this happens when we realize we have lost focus on the activity we have been engaged in. That realization comes from the meta-cognitive monitoring process. My colleague, Stephen Rennie, had a theory that there is an aspect of play that is meta-ludic. In other words, when children are playing they are somehow connected on a level that is not immediately identifiable, either physically or verbally. There appears to be some evidence for this in the following observation.

A pod experience

Brian Cheesman – playwork consultant

An observation at a pod, late March 2007

It is a bright and sunny early spring evening and I have arrived at the unlocked pod. One girl, aged 9 years, is waiting with her dad in his 'window cleaning van'. Two members of the playwork staff arrive, and suddenly five other children arrive, appearing to have 'beamed' down. One boy, age 11 years, races across the field to the pod, claiming he has been there an hour waiting for the pod to open. He turns immediately and runs back to the 'beck' (a small stream) from where he came. A friend arrives with three sticks. In the next 30 minutes seven more children arrive – two with parents the others without. Three boys continue to play in the 'beck' 200 yards away, but keep glancing back across the field towards the pod. The others, all girls bar one boy, continue to play close to the pod. Most of their play is generally self-directed, sporadic and sometimes fragmented. It is best described as being in a process of 'flow', constant movement.

Two children begin to get the fruit 'crusher' to work – batteries are connected – fruit is chopped and placed inside the 'crusher'. 'Smoothies' are in the process of being made and this becomes the centre of attention for most of the children. Roles are swapped, sometimes readily, other times with an argument, almost always with verbal negotiation.

At the back of the pod a den is made out of a parachute, into which a few of the not-quite-smooth 'smoothies' are taken. There is a slight altercation with one of the boys who seems to be unable to concentrate on one activity for more than a few minutes. Most of the other children deal with this disruptive influence by removing themselves from his vicinity. But he is determined to challenge them.

After the interlude with the argument and the 'smoothies', three boys return to the beck to continue their 'damming'. Some children from the other group join them in the process. Various discarded objects are pulled from the beck, including a useless chair and a rusty shovel. Both of these items are left on the side of the beck until one of the boys hurls the shovel back into the water. An onlooker would be amazed at the lack of conversation taking place. There are few words spoken but a great deal of furrowed brow concentration. Two parents cross the field to collect children from an after-school club, somewhat perplexed by the activities around and beyond the pod.

There are several striking features about this observation, not least the degree of shared understanding and cooperative activity, coupled with a lack of obvious communication. Perhaps Stephen Rennie has a good point. It is also worth noting the intense focus on the job in hand. Csikszentmihalyi (1980) identifies that as one of the main features of his concept of 'flow'. This, he says, is typified by:

- a merging of action and awareness
- centring of attention

- loss of self-consciousness
- being under one's own control.

He says these characteristics are not only typical of people who are playing, but also of the fully focused worker. He bases this idea on examples as varied as brain surgeons and rock climbers. Thus he throws doubt on the commonly held assumption that play and work are polar opposites. This also challenges the oft repeated sarcasm that play-work is an oxymoron. If we agree with Csikszentmihalyi then there really is no contradiction in the word at all.

From the perspective of the playworker, one of the main lessons from this observation is the value of standing back and allowing things to happen. That is also obvious in the final story in this chapter.

The car

Rionach Sarsfield – playworker

I was engaged in a bit of observational research at the Eureka! Children's Museum in Halifax, when I noticed three children playing together in the 'garage'. They were all communicating with one another and they were all telling one another what to do. One of the children was pretending to drive the car; another was pretending to put in some petrol; a third was pretending to fix the car. All of a sudden she shouted to the driver, 'Okay you're going to have to come and help me fix this. It's a bit hard.' At the same time she shouted to the other child, 'Put more petrol in – we need more petrol.' The children all worked along well together and involved one another. Eventually, one way and another, they all got a chance to pretend to fix the car, drive the car and put petrol in the car.

It's important to say that we don't necessarily understand what's going on in the child's mind when they are playing, and that we should not rush to judgement about it – for example, Rionach Sarsfield's observation at the Eureka! Children's Museum in Halifax. It would be easy to assume that this slightly chaotic approach to playing with the car shows the children are trying to role-play everything they know about cars, but don't really understand what they are doing in enough detail. However, that may be too simplistic an explanation. It might be that they do understand, but are very open-minded in their play, and are therefore happy to explore the possible extra connections. On the other hand, it could be that they are not really role-playing to learn about cars, but role-playing to learn about social interactions with other children. In other words the car is merely a tool in their play, and therefore the children are not particularly mindful of its use. The real focus of their play is one another.

Whatever is really going on in the minds of these children, several things are clear:

- they are having fun
- they are freely exploring their play environment
- they are flexible in their thinking and their approach to one another
- they are not restricted by an adult agenda.

3

The social world of children's play

Socio-cultural theories of play involve a study of the relationship between play and culture. Huizinga (1949) was probably the first serious theorist to address this issue. He famously suggested that human play behaviour pre-dates social culture, saying:

> Play is older than culture, for culture, however inadequately defined, always presupposes human society, and animals have not waited for man to teach them their playing. We can safely assert, even, that human civilisation has added no essential feature to the general idea of play. Animals play just like men.
>
> (1949: 1)

Huizinga argued that young dogs:
- invite each other to play through 'ceremoniousness of attitude and gesture'
- keep to rules regarding the level of violence in their play-fights
- pretend anger.

He said 'in all these doings they plainly experience tremendous fun and enjoyment' (1949: 1).

Thus, according to this line of thinking, animal play is similar to that of man, but animals have nothing similar to human culture. Since culture cannot exist in isolation from human society, Huizinga drew the conclusion that the drive to play is not dependent on any particular culture.

Later research into the neuroscience of the brain, by Pellis and Pellis (2009), has confirmed that the drive to play is almost certainly primitive in origin. However, the final sentence in the lengthy quote above reveals a flaw in Huizinga's argument. It might be true to say that animal play contains similarities to that of human beings, but it is extravagant to claim that 'animals play just like men'. Human play has become increasingly complex over time, culminating in play being used, for example, to enable children to come to terms with traumatic events (see Chapter 7). There is no convincing evidence that animals do anything similar to that.

Tinbergen (1975) disagrees with Huizinga. He says play is not a precursor of culture, but is actually governed by culture. Tinbergen suggests that two aspects of the difference between animals and humans are significant. First, the human child is far more immature at birth, and so in order to develop has to interact with the environment in an open-minded way. Second, the flexibility of the human mind has produced an ever more complex culture. In recent years genetic evolution has been struggling to keep pace, and each successive generation has to learn more than their predecessors. Tinbergen suggests that play is the mechanism that helps us cope with that ever-changing culture. Therefore, the effects of the prevailing culture in which children grow up should not be ignored.

The following story illustrates a further point about play and social culture – namely that children's play is not just influenced by the prevailing culture, but it also influences that culture.

Tango swings

Mick Conway – Play England development officer

'Tango swing', as another name for 'American swing' or 'Round the World swing', is beginning to enter the language – in some London adventure playgrounds at least.

Why Tango?

When their first American swing was built in Hornimans adventure playground, 20 or so years ago, the children created a series of swing games with rules. One was a version of cat and mouse, where the rule was that the cat had to hold on to one of the uprights, count to ten and shout 'Go!' before chasing around the circular platform after the mice on the two swings.

The counting speeded up until it became 'Tango!' and the rest is history.

Playworkers who used to work there now work in play area design and build. Older children who played there have grown up, some now have children and others have moved to other areas. Most of them have brought their name for that particular swing with them – an interesting example of how children can change the language and names for things.

I was at the new Roman Road play pathfinder adventure playground in Tower Hamlets a couple of weeks ago and was intrigued to hear the playworkers referring to their Tango swing. I asked them why they called it that and they just looked at me in disbelief (they'd been told that I was an 'adventure playground expert') and said that's what it's called. I told them the story of where the name came from, and they were delighted and amazed that a kid's game had given a new name to a type of swing that was now at the other end of London in a brand new adventure playground.

Parten (1933) described peer relations as being characterized by four forms of play: solitary, parallel, onlooker and cooperative. It is doubtful whether these are clearly identifiable stages, where children move from one to another as they get older. Nevertheless, the categories provide a useful description of different types of social play. Subsequently, Parten's fourth stage was expanded by Williams (1984), who identified three increasingly complex forms of cooperative play. For writers such as Bruner (1972), play is one of the most important aspects of social development. Learning during social play occurs on several levels. As well as knowledge, information and processing skills, children acquire an understanding of customs, rules and power relationships. The significance of play in that regard was identified by Suomi and Harlow (1971) in their research with monkeys. They state 'no play makes for a very socially disturbed monkey'. This is a finding tentatively confirmed as applying to human beings, as a result of a study of abandoned and abused children, conducted by Sophie Webb and myself (Brown and Webb, 2005). In the same study we also suggest that childhood play experiences enable humans to develop the crucial social skills of sympathy, empathy, mimesis and affective attunement.

Thus, play is now generally accepted as significant in both the socialization process and the gradual development of social skills. Hughes (2012) argues this is not only crucial for individual development, but also for evolution of the human species, because play is the mechanism that helps us cope with an ever-changing world – a process Sutton-Smith (1997) calls the human capacity for 'adaptive variability'.

The children in the following story are being collected from school and taken to an after-school club on an adventure playground. In the course of their short walk together they display a complex array of social skills. In particular the story shows the way in which children understand the different cultures within which they live their daily lives, and the different ways of behaving according to the particular setting they are in.

Walking back from school

Maggie Harris – playworker

I went to school to pick up the children. Only one child was booked in today.

A brother and a sister who don't usually come now, but who had previously come every day, came out and joined me. Nothing was said. They are 8 years and 7 years respectively. I asked the brother, who is the older, are you two coming to the after-school session tonight? He replied 'Yes.' That was sufficient reason to take these two. No adult advice or back-up was needed. I knew these children well, I knew I could trust them by their attitude to me and the way it was taken for granted it was correct. I trusted them and I trusted my judgement. They were coming to the after-school play session.

Another brother and sister gathered around me. They were clearly waiting for their mother who always came to the school. Their choice was always verified by her. She appeared very soon after. At first she had a row with the daughter, something to do with her being 'cheeky' in front of an audience. 'If you are going to behave like that you're not going.' The daughter stood to one side, embarrassed but smiling nervously. The mother behaved as though she was only going to pay for the brother to come but I knew she needed/wanted the daughter to come too. I didn't respond in any way as far as I know. She said to her son 'Are you going?' Pause, 'Yes.' She pretended that was the whole transaction, ignoring the daughter.

Another girl came to me, the only child who was booked in that day, and started to tell me about her spending money. I said 'Is this your spending money?' It was obviously more complicated than that. I could tell by her big intake of breath that a complicated story about the money was going to follow. She started, 'No, my sister has . . .'. I missed the rest because the mother of the girl who wasn't/ was coming started to talk to her daughter again. I wanted to pay attention. I wanted to know if the girl wanted to come or not. She clearly did. She was smiling, but in a nervous, awkward way. Her mother told her to stop smiling. 'You can stop that. Are you going to behave? Do you want to go? You can stop that silly smiling.' The girl could not stop 'that silly smiling' but the mother wanted/needed her to go to the after-school session and pulled the daughter forward. The girl was coming.

Then I noticed two brothers standing by me. One sometimes came to the after-school session but didn't seem happy at the playground, although he sometimes seemed to want to be there. His older brother was more definite about his decision to come; when I asked 'Are you coming to the after-school today?' he replied, 'Yes.' Their mother appeared very soon after. I wasn't sure until then because of the younger brother. I would have accepted the older brother's answer straight away. He was a reliable boy, but I knew the younger one would only be coming through an arrangement with his mother, so I waited. His mother said she would pay for them both when I brought them home. She knew this arrangement was OK because we had previously offered that as an acceptable solution.

The older boy was very happy, the younger one was a bit unsure. On his last visit to the after-school session he had been upset by something that happened with another child, and returned home without saying anything to anyone. However, I knew we had all discussed this and didn't feel I had to concentrate on that at all.

Another girl came and asked me if she was 'down to come with me'. I told her 'No' as she wasn't. She comes the same two days every week but this was not one of them. However she sometimes comes on other days, but usually her sister or mother come to the school and tell me and pay at the school. She looked a bit lost so I told her to pop home, which was nearby, and check if she was coming and if so to stand at the bottom of her street, which we passed on the minibus route to the playground, and wave to the minibus to stop. She has done this before without being prompted. I find it quite funny, as if we become a bus service with stops along the way. She was happy with this solution and set off home.

Meanwhile the larger than average percentage of boys were getting very excited about the fact that they formed the majority. We left school with three girls and four boys.

The minibus was waiting at the gate, partly full. The playworker said there was space for three children. All the children said they didn't want to go. They gathered around my car, which was parked near the school, saying 'We want to go in Maggie's car.' I said 'I'm not taking my car to the playground, you either go in the minibus or we walk.' 'We don't want to go in the bus.' It was starting to rain.

I had noticed that child B was very tired and tearful. I suggested to B that she went in the bus, '. . . it's starting to rain and it's a long walk to the playground'. She agreed. I looked at all the other children. Their body language and their verbal language told me they didn't want to go on the bus. The bus driver offered to walk with them if I drove but I wanted to walk with them so I said no thanks.

We set off walking. I stopped at my car to get four umbrellas I had. The boys were very vocal about walking in the rain: 'We're real men' etc. I offered a brolly to the two girls, who were pleased and managed to open them (they were tele- scopic umbrellas) without any instruction or help from me. I offered umbrellas to the boys, who refused them, saying 'We're real men, not poofs' about half a dozen times. I didn't respond to that other than to ignore it. Then they started to say, 'Me and my ma and my pa and my grandma and my grandpa had sexual intercourse.' At first I thought they were trying to say something about incest, I listened more closely the second time to what they said. Although they struggled with the words 'sexual intercourse' it was obvious that was what they wanted to say and was not a mispronunciation of incest. I didn't respond. This became a chant for quite a few minutes, interjected with 'we are men not poofs'.

The fourth boy, who was usually shy about coming to the playground, did not join in.

I had a black umbrella so I said to the boys 'Do you want this man's umbrella? That's what this is, a man's umbrella.' They declined en masse but the shy boy looked interested. I asked him 'Do you want the man's umbrella?' He nodded, took it from me and walked with the girls. One of the girls then asked me to swap her umbrella for the last one I was holding. I swapped them and she opened the new one exclaiming, 'Oooh this one is very big.' It was the same size.

The two girls and the boy with the brolly walked together, testing the brollies in different positions and feeling the wind against them, putting their brollies up and down and pushing into the wind. The other boys carried on with the 'poofs' chant and the sexual song. We had a good journey back to the playground. The children stopped at each corner for us all to cross the road together. We arrived at the playground shortly after the minibus. Everyone was happy and had enjoyed the walk in the rain.

This story shows the children using wide-ranging and sometimes quite subtle social skills (verbal and non-verbal); for example, when it comes to negotiating with their parents and their playworker. As a result, although the playworker is expecting to collect just one child she ends up taking seven with her. The children also show an understanding that different rules can apply in different settings, and also that their playworker will treat them differently from almost any other adult. For example, it is reasonable to assume that these children would not expect to get away with the 'we are real men . . .' chant in front of their teachers in school or their parents at home. They know there is a much more relaxed attitude on the adventure playground, and also that their playworker is not there to judge them.

This attitude on the part of the playworker has been termed 'negative capability' by Fisher (2008: 178). She enlarges on the concept thus:

This is at the heart of what I understand playwork to be. It describes the paradox, that by sometimes appearing to do nothing, we enable ourselves to do most. By hurriedly reaching to 'solve' situations we limit our capability, but by actively 'being with' a situation, without trying to change it, influence it, explain it or understand it, we keep all options open – anything is possible and nothing is closed off. Negative capability is not passivity; it is not sitting back, spacing out and doing nothing. It is really being aware of the situation without jumping to conclusions and leaping to intervene.

Children use play to find out who they are, their status in the group, the different roles they might play, etc. These may vary from one group to another. Essentially they are developing their sense of self, and the playworker's open-minded, non-directive approach doesn't get in the way of that.

In the covering note that came with this story the writer commented,

There were some hugely memorable walks from school to playground – some quite mad, but not written down. I wish I had, it really took me back to that day when I read this again. Just writing that reminded me when I first approached parents outside the school about whether they would be interested in an 'after school' provision, one of them asked 'How do we know we can trust you with our kids?'

This touches on the value of reflective practice (Palmer 2003), but also shows the importance for playworkers of getting to know their community. The relaxed way in which the number of children going off with Maggie changes from one to seven in the space of a couple of minutes, shows the trust that has developed between the play-worker and the local community. That sense of a playworker knowing the community and exactly what he can and can't do is shown in the next story.

Banned?

Jess Milne – play consultant, lecturer, builder and trainer

On the Adventure Playground, among the 150 regular children and young people that came every day, there was always one that stood out, even more than all the other characters. Such was Andrew – stubborn, opinionated, angry, with a huge sense of injustice and a temper that was legendary, all wrapped up in his 8 years. We had many a run-in, and one day I had to tell him he was not getting hammer or nails until I had the other tools back from his camp. He got very angry, blaming everyone except himself, so I walked away.

Later on I was sitting in the office taking a phone call when Andrew ran up and threw half a house brick through the office window aimed at my head. The large pane of glass shattered, covering my desk and me with glass. This was too much, and I ran outside, grabbed him and said, 'Right we're going to see your mum.'

Asking the other worker and an older youth to look after the place, I dragged Andrew up the street to his house. We were arguing furiously all the way until we got to his door. He went quiet. Knowing it was useless to knock we entered and went through to the kitchen where Andrew's mother was peeling potatoes. 'Ah, Jess,' she said, 'what's the little bastard done now?' As she said this she threw the knife at Andrew, a sort of angry flick. The knife struck the door by Andrew's head.

Immediately, I said 'Nothing that bad Mrs H. I was just going to tell you about his language, and now I'll take him back to the Adventure. I can see you're busy.' Turning, I caught hold of him and we left, walking through the house and out on to the street. 'Reckon your mum's got a temper like you,' I said. 'You had better come back to the playground.'

Andrew stopped and, looking up at me, said 'I'll bring the tools back.' That's all he ever said about the incident. Did he have less volatile relationships after that? Well . . . no . . . not really. The local school often used to ring me to come and quieten him down. He kept coming to the Adventure every day though.

This story reminds us that the playworker's priority is always the child. If Jess had gone through with his original intention he might have given himself the short-term relief of a peaceful evening – one where he didn't have to cope with this difficult child. However, faced with the reality of the boy's home life, his priorities changed in an instant. At its heart this is a story about the real lives of the children with whom play-workers work on a daily basis. There is something about the playwork approach that gives access to those lives on a level that is almost unique, albeit it is sometimes quite shocking (as in this case). In all probability the playworker's non-judgemental, non-directive approach to working with the children seeps through to the community at large, and just as the children develop a sense of trust in their playworkers, so too do their parents and other significant adults.

The relationship between children and most adults in their lives is rather different from the child–playworker relationship. The former tends to be based on status and hierarchy. At its best the child respects the adult; at its worst the child is just frightened. Either way, the adult retains all the power in the relationship. In contrast the child–playworker relationship is firmly rooted in trust, and the power is substantially shared (Williams 1984). The playworker's role is not to instruct or direct the child, but rather to offer children play environments that enable them to find out for themselves.

The all-pervading influence of non-playwork adults was clear in the findings from my own PhD research (Brown 2003c). When conducting carefully unobtrusive observations of children's use of fixed-equipment playgrounds I found that, in the presence of adults, children used the equipment in exactly the way it had been designed to be used. If there were no adults around, children had a strong tendency to invent their own ways of using the equipment. For example, I rarely saw a child climb up the steps of a playground slide and slide down it. It was more common for them to climb up the shiny slide and slide down the steps with their legs on either side of the guard rail. The most common use of a pair of swings was as a place to sit while having a chat. I once saw a child climb up the frame of a swing and balance across the top bar!

The reasons for the children's differential approach to the playground in direct relation to the presence (or not) of adults, are complex and varied, and may be dealt with elsewhere. For now, the most straightforward point is that children do behave differently in the presence of adults, but much less so in the presence of playworkers. Sometimes the social rules set by adults are so powerful that children apply them to a setting despite the absence of the adults who invented the rules. This is especially true of the school environment. Sometimes this even impacts on the relationship with the playworkers. For example, it is often the case that children will abide by school rules even when they are in an after-school club that has far more relaxed rules.

Shoes off

Alex Casey – playwork student

I took part in a session the Play Rangers offer during lunchtime in a local school. When we got there we set out a range of equipment on the playground. These included a large variety of loose parts such as wheeled toys, hockey sticks, balls, soft play, a basketball hoop, soft interlinking play mats, long wooden planks and blocks. The playworkers supervised the play and let the children lead, only intervening when offered a direct play cue, an action that invites play (according to Kilvington and Wood 2010), or when safety became an issue. The children very quickly built up an obstacle course and took turns; they didn't push and shove to go on, but instinctively formed an orderly queue so that everybody had a fair chance to facilitate the game. What surprised me about this game was that all the children took their shoes off. It was an extremely cold day, but all the children felt happy and comfortable to do this! We did intervene at this point, but the children wouldn't put their shoes back on.

In another area of the playground some children had put together the rubber matting and the children had made a safe pathway for them to cross, which also had areas that were danger zones, if you went into these areas then you lost lives. These children also took turns. In both these games the children were deeply involved and had total control of the activity, and yet they still adopted rules that were clearly derived from their experience of the school's regime, e.g. lining up, taking their shoes off, etc.

How should playworkers deal with this apparent contradiction? Hughes (2012) places great emphasis on the idea that playworkers need to make it clear that certain types of activity (such as digging holes, lighting fires and rough-and-tumble play) are allowed, because children will tend to assume that things are not allowed.

Sometimes the subtlety and complexity of the interactions between children at play are a delight to behold. It is often the case that older children will make all sorts of allowances for younger children – the sort of allowances that would not be made during non-play activity. This can be important for the younger child's self-esteem, because being able to play with older children successfully is regarded in children's culture as an indicator of status. This applies at almost any age during childhood.

Let battle commence

Suzanna Law – play ranger

He can't have been more than around 7 years old, but clearly he had decided that I would be the perfect opponent. Taking a short cardboard tube of around 2 foot long, he made eye contact, pointed towards me and then ran away. Taking the cue, I picked up the other half of the once 4-foot tube and met him at the clearing where he had selected our battle to take place. Immediately, he drew his weapon, made a war cry and struck at mine. Countering his attack, I returned with a slash of my tube in the same intensity as his, and repeated the sound that he had made.

After a few exchanges, a little boy of around 3 years arrived near the battle-ground. He had dragged along with him his weapon of choice: a 4-foot-long tube that he could only just about pick up. Gesturing with all his might, he also repeated the war cry, and taking his cue, the older boy ran in his direction and lightly tapped the little boy's weapon. The little boy didn't miss a beat and on contact, repeated the sound that had drawn him towards the battle. The older boy continued to battle with me, doing an elegant dance around the younger boy so that he would feel included and would occasionally make contact with the 4-foot tube to ensure that the little boy felt welcome in the exchange. I took his lead and also tapped the younger boy's tube, noticing all the while that I was rapidly running out of energy and breath. Very soon, I had to feign death to give my body a chance to recover.

This did not stop the battle. The little boy had then discovered that he could use his tube as a war horn, and the older boy told me, just after I 'died', that the sound of the horn would bring me back to life. So, up I got and continued the war-dance around the little boy, blocking and parrying with both boys. Using my fake death in another way, I decided to 'stab' my opponent, who also feigned death and gave me a chance to catch my breath again before the little boy again brought him back to life, and the battle continued. Crash after crash our swords met, and alternately our lives would end only to be resurrected around three seconds later. It was wonderful, exhilarating, and the boys both let out their war cry with increasing ferocity as the battle went on.

I am not sure how long our battle lasted, and I can't remember how it finished but I know that the boys sat down with me on the grass with beaming smiles. As quickly as the fight started, so too did it end. The smell of food was in the air. The kids were summoned to eat their block party pulled-pork sandwiches, and I took a moment to reflect. As I tried to soothe my screaming arms and legs, I wondered whether the two boys knew each other since they were children from the same neighbourhood. I also wondered whether they will remember today, the day of our epic battle, the battle where we lived and died, and lived again.

Children will often make similar allowances for those less fortunate than themselves.

Tortilla chips

Morgan Leichter-Saxby – pop-up playworker

Today Mourad learned about slapstick. Mourad is usually the loudest member of this little group, almost always kicking a box in front of him and shouting, 'Woop, woop. Woop, woop.' But today all he wants to do is smash tortilla chips against people's heads. We don't know where this came from, but the first time he did it he laughed so hard he farted and fell over. He puts a tortilla chip in his palms and slaps all of us playworkers in turn, upside the head, sometimes quite hard. Soon we all have bits of corn and salt in our hair.

Mourad begins to look for new targets, but most of the other children either ignore him or move quietly away. Eventually he spots James on his back on a crash mat. I'm with James one-to-one. We don't know how old he is, what his specific issues are or even how much he can see. He looks like a little baby, and actually gets called 'baby' by some of the other children, who seem disappointed that he doesn't seem to grow. Mourad approaches, 'Woop, woop. Woop, woop.' I'm still feeling the slap he gave me and am wary of how careful he'll be with James, but I sit back and wait to see what happens.

Mourad takes a tortilla chip from his pocket and places it gently, almost reverently on James's forehead. James looks confused. Mourad leans down, and with two fingers and the lightest of touch I've ever seen, cracks the chip in two. He laughs – laughs so hard that spit bubbles collect at the side of his mouth. James starts laughing too – a high giggle that shakes him like jelly. That sets Mourad off again and with a last hysterical 'Woop!' he collapses on the floor beside James, and they laugh and shudder together.

To some extent these examples demonstrate the development of important social skills. Our own experience of play enables us to develop the human attributes of sympathy, empathy, affective attunement and mimesis, and so make appropriate responses to children's play cues.

Adam Smith (1759) suggested that human beings are innately sympathetic to one another, and that it is the human capacity for *mimesis* that makes this interpretation possible. Through fantasy, invention and symbolic play, humans are able to use parts of the body to describe almost anything. For example, we all know what it means if a child is running round the playground yelling 'brooom, brooom', and we can easily interpret the accompanying actions. To quote Donald (1991: 168–169):

> Mimesis rests on the ability to produce conscious, self-initiated, representational acts ... Thus, mimesis is fundamentally different from imitation and mimicry in that it involves the *invention* of intentional representations. When there is an

audience to interpret the action, mimesis also serves the purpose of social communication.

Human beings are probably the only animals able to symbolize meaning in their actions in this way. For Trevarthen (1996) mimesis is a talent that gradually develops, and play is the catalyst. In other words, we learn how to interpret other people's play cues while we are playing. This is a skill that is fundamental to effective playwork practice (Sturrock and Else 1998).

Similarly Daniel Stern's concept of *affective attunement* (1985) may be something that we learn through our play. Stern did not suggest that. He focused instead on the mother–baby relationship, and was interested in the way mothers attune with their babies' rhythms. This makes it possible to demonstrate to the baby ways in which its actions might be further developed. For example, if an object is just out of reach, a baby may have to make a double movement in order to grasp it. The mother is likely to clap her hands twice, or make a sound 'ah-ah', in exactly the same rhythm as the baby's grasping action. This apparently simple interaction contains some very complex subtexts. The obvious message is, 'I am in tune with you', but there is a more subtle and far more powerful message: 'I can help you translate your actions into a different form.' Stern linked most of his ideas to the mother–baby interaction. However, we have evidence from the work in Romania that affective attunement can easily be achieved by a sympathetic adult working with a severely disturbed child (Brown and Webb 2005).

Sympathy, empathy, mimesis, affective attunement and the sensitive interpretation of play cues are skills and abilities that are essential for a well-adjusted social being. Children develop these skills while they are playing. It is doubtful whether they could be learned in the classroom. They are all also skills that are essential to the playworker.

Nicolae's play cues

Author's observation

I once watched a playworker playing with a 10-year-old boy called Nicolae, in a hospital ward. The pair were engaged in a game of chase. Nicolae was chasing the playworker, but seemed to want her to chase him. As they were running round the cots, Nicolae stopped at a table and banged it noisily twice with his hand. The playworker kept on running; having missed the play cue she had just been given. Nicolae resumed his chase. Next, he knocked over a mattress, and clasped his hands to his face in mock horror. He even said 'Oh dear!' This was a much more obvious play cue, and yet the playworker missed it altogether and continued to run away from him. That left Nicolae with no option but to take his cue from the playworker, and so he started to chase her again. Almost immediately he ran past the playworker's coat, which was hanging from a door handle. He stopped and put his hand into the coat pocket, pretending to steal something. At last the play-worker got the message, and started to chase him. Nicolae yelled excitedly. He allowed himself to be caught quite quickly, and the pair ended up rolling around on the floor with Nicolae giggling triumphantly.

The unstated meaning of the play cues in this example is fairly clear – 'Stop running away, and start chasing me.' When the playworker eventually responded, Nicolae's reaction was not to start running away. His excited yell showed a real sense of accomplishment, and the fact that he allowed himself to be caught seems to reflect a desire to confirm his achievement.

Sturrock and Else (1998) emphasize the importance of the playworker's ability to interpret children's play cues. They suggest that a consistent failure to do so may have a damaging impact on the children concerned. Play cues are often quite subtle, which means playworkers have to be highly sophisticated in their ability to interpret the meaning of each child's behaviour. However, it is fortunate that one of the benefits of play is that it provides us with the opportunity to engage with the non-verbal messages of other human beings. Through play we develop those interpretative skills (Brown 2008). Therefore, so long as the playworker has had a reasonably well-balanced childhood, there should be no problem interpreting children's play cues.

It is also significant that Nicolae had been born ten weeks premature, and weighing less than two pounds. He was abandoned at birth, and subsequently spent most of his life tied in a cot. He had considerable brain damage, although it was not clear whether this was the result of his genetic make-up or his life experience – probably a combination of the two. At the time of my observation, Nicolae had been free of his abuse for only about nine months. In that time he had learned to walk, developed some rudimentary language and was now engaged in social play. His use of quite sophisticated play cues was a further indication of his development through play.

The final story in this chapter reveals a great deal about the playwork approach, and the fact that it can be applied in some very unlikely environments, in this case a nursery in a private school in the middle of London. However, that is not the reason for its inclusion here. Instead, it has been included as an example of a playworker using the children's play cues as the basis for an extended fantasy play session.

The troll

Katherine Press – playworker and Montessori teacher

It is snack time, and picking up on the relaxed atmosphere, I lie on the floor in the middle of the children while they have their snacks.

Gerry: 'Look Katherine has fallen asleep!'
I open one eye and look at Gerry.
He laughs and runs back to his seat.
Martin: 'That's not Katherine – it's a troll.'
I then begin to snore loudly: zzzzzzz . . .
The children laugh and start to get excited.
Two children come over with their apples and put them on my tummy.
As I move to get the apples the children run back to their seats.
I pretend to eat the apples but sit up and start to sniff.
'I think there must be children moving around!'
'I can smell children when they move close to me!'

Yum yum!'
They all scream and run back to their seats.
Lisa creeps into the home corner.
'Let's get some pretend food for the troll.'
She puts the food on a plate and pushes it towards me.
I sniff again . . . 'Oh yuck that's not my food. My food's children!'
Lisa laughs.
Then Jodie gets a teddy from the cuddly toy box.
She creeps up to me with the toy and puts it by my head.
'Here you go Mr Troll, I got you a teddy.'
She sits back.
I slowly start to stroke the teddy.
I start to smile and cuddle the teddy bear.
I sit up slowly and, still cuddling the teddy, I walk out of the classroom.
I come back in as Katherine.
'Hello everyone I just saw a really funny troll holding a teddy, did you?'
The children start to tell me about their adventure with the troll, and how he could smell them and wanted to eat them if they moved! Not one single child said that the troll was me.

That last sentence contains much for us to ponder:
- the playworker's statement about having seen a troll allows the children to continue their fantasy and bring it back to the reality of the classroom
- the children's collective consciousness (Durkheim 1893)
- the children's apparent ability to mix fantasy and reality to create another experience, i.e. the discussion with their teacher
- the cooperative nature of children's play, even at a young age.

4
Playful physical activity: challenge, risk and danger

Physical activity has been shown to be beneficial for health reasons. Energetic physical activity is known to release oxygen to the brain, which Gallahue, Ozmun and Goodway (2011) tell us helps to create physical and mental health, and a general sense of well-being. Not surprisingly, it was the physical aspect of play that exercised the minds of the 'classical theorists' (Hughes 2010). The first of these was Spencer (1873), who developed Schiller's earlier surplus energy theory; the second Lazarus (1883), who suggested that play was used to re-create lost energy. There is little scientific evidence to support either of these theories. However, there is plenty of evidence of the biological and physiological benefits of active play – the most obvious manifestation being the development of motor skills (Johnson, Christie and Wardle 2004).

Goodall's (1989) work with chimpanzees led her to suggest that youngsters sometimes engage in physical acts simply for the pleasure of performance. However, she also suggested that youngsters need to learn about the environment at a time of life when the body is supple enough to cope with minor falls. That is achieved through playful physical activity.

In fact Mackett and Paskins (2008) have shown that children are more active, and use up more calories, when playing than when engaged in organized activities. This is because playing is generally a non-stop event, whereas structured activities usually involve time spent getting changed and standing around listening to instructions. They have also shown that children who walk to school (as opposed to being driven) are generally more physically active throughout the day. Also, if they walk to school without their parents they engage in a lot more exploratory activity.

These findings are confirmed in Nielsen's (2011) study of the physical activity of 500 Danish children. He found that the highest levels of physical activity took place in self-organized play, rather than in organized sport. Outdoor child-initiated play was more beneficial than organized sports or activities, as that form of self-organized play was more intense and burned more energy than any adult-directed activity. Nielsen found a correlation between the number of play facilities provided in institutional settings for self-organized play and the children's overall physical activity level. He also found these activity levels were independent of gender – a finding that confirms my own observations (Brown 2003c).

However, according to Griffiths *et al.* (2013), only half of 7-year-old children in the UK achieve recommended levels of physical activity. They suggest that:

> Longitudinal studies are needed to better understand the relevance of these (in) activity patterns for long-term health and well-being. In the meantime population-wide efforts to boost physical activity among young people are needed which are likely to require a broad range of policy interventions.

Sadly, the response of most politicians to the growth of obesity in the child population is to encourage more *organized* physical activity in schools. When coupled with an increasing emphasis on academic achievement, the result is that many schools are actually reducing time spent in free play. This is an extremely worrying development, and there have already been several campaigns aimed at persuading politicians to change their priorities, but these appear to have made no impression thus far. Perhaps the idea of giving children more freedom to roam around is just too frightening for the average politician.

One of the aspects of children's physical activity that adults find especially difficult is the idea that some things children choose to do may bring them into danger. Indeed the complex issues of challenge, risk and danger have exercised playwork theorists for many years. Hughes (2012) suggests that taking risks is a fundamentally beneficial part of children's play. It is only by testing the boundaries of their play environment that children will learn where the limits are, and where danger lies. If children are unable to experience the challenges presented when they engage in exploration, then they will struggle with those concepts in later life. Here is a child struggling with a challenge offered by his environment.

Climbing a tree

Stevieleigh Copcutt – playwork student

At the Adventure Playground I observed children trying things out for themselves and experiencing complex outcomes from what they were doing. During one session a child wanted to climb a tree but couldn't reach the first branch to help pull himself up. He went into the playground building and came out with a bucket. He placed the bucket upside down next to the base of the tree and climbed on to it, stretching up towards the branch, but he still couldn't reach. He took the bucket back inside and replaced it with a chair. As he climbed on the chair it began to move away from the tree, because it was on wheels. As it moved he jumped from the chair and tried to grab the branch but missed and fell to the ground. He tried this again and again, until he eventually managed to grab the branch. So, at last he was able to climb up the tree.

In this story it is clear that the child wanted to climb the tree, although we cannot assume that was his ultimate aim. After all we are not told how high he climbed, nor what he did when he eventually reached the top of his climb. On the one hand, he may just have been thrilled to be climbing; on the other hand, he may have had a target in mind – perhaps he wanted to make a tree house and was checking out the possibilities. There is no way to know. However, we do know from this one short description that he has overcome more than one challenge – first the physical challenge of how to climb a tree; second the intellectual challenge of how to reach the first branch. At the same time as exercising a number of muscles, he has also engaged his problem-solving faculties.

Originally the story-teller suggested this was a 'terminal game' (Salter 1980), i.e. a game where the aim is purely to avoid a negative outcome, which is potentially painful, and sometimes disastrous, but nonetheless inevitable. After some discussion we decided it was not a very good example of that phenomenon as it was not likely the enterprise would end in disaster. The following stories are more typical of this phenomenon.

Three terminal games

Author's observations

Children's Centre

I was standing at a window on the second floor of a school building. In the play-ground below, a boy was riding round and round his little sister in ever decreasing circles. The game he was playing was obviously 'How close can I get to her before I knock her over?' Eventually he got too close and knocked her over, with terrible (but totally predictable) consequences. His sister started crying loudly, his bike was damaged, and his mother came and shouted at him. Maybe he had calculated all this into his subconscious cost–benefit analysis of the game. Perhaps the adrenalin rush of getting closer and closer was enough to outweigh the certainty of punishment once the game was over.

A primary school playground

Three children are playing a game on the giant xylophone. At first sight it appears that two boys are using the mallets to strike the bars of the instrument, while a girl watches them. In fact the girl is placing the tips of her fingers over the edge of the xylophone and the boys are attempting to hit them. Eventually they succeed, with fairly predictable consequences. The girl lets out a scream and starts crying. She is in so much pain she falls to the floor. One of the teachers comes over and comforts her until she stops crying. As soon as the teacher moves away the girl goes back to the same game. There can now be no doubt that all participants understand the potential negative outcome of the game, but that does not deter them.

Roma village in Transylvania

One of the main characteristics of play in the village is the very physical nature of the interactions. There is a lot of falling over because of the rough terrain, and lots of shouting and tears, but these are pretty hardy children, who get back to playing as soon as the tears stop. Very often they return to playing the same game as the one that resulted in the accident in the first place. This sort of boisterous physical activity seems to be taken for granted by the children. For example, I witnessed small children playing a game that involved trying to slap one another's faces while at the same time dodging out of the way of one another's hands.

The great ethologist Robert Fagen (1981) identified a link between the survival probability of a species and the amount of risk it is prepared to tolerate in its play. When survival probability is low, then free play is too risky, because of the risk of predators, starvation, overcrowding, etc. The human species is not at any great risk (except from itself), and so its play is characterized by substantial risk-taking behaviour. Sometimes these extremes of play are revealed in a type of play that Bentham (1802) termed 'deep play', i.e. play where the stakes are so high it is irrational to participate. Bentham, the father of utilitarianism, thought that deep play had no purpose, and that anyone engaging in it was socially irresponsible and should be locked up. The concept was further developed, but in a less dogmatic way by the anthropologist Clifford Geertz (1993), and more recently by the playwork theorist Bob Hughes (2012). The Hughes interpretation of deep play is akin to extreme risk taking, and he suggests it serves the function of helping us to develop survival skills and come to terms with our fears.

Fireworks

Jackie Jeffrey – community edupreneur

Around bonfire night last year I had the pleasure of being at the Somerford Grove Adventure Playground in Tottenham, running a playful youth session. But it was not what was happening inside the adventure playground that forms the basis of this story but what being there enabled me to see.

Not sure what you know about Tottenham but to many it's hell on earth. For us who live and work in the community it's a cool place to be. For the young people growing up in the area, they have multiple issues to contend with, and respond and react accordingly. The playground provides a neutral space that we are trying to open up outside of core hours to young people.

Enough of the fluff: it's around bonfire night and I can hear fireworks going off all around the outside of the Venture and young people shouting loudly. I hate the sound of fireworks but the sound of the shouting intrigued me so I found myself a space on top of one of the structures to observe the play taking place outside.

From this space, I could see young people playing with fire. Not controlled by anyone else but themselves – what we would call 'deep play' but felt more therapeutic to me. They threw fireworks at one another and ran in multiple directions, giggling so hard that it literally paralysed their movement. Some ran, stopped and knelt on one knee to fire rocket launchers from their shoulders; others just lit fireworks and threw them at their friends, laughing all the way. The explosion of light seemed to make the situation even more exciting and created a crescendo of sound. This continued for what seemed an age. All of a sudden the sounds of exploding fireworks and giggling were joined by the sound of the police sirens. If you know the area you will know there is a green space that prevents vehicle access so when the police arrive the young people simply move beyond their reach. I was disappointed to see them. I imagined them running out of their vans with batons chasing the young people across the green. I also imagined the young people throwing fireworks at the police. But none of that happened. The police parked their vans at the edge of the green and although a few fireworks were aimed in their direction the young people just stopped and waited for them to leave. In the time that took, I had time to reflect on this.

From my vantage point, and as a playworker, I could see the beauty of this play, but I was also aware (especially mindful of my personal dislike of fireworks) of how people walking down the street would have felt if they happened upon this scene or how the others observing this scene from their windows might also view what I felt was just an example of playful youth.

This story illustrates the possibility of a single event engendering different perspectives on risk in children's play, depending on the value systems of the viewer. Some would see the children's firework play as being dangerous and irresponsible, whereas Jackie Jeffrey clearly thinks it is beneficial, and even beautiful.

The following is an example of how different perspectives can confuse the issue and prejudice the adult view of what children are doing.

Spider's web

Author's observation

Once, when my wife was away in France, I collected my 5-year-old grandson from school. As a special treat we went to Rowntree Park, where there is a variety of brightly coloured adventurous play equipment. He went straight to the top of the 'spider's web' (about 10 metres off the ground). Admiring his agility, I sent a text message to my wife telling her of our grandson's feat. Almost immediately I received a reply saying, 'Are you mad? Get him down!' In an instant my whole perspective on the situation changed, and I began to encourage him to come down. He was halfway down when a girl, at least three years his senior, passed him on the way up. Of course, he turned round and followed the girl back to the top. When she reached the top, the girl leant through the ropes, grabbed the central pole and slide down to the ground. My grandson started to copy what he had seen (and I started to panic!). Reaching through the ropes he placed his hands on the central pole, but on surveying the scene, he pulled back and climbed back down the net (much to my relief).

The lesson from this story is that, even at the age of 5, my grandson was perfectly capable of his own risk assessment. He was able to judge what he could and could not manage. The irony is that if he had been within my reach I would have intervened. Such intervention would have had purely personal motives, and would not really have been in the best interests of the child. In the words of Bob Hughes (2001: 54):

> Most children are neither stupid nor suicidal. They are not going to deliberately go beyond the limits of their known skills. But to evolve at all they must take much of what they do to that limit and test it. When we see a child engaged in something 'dangerous', we are making that judgement from our standpoint, not from theirs.

However – and this is where the playworker comes in – there are circumstances when the child's natural sense of danger may be compromised; for example, when they are being bullied, or simply encouraged, to do something by older peers. The pull of the social group is powerful, especially when it contains older peers. Children who want to be part of a group will often compromise their personal boundaries in ways that are actually dangerous, rather than just risky. If my grandson had received 'encouragement' at the top of the 'spider's web' from older children, he might have been more inclined to attempt the slide down the central pole – a feat that was clearly beyond him at that time.

Sandseter (2009: 93) talks about risky play as being 'thrilling and exciting forms of play that involve a risk of physical injury', and suggests that some children deliberately seek out such forms of activity. If that is the case, why would children do such a thing? The most common explanation is that they are curious about the unknown, and about the limits of safety, the environment and their own abilities. This leads them to explore and experiment with activities they have not tried previously (Apter 2007).

A second explanation is that children enjoy the thrill of extreme emotion, being on the edge of fear and fearful situations (Sandseter 2009). According to Adams (2001), exploring risk and challenge can be a significant part of a child's development. It may even aid survival in later childhood, when adults are less likely to be around (Apter 2007). After all, when they push their behaviour to the limit, they presumably develop a clearer understanding of exactly where those limits are; at the same time developing an understanding of which behaviours are essentially safe. Thus, it seems this type of behaviour has many benefits. Not only does it enable children to master risky situations, but in the process they learn the skill of risk assessment, and therefore gain a personalized view of what constitutes a risk for themselves (Aldis 1975; Ball 2002).

Given the weight of evidence suggesting the value of risk-taking behaviour, coupled with the fact that children seem to feel the need to take risks in their play, perhaps we should make sure this is a possibility within the play environment. Sandseter (2007) makes the rather simplistic proposition that it is possible to identify six categories of risky play – height, speed, tools, elements, rough and tumble, and disappearance (getting lost). This is an interesting categorization of physical risk in children's play, and if playworkers wanted to ensure that children have the opportunity to explore their own risky play, then this list might be used to guide the basic design of a playspace. However, we should not be in the business of deliberately creating risky playspaces. That is potentially dangerous, because each child's concept of risky behaviour is different. The role of the playworker is merely to ensure that children have the opportunity to take risks if they so desire, not to deliberately put them in harm's way.

Some children will happily put themselves in harm's way, though, usually for the sake of impressing other children.

Hot pants

Joe Frost – Professor Emeritus University of Texas

During the latter years of the Great Depression I was growing up on a small farm in the Ouachita Mountains of Arkansas. The native stone school for first through twelfth grades was built by President Franklin Roosevelt's Works Progress Administration (WPA), on an exceptionally well-chosen site with a creek and mountain behind the school and a cleared space in front to accommodate three recesses each day. In the main, teachers stayed indoors, and children of all ages planned their games, chose their sides and picked the play sites.

The heavily forested mountain was ideal for war games – forming battalions, meeting across open spaces and striking dead pine tree branches across tree trunks. The ends of branches would break off and zoom towards opponents – much like arrows when storming castles in movies. The creek was used for building dams to wash out opponents' dams, and the open space in front of the school was for all sorts of contrived games. On weekends we would hold rodeos in barn lots with large calves, play cowboys, and race our horses, which also served as work stock.

All the boys carried knives used in their work on small farms and for mumble peg games, but no one used them for aggression against others. Even a threat would have resulted in quick, painful action by principal, teachers and parents.

This was a creative lot. One game in the open space was called 'hot pants'. Since boys were instructed to play on the east part of the mountain and girls on the west, the game was created in part as a way to attract girls as onlookers (admirers). First, two of the older, more vocal boys chose up sides from everyone wanting to play. Then two parallel lines were formed, a small piece of paper was inserted in the back pocket of each boy in front of the line and SET ON FIRE. Both would run as far as they could before whipping out the fire with their hands. Progress was marked and the second boys in line took their turns, and so on until all had an opportunity to participate in the fun. The side travelling the longest distance WON and were the 'top dogs' of the day. The game later ended during its second run when a teacher spotted it from a classroom window and reported us to the principal.

Although the focus of this story is clearly the pants-on-fire element, Joe Frost's passing remark that 'all the boys carried knives' is interesting in itself. This shows the importance of cultural context. Clearly, in 1930s rural America carrying a knife was taken for granted. Eighty years later, in most inner-city areas that would be a reason to be arrested.

The point about cultural context is further reinforced by a photograph I took when we were building an aerial runway on an adventure playground in the 1970s. An adventurous teenager climbed to the top of a telegraph pole and, balancing right on the top, made himself into the shape of a star. When I took the photograph the only thought in my mind was that it made a remarkable image. Looking at that same photo now I find it truly scary. It's not that I'm older and wiser, but rather that social norms have changed. If I saw the same boy do that today I would be trying to persuade him to come down. In fact that might make matters worse – it would probably be better to leave him to come down in his own time.

The final point to make about this subject is that, contrary to Sandseter's categorization, risk-taking during play is not just about physical risk. As Gladwin (2008) points out, it can also occur in relation to other aspects of play. It sometimes involves social risks – for example, jumping out from a hiding place and yelling 'boo!' is risky for lots of reasons. Stealing apples from a neighbour's garden is risky. What if they catch you? What if your parents find out?

The lovers

Brian Sutton-Smith – Professor Emeritus University of Pennsylvania

One of the other great childhood New Zealand amusements was that, after the First World War, a lot of people were out of work and so on; they put them to work planting trees, pine trees, so all round the hills around me were pine trees. When we started exploring the pine trees we found that these were the place where lovers went and if you went quietly through you would find lovers doing their thing. We would be laughing and we couldn't stop ourselves. We'd take pine cones and we'd throw them at the lovers. Several times we'd have great contacts; a pine cone hits the back of the man doing his thing. Sometimes it would be OK, but sometimes the man would get up and he would chase us full of anger, and we would run screaming down the tracks. They had tracks going through these pine trees and we would disappear, lying behind a tree and hope we didn't get caught.

Challenge, risk and danger have been fundamental elements of children's play throughout history, and it is therefore not unreasonable to suggest that there might be a good reason for that – most likely in enabling children to explore the physical and social boundaries of the society in which they live, and also their own personal limits. We need to consider what might be the implications of the current trend towards overprotecting our children.

5

Environmental cognitive stimulation

The significance of play in the acquisition of information and knowledge was first identified by Plato and Aristotle. Locke (1690) described the mind at birth as 'white paper', awaiting ideas from experience – a process that was to be stimulated by adults. Not surprisingly, 'Locke's Blocks', the first example of toys specifically intended for children, were designed as an educational device. Subsequently, there are numerous examples of educationalists recognizing the significance of play in the learning process, from Froebel (1888) through to Steiner (1965) and A.S. Neill (1968).

Piaget (1951) is often credited with giving this approach a solid foundation, whereas in fact he regarded play as having a subsidiary role in cognitive development. In his view play was 'only a happy display of known actions'. He thought play was largely 'repetition, reproduction and generalization'. Piaget saw play as a mark of immaturity, with its significance reducing as more logical and adaptive thinking emerges.

Not everyone is so dismissive. Millar (1968) suggests fantasy play is used as an aid when the mental capacity to understand something is lacking. Sylva, Bruner and Genova (1976) provide evidence that play is a tool for understanding the qualities of objects and situations, and that play encourages serial ordering. According to Singer and Singer (1979), make-believe play opens children to experiences that stimulate curiosity.

My own feeling is that there is much to be said for Vygotsky's (1966) view of play, and that will be explored later in this chapter. In the meantime the following story reinforces the idea that children learn and develop while interacting (playing) with their environment. It also provides a good example of Nicholson's (1971) *Theory of Loose Parts*, which will be explored in more depth in the next chapter. Finally, the story illustrates the very fundamental relationship that Hughes (1996, 2012) says small children appear to have with the classical Platonic elements of earth, air, water and fire. Of course we now know that these are not really elements in the chemical sense of that word, but that doesn't detract from Hughes' idea.

Dirt, water and nature

Susan Caruso – Sunflower creative arts director and teacher

A new building was taking the place of our old, much beloved playground. In spite of carefully planning to protect the children, workers arrived early one morning without warning and started chopping and tearing down everything, including the gorgeous old climbing tree and playground equipment (which was supposed to be saved and moved to the new site) right before our eyes. As we scuttled the children safely off to the park I realized that for the next year our play area would consist of a very unfriendly rectangle of sandy rubble.

I ordered a truckload full of sand, which was dumped at one end of the yard. A huge mountain! Two very long hoses offered a water supply. Then we invested in a dozen potted ficus trees that the kids could move around on their own. We also discovered an unused natural area on the property, complete with a drainage ditch and old trees. We fenced it in and named it the 'Valley'.

We had a magical year. The kids endlessly created forests, forts, stores and houses. Rivers, ponds, dams and waterways were constructed daily. The sand mountain was carted, shovelled, slid down and explored in the hundreds of ways that children will find when left alone.

We had all we needed: dirt, water and nature.

The significance of the key elements in children's straightforward interaction with the environment is also shown in the following observation.

On The Beach

Chris Taylor – consultant and trainer: play and playwork

Observed on an adventure playground in Tower Hamlets

Sandall House, a 20-storey block of high-rise flats, with unintended irony, overlooks the playground sandpit: The Beach.

A rectangle of telegraph poles contains the sand, several natural tree stumps are suggestively placed to desert-island effect. There is a stop tap at one end. This has been running for some time and has filled the top half of the sandpit, creating 'the sea' on which a surf board and a plastic box are floating: an inner-city treasure island.

A boy with ginger hair has a spade. He is digging on the shoreline, where the sand and water meet. He is engrossed, shovelling sand from here to there; carrying a tyre to float in the water. He is absorbed and alone.

'Hey look, I made a wallet, I've made you a wallet, you can make one, and it's really good.' The boy is distracted by his friend's announcement and gains a new interest. He goes ashore to make a wallet.

Tyler, Ginger and Mona come to the beach.

Leanne the playworker is with them.

'How deep is this? Are you sure I'm not going to drown?'

Tyler sits in the plastic box, her friend takes a photo on her phone . . . several.

Tyler splashes, Mona screams and jumps into the water, laughing and splashing.

Easy transitions from absorption to self-preoccupation to absorption . . .

Now there's a 5 year old in the boat (plastic box).

Progress is precarious and it's very wobbly.

He shouts to the playworker.

'Ifkey, it works a little bit.'

'Yes.' She smiles, non-committedly.

Interest wanes, the sea empties and the beach clears.

Ginger returns and plays with the tyre, twisting and turning, and watching the swirl and wave creation . . .

Two teenage girls walk past. 'Hey Ginge,' one shouts, 'You know every fox on the estate has shat in that pond.'

Ginge grins. They go on their way, laughing loudly.

Towards the end of this observation there is a fascinating bit of banter. We are not told the age of the boy in the water, or whether the two teenage girls actually know him. We do not even know for certain that their statement is an invention, although that seems likely. Nevertheless, this playful exchange contains a number of lessons. First, and most obvious, the girls are having a laugh at the expense of the (presumably) younger boy. However, it is a light-hearted sort of laugh. They probably don't expect him to believe them, but that doesn't really matter. Here we are entering into the realm of 'what if?' (Lester and Russell 2008). It's the thought, 'what if it were true . . .?' that makes the statement funny. Even the boy in the water seems to understand that. That sort of complex double meaning is common in children's play, and we generally take it for granted, but it is all part of the gradual process of learning about the complexity of our language.

Another thing that comes across from this exchange is that the two girls are, in a very subtle way, affirming their status. They are old enough, and have enough status, to make a joke at the boy's expense. He obviously knows that, and is obliged to accept it. He may even be flattered to be the butt of their joke – feeling somehow more important as a result. Vygotsky (1978) suggests younger children's interaction with older children is often a key element in their development. However, it is not always age that is the crucial factor, as is shown in the following observation.

Treasure hunt

Kitty Press – playworker

Josh (3 years) walks into the classroom and asks, 'Where's Rosie?' He smiles when he sees her and walks over to her. They bounce up and down, facing each other.

> Rosie (3 years) takes some books from the table and drops them on the floor. 'Let's go for a walk with books!' she says. Holding hands they walk around the classroom carrying the books. 'We are walking, we are walking,' they proclaim.
>
> 'Let's make a map of where we've been,' says Josh. They get paper and crayons and scribble a map. Then Josh rolls up his paper into a tube. 'Roll your paper,' he tells Rosie. 'Let's go looking for treasure.' Rosie can't roll her paper and asks me for help. I suggest that Josh helps her. 'Okay,' says Josh. They hold the 'telescopes' to their eyes and walk around the tables chanting, 'Treasure! Treasure!'
>
> Rosie says, 'I am Princess Rosie.' Josh says, 'I am a pirate.' Rosie collects a basket of beans (from the 'transferring exercise' equipment) and tips these on to the floor. She asks me to help her dig for treasure.
>
> At this point the teacher chastised Rosie for tipping the beans on the floor, and told Josh to go and do something more constructive.

The teacher's lack of respect for the rich nature of the children's play is shocking, but that sort of adult propensity to intervene inappropriately will be addressed in Chapter 9. For now, this observation raises many interesting questions. For example:

- What function did the 'bouncing' greeting serve?
- Why was walking with books such a fulfilling experience?
- Where did the maps/treasure/telescope/princess/pirate ideas come from?
- What made them link the concepts of maps, telescopes and treasure?
- Why did Rosie collect the beans and tip them on the floor?

Whatever the specific answers to these questions, this play sequence clearly has meaning for the two children, and it is arguable that this one small observation provides a wide-ranging insight into children's development during play. There are clear social, physical, intellectual and creative benefits for the children. There may even be elements of self-discovery and enhanced self-esteem. However, the interaction also raises a very fundamental point about the cognitive process involved when children are learning while playing.

Most teachers will be aware of Vygotsky's (1978) concept of the zone of proximal development – that is, the difference between what a child can achieve on their own and the level they might achieve with the assistance of an adult or more capable peer. Vygotsky greatly favoured this sort of assistance as a learning aid, and his theories have sometimes been used as a justification for a didactic approach to teaching. However, this observation illustrates a far greater truth, namely that the simple act of social play can also benefit children's learning. In this example, Rosie had no prior knowledge of telescopes, nor did Josh set out to educate her about them. Rosie was introduced to the concept only because she happened to be playing with a child whose older brother had been learning about telescopes at school. Thus, through unstructured (unscaffolded) play with another child, Rosie improved her understanding of telescopes. Indeed Vygotsky himself said:

Play also creates the zone of proximal development of the child. In play a child is always above his average age, above his daily behavior; in play it is as though he were a head taller than himself. As in the focus of a magnifying glass, play contains all developmental tendencies in a condensed form; in play it is as though the child were trying to jump above the level of his normal behavior.

(1978: 102)

Vygotsky was in part highlighting how inventive children can be when they are playing. In the following example the children have no boiling oil, but through the use of symbolic play (Piaget 1951) they easily overcome that minor obstacle. However, it is interesting that Gladwin suggests the children are just as fascinated with the physics of their creation as they are with the game itself. The creative learning aspect of the story is amply demonstrated by the fact that, a week later, the same physical actions are used to create rain, rather than boiling oil.

It's raining sand

Mark Gladwin – play researcher

Three boys have found a large tree branch that they call a rocket. They straddle it, one behind the other, and walk it up to the fort, where they prop it up in the doorway. Then they march it round the fort. One of the playworkers comes and takes it away from them. The boys go and find a slightly smaller plank of wood that they carry up to the fort and then use to barricade the door. The game turns into an elaborate 'Attackers vs Defenders' drama that involves transporting sand in containers from the sandpit. Sand is dropped by the defenders through gaps above the fort doorway, supposedly as a weapon against attackers – in lieu of boiling oil. Actually, just playing with the sand and watching it fall through the cracks seems to be the main point. The staff try to stop children carrying sand up to the fort; one child even gets banned from the playground for disobedience, but the game carries on despite staff discouragement. The game reappears in a new guise the following week. Buckets full of sand are fetched from the sandpit and poured through gaps above the fort gateway – 'making it rain'.

It would be easy to be critical of the playworkers in this story. Why did one of them feel the need to take the branch away from the children? Why are they not keen for the children to transport sand around the site? However, we are not given a complete context, so it is not possible to know the reasoning behind such actions. Setting that aside, it is significant that these efforts on the part of the staff appear to be wasted, since Gladwin reports that the children are creative enough to find a way of carrying on with their game.

Children's propensity to be creative can often take surprising forms, as with the following observation, wherein the children are entertaining themselves (and others) through detailed re-enactment of an observed experience. At the same time as they are having fun, they are also learning about the complexity of social interaction, as well as the potential of loose parts to represent real things. They are also learning more about the rules of the game of rummy and the associated forfeits.

Rummy

Author's observation

Colin Ward (1978) suggested children will play everywhere and with anything, which is clearly the case with these Roma children. However, their attitude to property may be even more anarchistic than Ward envisaged. Regardless of ownership, they wander from yard to yard in a fairly indiscriminate manner. That opens up all sorts of play opportunities that would not be available in cultures where the concept of private property is generally understood and accepted.

I witnessed an example of this on one of my last days in the village, when children acted out an elaborate role play in the front yard of the house next door. The Romanian version of rummy is played with a set of 'bones' (plastic tablets with card symbols on one face), and involves making similar combinations to poker (numerical runs, three of the same number, collections of the same suit, etc.). Each player has 14 bones, which they arrange on a wooden rack. The object is to collect sets of three or four bones until you have used all 14. Players take turns to pick up bones from the stack and throw away unwanted bones. I watched a group of men playing this game one evening, sitting around a table in the yard next door to my usual observation point. Each time someone lost he had a garland of leaves placed on his head. The more he lost, the more leaves were added to the garland. There was a lot of laughter, and a great amount of arguing and shouting involving participants and audience alike.

The next afternoon a group of children wandered into the same front yard, and positioned themselves around the same table and began to play a mock game of rummy. They role-played exactly what I had witnessed the day before. They used old roofing tiles as a rack for their non-existent 'bones'. They did a lot of shouting, and penalties were awarded, by making the 'losers' wear a garland of leaves (just like the adults). The 'game' of rummy was not in any way real, but was played for more than an hour. Even more amazing was the fact that they gathered an audience of young children who stood and watched the game for the last 30 minutes, joining in with the arguing and shouting.

This example is both charming and instructive. Obviously it provides an illustration of the children's imagination and creativity. It also demonstrates something quite fundamental about the nature of play, namely the value of freedom. The children were free not only to come and go as they pleased, but also to control what Hughes (2001) calls the intent and content of their play. Their role play could not have happened in a culture where 'an Englishman's home is his castle', where people who come through the garden gate uninvited are regarded as intruders, and where 'children should be seen and not heard'. The fact that the children felt free to occupy the same space that had been the scene of the original game, made the role play that much more real, both for them and their 'audience'. Thus, in some small way, we have an example of children learning that they are capable of controlling what Sutton-Smith (1972) calls 'their own little microcosm of the world'. The same is true of the following story, and of many of the stories in this book.

Street party food

Suzanna Law – play ranger

Thursday, 7 June 2012 – Jubilee Day street party

All the other children had run off to the only garden on the road with a slope, and were running around with apparently purposeless glee, enjoying the company of children they had never seen before. But one little girl was playing, in the middle of the road, with the boxes. I approached quietly and was immediately greeted with:

'This costs 10p.'

'Oh really? So how much is this?' (pointing next to where she pointed).

'Oh that's free.' She disappeared into the giant box-house with a lot of chatter to herself, and brought out a polystyrene tray of bits and pieces. Then she pointed at things and told me what they were, after which she started to poke, jab and move the contents of the tray around. Finally she put the tray into a big box. I squatted next to her.

'What are we waiting for?'

'It's in the oven.'

'How long does it need to be in for?'

'One minute, and then we have to fry it.' So we did – in the 'house'.

She took the tray out of the fryer, and picked up each item in turn to explain what each of them was. There were noodles, red chicken, sweets and burgers.

'We need more – I have one!'

So then she started making an extensive list of things – the best list of things I have ever seen. It included: 'noodulz, blooberiz, sdorberees, kookumbroz, plumerz, orinj, apul, peech . . .'.

She wrote her version of each word, and then looked up saying:

'That's a good one – what else?'

Each time, there was a little pause while she thought, and I waited.

'I have one!' she would say, and then she would put her entire concentration on spelling the next word, and the process would repeat.

One of the neighbours walked past at this point, looked over and silently laughed. I don't think he was laughing about the spelling, although he saw it. He was laughing at her seriousness, her absorption, and the intensity of the play – and the genius of the spelling. This was serious stuff.

The list continued for three sheets of A4. It was a very long list. I left her to write as I mingled with the adults briefly, but then there was a light tap at my side and there she was, presenting the tray to me.

'We need to give out the food – it's free!'

The little girl took me to almost every adult at the street party and asked them if they wanted a blueberry drink; or a noodle; or a sweet.

'It's free!' she cheerfully announced after each item was taken.

The magical part of this was, every adult said yes. Every person took something and pretended to eat it. Everyone played along with this little girl and allowed for her play to continue. They understood that it was important so they dropped their adult agendas for a minute and allowed the child to direct her own play. This was around 30 adults!

Eventually, she decided she needed more food and ran off to collect more bits and pieces from the boxes on the floor. Then she approached the larger group of little girls and they were talking. I don't think most of it made sense, but they were all so serious, and they were so involved with the moment. I think she was explaining about every item on the tray.

And then? One little girl in a spotty dress took a 'sweet' and pretended to eat it. Everyone smiled and then disbanded. If you had blinked you would have missed it.

After a while, the little girl appeared next to me again. 'I'll let you keep that one, it's a good one,' she said, handing over the blue list of things she had written.

Tucked away in this story we find two very interesting observations. First, Law says about the adults, 'everyone played along'. Given the right circumstances most adults can get into play mode. In this case it's a street party, and everyone knows you have fun at a street party, so the adults are already feeling playful. Thus, when confronted with a playing child they cannot help but play as well. Arguably, the human drive to play is so powerful that we cannot help ourselves. When we are invited into a child's play we find it hard to resist (and why would we want to!). Second, there is the magical moment when the actions of another child (in going along with the pretence) round off the game perfectly.

We cannot be certain, but it is very likely that the little girl was re-enacting her experiences prior to the street party. She had probably seen a grown-up doing a lot of cooking for this special event, which she then imitated. Perhaps the adult, at some point, made a list of some sort. Again the child copied that behaviour. Maybe she had been told at some time that the food was for sharing, and so she did just that. Does this mean that the child was practising adult roles in preparation for later life, as suggested by the theories of Groos (1898, 1901)? That is possible, but it is more likely that she was merely using her recent experience to provide an agenda for her play in the here and now.

This raises the issue of the extent to which our childhood play behaviours provide a stimulus for later skills and careers. Is this little girl going to grow up to be a cook or a chef? It is quite a common perception that the way we play as children has an impact on the way our adult life develops. That brings to mind the Jesuit maxim: 'Give me a child for the first seven years, and you may do what you like with him afterwards' (Lean 1902), and also Lenin's statement that if he had a child for eight years he would make him a Bolshevik for ever!

Certain toy manufacturers would have us believe that, if you buy a toy trumpet for a child, then s/he will grow up to be a musician. There is no research evidence to support this. It may or may not be true, and there is too much genetic and experiential diversity in our population to be absolutely certain. Nevertheless, it appears that childhood behaviour patterns do live on in some adults. Take the following example:

The bike racer

Ingrid Wilkinson – Play England development officer

This is just about how my son used to play. He used to spend a lot of time leaping off the sofa, and doing whatever risky challenging play he could do. I never stopped him, as long as it wasn't life threatening. He used to go to the speedway with his dad from a very young age. He had a little quad bike, and then a pedal bike, and he used to dress up with a little helmet on and the full gear. If we went out anywhere the helmet had to go on, and the boots had to go on, and the whole shebang. We lived like that for several years, and it just continued for a long time. He used to pedal his bike along, and then he'd crash his bike and just copy what he saw at the speedway. He's now to the point where he's the British number-two trials rider.

Another way in which children learn and develop by playing with the environment lies in something Hughes calls attention to in *Play Environments: A Question of Quality*. In Quality Indicator No. 14 he refers to the need for children to 'show a widening of ecological/non-human horizons' (1996: 53), and sets great store by them having the opportunity to interact with the animal kingdom. He is not just talking about keeping pets here, although that is to be encouraged. His enthusiasm for this sort of experience is rooted in his belief in the significance of Haeckel's (1901) theory of recapitulation, which suggests that children need to play through the behaviour patterns of their ancestors before they can feel truly comfortable in the modern world. Although this theory has largely been dismissed by those in the world of biology, it continues to have some credibility among cognitive development theorists.

Sometimes children's interaction with animals can descend into actions that most adults would regard as cruel. This poses a dilemma for playworkers. Killing a wasp or stamping on ants may go almost unnoticed, but how about pulling the wings off a crane fly? My ex-colleague Stephen Rennie often challenged students to discuss what they would do if they came upon a group of children cutting up worms. For most of us our instinct is to intervene, but don't we have an obligation to enable children to learn from their interaction with the environment? It is also worth considering that we may have done this sort of thing ourselves.

The following story is not so much about cruelty, as opportunity and curiosity, and maybe even hunger.

Skinning a rabbit

Louise Kennedy – woodland playschemes coordinator

It was October half-term and it had started as a usual playscheme day – that was until we were on our way to meet the children! It was quite a bright day, my colleague and I had set up camp in the woods. It is not every day that I take my dogs to work. However, this particular day I had the Labrador and two Jack Russell terriers. They love coming to the woods, as it means charging around with the children and clearing up stray bits of food!

It was time to wander down the track to greet the children and parents. We were close to the gate and could see a couple of children sitting on the fence. At that moment, it was so quick that I hardly saw it happen, a rabbit must have run across the track – or at least tried to. It ran into my terrier's mouth and that was the end of the rabbit, all very quick. It then dawned on me that the children and parents who were waiting had seen the whole thing. I glanced at my colleague as I wondered what to do with the dead rabbit – pretend it had not happened, or acknowledge it and deal with any consequences – that is, once I had managed to retrieve it from the dog's firm grip. We placed it on a log pile and wandered down to meet the children.

A few of the boys said they saw Roo catch the rabbit and that I had hidden it on the logs, so we had a quick conversation about it, said cheerio to the parents and headed for camp. The children wanted to look at the dead rabbit. There was some 'yuk it's gross', 'it smells', 'that poor rabbit' and 'wow look at its eyes'. They wanted to take it back to camp.

What occurred next was a real mix of emotions, some of the children were quite dismissive of the fact I was carrying a dead rabbit, while others were fascinated in looking at it, talking about it. Then a question I was not expecting – 'Can we skin it?'

Umm ... without wanting to alter the experience, I thought about it for a second and replied 'Yes, why not' but thinking 'Oh my life I have only done it once myself!' I went to hang the rabbit in a tree away from the dogs. On doing so and hanging it upside down it looked like the rabbit was weeing ... the children burst out laughing and there was lots of hilarity over the fact it was weeing on my tool bag, yet it was dead – quite a weird concept to get your head around!

By luck we had a book that explained and demonstrated how to skin a rabbit. A few of the children were not interested and went off building dens, while some came and got their hands stuck in – literally. Step by step we skinned and gutted the rabbit, as doing so one boy asked another question I was not expecting – 'Can we cook it?' At first the two boys approached 'taking the rabbit's jacket [skin] off' with fine pincer movements and quite gently. It was only after a while when they needed to use a bit more strength that they really got stuck in.

There was one boy who was 8 years old and autistic; his reactions to the experience were differing and seemed complex. He thought it was funny as it looked funny, he didn't like it when the rabbit's eyes were open. He got very cross with the dog, and said she was bad, horrible and a killer. He wanted to give the dead rabbit a hug before we skinned it to say goodbye, and was very sympathetic and empathetic towards the rabbit and stroked it very gently before carefully placing it back down. I was fascinated with the idea that all the children did not like skinning it while the rabbit's eyes were open, so after a while we did close them.

When we came to gut it, it started off fine and one boy said 'I don't know what my mum will say when I tell her what I have done.' This particular boy comes to the woods regularly and is quite a thoughtful, quiet boy. We were having problems getting all the guts out but the various parts were identified as they came out, such as 'err, that's the kidney', 'Wow, is that all the intestine?', 'I've found the heart.' There was another lad who was off den building who made the comment that he does this all the time with his dad at home when they go rabbiting, and we were told many stories of his various adventures. At this point we asked him to come and help, he said the best way to get all the guts out was to hang on to both ends of the rabbit and swing it fast and they will all fall out. Easy we thought – he did it and made sure we were not in the firing line, he took a warm-up, grabbed the rabbit and swung it fast . . . the guts flew through the air landing on branches of trees and bushes. Again there was a roar and outburst of laughter, giggles and yuck remarks! Obviously the dogs were lying in wait and cleaned it all up . . . another yuck!

The only bit that was left of the insides was the rabbits 'pooh trail', as the boys called it. One particular boy found this amazing; he said that the rabbit pellets looked the same inside as they do when you see them on the grass, the same colour and shape. He then seemed to be amused by flicking the individual pellets at the other children and shouting very loudly about what he had found, getting everyone to come and have a look.

It was now time to get the meat off the carcass and prepare to cook. The children who did the majority of the skinning and gutting wanted to help prep the veg, and a few others joined in too, chopping the onions, garlic and butternut squash that by chance I had brought in case anyone wanted to make pumpkin soup. I did not think we would be making our own *rabbit stew* instead!

Clearly the children were able to learn a lot from this experience. Nevertheless, given the way social mores have changed in recent times, I felt obliged to ask this contributor what sort of reaction she received from the children's parents. Her response was both instructive in terms of the playwork experience, and surprising in terms of the parents:

For me, it was a totally amazing play experience that highlighted why I do what I do. Not because of the dead rabbit, but it was a totally unexpected and unplanned situation that was responded to in a spontaneous way, it felt like it all just happened and was quite easy. The children were totally in control of their level of engagement in the process, some of which was horrible and smelly. I was pleased that on a moral note the rabbit was not wasted; the dog had killed it, which is something that happens, and we used that situation to our advantage. Not all the children took part in the actual skinning, but they all interacted at some level, and everyone tasted the *rabbit stew* and were pleasantly surprised how good it tasted, with many coming back for more!

I have reflected on this particular experience a lot since it happened and I am still amazed, none of the children appeared to be particularly phased by the event. At the end of the day when we were going back to meet the parents, some of the children wanted to take the skin home, but we have kept it drying. The children did mention to their parents what had happened; I must admit that although I was comfortable with the play experience as it occurred I was, however, a little apprehensive as to how the parents would react. All seemed fine and happy at the time.

A week later I received an email from the boy's mum who made the comment about not knowing what his mum would say. My heart sank on opening the message wondering which way it would go. She was writing to thank me for allowing such an amazing experience for her son. He had not stopped talking about it for days. She had received a blow-by-blow account of the skinning/gutting/cooking/eating process, and a really detailed account of the rabbit's insides. She works in health nutrition and apparently they had an in-depth conversation about the comparison of rabbit's insides to a human – she called it a 'real biology lesson in action'!

Perhaps the world has not become as litigious as we assume. Unfortunately, I don't think that's true. Gill (2007) says children are a declining species in the great outdoors. He says if these were birds we were talking about, we would be forming a committee to protect them. We live in a rapidly changing world; a world where the needs of the motorist dominate our outdoor environments, and where children are 'protected' at every turn. No longer playing out in the street, they are taught to be fearful of any stranger (especially males) and they are not known by the local community, nor do they have a mental map of their neighbourhood. Of course the irony of all this is that children are more at risk from dangers inside the home and family.

In light of all this, it is interesting to reflect on the following account from a first-year student on the BA (Hons) Playwork degree at Leeds Beckett University. The students were taken out of the university on a field trip and introduced to a range of popular play activities, after which they were invited to record their thoughts. Here is one such reflective account.

Reflective account

Mahmuda Khatun – playworker

The farm was a new experience for me. I have never helped make a fire before. I really enjoyed that as I've never even seen a fire lit before, let alone helped to light one. I now understand the buzz the children get and why it is so popular. As a child I was not allowed near fire. I suppose the risks weighed up by my parents outweighed the benefits. Now from first-hand experience I see that allowing children to learn from their own experience can only benefit their understanding of the world around them. Seeing the fire flame up, feeling the heat, smelling the fire helps the child learn about the dangers as well as the benefits of fire.

At the farm we were set another task of den building. Den building, along with starting a fire, helps children gain people skills and problem-solving skills, working in a group, taking the best points of everyone's input. Working together in the natural surroundings allows you to engage in play and interaction with natural objects, rather than ones that you should keep neat and clean. It allows you to become adventurous in your environment. The team I was in didn't win, even though I did think the den made by our group deserved the title of best den.

The group returned to the city, where we were shown three settings where children could come and play in the busy city centre. In contrast to the experience on the farm these places showed how children and young people are greatly let down by the adult perception of how the city should be seen. The settings showed how children were being failed and insulted at the same time. The few provisions for the children in the city centre were very basic and stood out for all the wrong reasons.

Overall the day was an eye-opener to all the beneficial aspects of nature and nature's tools, and how children could risk-assess for themselves, and do the same activities as adults without getting hurt. The day also showed how children are being let down in a way that has become accepted by society.

The outdoor environment offers rich possibilities for exploration and experimentation, but in the past 30 years our children have become less and less likely to become fully engaged with it. We don't yet know the consequences of this, but it is hard to believe they will be anything other than damaging.

6

Creativity and problem solving

When playing, without adult supervision, children often choose creative activities. Spencer (1873) felt this sort of artistic, aesthetic play was the unconscious product of inborn instincts. Indeed, Winnicott (1971) suggests that play is the only setting where humans are free to be creative. A distinction between two types of creative play was drawn by Hutt *et al.* (1989): epistemic (exploratory) and ludic (imaginative) play, which leads us to the structure of the human brain. Weininger and Fitzgerald (1988) suggest that symbolic play is the mechanism that enables the transfer of information from one side of the brain to the other. Symbolic play is a creative process that integrates familiar objects and behaviours into unfamiliar settings. When children begin make-believe play and use objects to represent other things, meaning gradually becomes separated from reality, and the capacity for abstract thought starts to develop.

Play often involves the use of actions to represent meaning – something Donald (2002) calls 'mimesis' – but that meaning sometimes contains ambiguity, which led Bateson (1955) to describe play as a 'paradox'. Play texts become increasingly complex with age (Fein 1981), as play offers opportunities to explore alternative solutions and combinations of behaviour. This is explored to great effect in Singer and Singer's beautiful text *The House of Make Believe* (1990). Such exploration of ideas appears to lead to the development of creative problem solving (Bruner 1972). In fact, Sylva suggests, 'What is acquired through play is not specific information but a general [mind]set towards solving problems that includes both abstraction and combinatorial flexibility' (1977: 60).

Hughes (2012) argues that a child's interaction with the environment is fundamental to their future development, and that this needs to take place at a very basic elemental level. For Hughes, and many others in the playwork world, a healthy play environment contains lots of opportunities for children to dig holes, light fires, interact with animals, etc. The following observation occurred during a study of the play behaviours of Roma children in a Transylvanian village (Brown 2012).

Turkey racing

Author's observation

In the village, opportunities to interact with the environment exist in abundance, and the children take full advantage. These children play with anything and everything. For example, there is a woman in the village who keeps ducks, geese, turkeys, cows, etc. The turkeys in particular roam around the top end of the village unhindered, and the children clearly regard them as 'fair game'. On this occasion two boys created a race track and invented turkey racing. The boys spent nearly an hour delineating their race track with bits of wood, string and rocks. They then disappeared around the back of the houses and returned carrying one turkey each. The turkeys were held at the start line until one of the two boys gave the signal to start. The children then 'encouraged' their turkeys to run along the track, sometimes merely by standing behind them clapping, some-times by tapping them with a stick. Each race took about 10 minutes, because the turkeys were not especially cooperative. The boys tried out several turkeys with varying degrees of success. Later the same day, they tried a similar game with ducks, only to find the ducks were even less enthusiastic than the turkeys.

The summary of the benefits of turkey racing shown in Table 6.1 is not entirely tongue in cheek.

It is possible to see all these elements and more in this short example, and that is true of most instances of children's play. Although we tend to trivialize play with phrases like 'it's child's play', in fact play is complex, and the benefits are multi-faceted.

Table 6.1 Some of the benefits of turkey racing

Nature of the experience:	Leading to:
interaction with the environment	deeper understanding of specific materials and the potential that they offer
social interaction	reinforcing of friendships and internalizing the value of cooperation
interaction with other species	greater understanding of the characteristics of specific species
physical activity	health, fitness and the development of motor skills
cognitive challenge	stimulation of the imagination and creativity problem-solving skills
being in control	self-discovery and a recognition that it is possible to influence the world around you

Simon Nicholson's *Theory of Loose Parts* holds that

> In any environment both the degree of inventiveness and creativity and the possibility of discovery are directly proportional to the number and kinds of variables in it.
>
> (Nicholson 1971: 30)

In this village the 'number and kind of variables' is enormous in one way, and minuscule in another. On the one hand the children seem to regard anything left lying around as something that may be played with. On the other hand they have no personal possessions such as toys or board games. The artefacts they play with are almost entirely recycled scrap. This may be slightly dangerous at times, because of the splinters and sharp edges. Clearly, rooting around in a skip for your next plaything carries with it health and safety risks. However, it also means the children have all manner of unusual opportunities to combine materials that would not be available to their counterparts in modern housing estates. Sylva says 'the essence of play lies in … combinatorial flexibility' (1977: 60), which Bruner (2006) suggests is the initial building block for human creativity. He says:

> Play and playfulness free us from the narrowing immediacy of pressing demands, enabling us to better explore the combinatorial possibilities that are opened to us by our cognitive powers.
>
> (2006: 5)

Here is another example.

Skittles

Keith Ramtahal – inspector for early years

During a half-term break, while employed as a teacher in Cairo, I visited a recycling site run by the Zabbeleen, a group of mainly Coptic Christians who collect Cairo's rubbish and recycle almost everything thrown out by the residents of Cairo and old and new businesses that are sprawling up throughout the city and beyond. The Zabbeleen receive no income for collecting the refuse and have a monthly household income of 11.5 US dollars per month, which comes from recycling the refuse they collect daily.

I suddenly heard a lot of cheering, screaming and slapping of hands. I looked across the rows of overflowing skips that held the refuse waste, as well as doubling up as beds for the night for some of the families from the Zabbeleen community. At the end of the row of skips, on a tiny patch of waste land, I saw a group of Zabbeleen boys and girls playing a version of skittles using old Baraka water bottles filled with a minuscule amount of grit at the bottom and using greasy tin foil rolled into a ball shape as a ball. Every time someone knocked over all five bottles the children whooped, cheered gave high-fives, and jumped and skipped around.

No factory-made skittles kit was needed, nor a referee with a whistle, clip-board and pen. No cautions were given or players reprimanded for having loose shoelaces. They were just having fun!

Colin Ward (1978: 204) said 'children play anywhere and everywhere'; also that they regard anything as a potential plaything. During the observation period associated with my research in the Transylvanian Roma village, I witnessed numerous examples of that, and of children making use of loose parts in their play. These examples were originally highlighted in an article for the *International Journal of Play* (Brown 2012).

- An old bicycle tyre was bowled along like a hoop, and subsequently used as a hula-hoop. Eventually it was discarded, and later claimed by two children who twisted it into a figure of eight around themselves. Then they hopped down a hill, eventually tumbling into a heap at the bottom. Despite the cuts and bruises they repeated this at least a dozen times.
- A piece of corrugated-iron roofing was used as a channel to get water from one bucket to another, and then back again (for no obvious reason – maybe just as a sort of practice play).
- An upturned dish doubled as a hat.
- Fertilizer sacks helped create a competition – not by hopping along in the sack like a traditional sack race, but with the sack covering the head while negotiating an obstacle course. Later the sacks were used to collect nettles, presumably for soup.
- A long length of bright-blue string was used to delineate the playing area, and also the net, for a game of football-tennis.
- Grass was tied up as a sheaf, with one end whipped tightly. When tossed into the air the whipped end naturally made the whole thing fall to earth like an arrow. This was also used as the touch mechanism in a game of chase – the sheaf being thrown by the chaser.
- A large piece of polystyrene foam was used as a goal post, but blew away when the wind rose. It was also used to model a face.
- The lid from a tin of paint substituted quite well for a frisbee in a game of frisbee football.
- A plastic bottle with a string tied around the neck made a musical noise (sort of) when swung round. Alternatively, the string was held in one hand, while the bottle was kicked away from the player. On another occasion the string was tied fairly tightly round a telegraph pole. Flat nails were hammered in a circle around the pole to stop the string from slipping down. The bottle was then used like a 'swing ball', but played with feet, rather than a racquet. This didn't work very well, but certainly illustrated the creativity of the players.

The key to this is flexibility, a theme that permeates the whole of this book, and that will be explored in some depth in the concluding chapter. The following story reinforces the point, while at the same time reflecting Hart's statement that 'traditional playgrounds with fixed equipment are most interesting to children when they are being built or dismantled' (Hart 1992: 19).

The construction site

Tobias Voss – youth worker

When I was about 3 or 4 we moved to a new house, and the area was basically a construction site. That continued for about three years. I think that was the best of times. We didn't have playgrounds or anything. We just had the construction site and a big mud hill. We made our own campfires out of the wood left by the construction workers. The mud hill was quite close to our house, and that was where we built our castle towers from the timber and things 'left over' on the construction site. So, we had our own construction site, and once the builders had finished all the gardens, they said they would build us a playground, and the people from the City Council came and asked us what sort of playground we wanted. We told them all kinds of things, but after the playground was finished we didn't really play on it. We just wanted to have our construction site back.

Of course, children in modern urban environments (and contrary to popular belief even in some modern rural environments) are generally starved of the opportunity to interact with their environment in this way. As we have already seen in Chapters 4 and 5, the opportunity for children to play outside and explore the world (natural and industrial) is disappearing fast. Playwork is in part a response to this. Hughes (2012: 38) suggests playwork may be seen as a compensatory discipline, meaning that:

> Playworkers could learn to identify any perceived deficits in children's experience of play types, for example, and make compensatory responses for them, using environmental modification.

The role of the playworker, as defined by Playwork Principle 5 (PPSG 2005) is 'to support all children and young people in the creation of a space in which they can play'. Clearly, in any playwork setting the playworkers have a responsibility to provide materials that offer children opportunities to be creative. Here is an example:

The large black tube

Aled Evans – play development worker

At one of our play sessions we were given a large black tube, and several large cardboard tubes. On the first day we waited to see what would happen. At first the children either climbed inside the large tube or rolled it around. The smaller cardboard tubes were generally tossed around. After a couple of days one of the children rolled the large tube to the top of a hump and rolled down inside it. This gradually developed into a string of games, including who could roll the furthest. They also played 'skittles', with two teams taking it in turns to go inside, roll down the hump and knock over the cardboard skittles. This is still the most used, most inexpensive bit of kit we have.

It seems the playworkers in this story did not know what to expect when they introduced the tubes into their play sessions. However, they knew intuitively (or perhaps from their training and/or experience) that the tubes would be popular and would stimulate creative thinking on the part of the children. This is a good example of the non-directive nature of playwork in practice – provide the environment and the materials, and then stand back. Here is another example – this time more complex:

Box town

Janice Smith – playwork student

The children arrive in the playwork setting and as normal are invited to choose what they would like to play with. In the store room there is a variety of different-sized cardboard boxes and all kinds of loose materials, such as wood, blankets, dressing-up clothes, etc. Most of the children ignore these materials and choose equipment they have played with previously. Two younger children spot the materials and ask the playworker whether they can have those. Once they have the materials they start a discussion on what they might do with the boxes. They go through the usual suggestions like making a boat or creating a theatre for a puppet show. The younger of the two children says, 'I know, let's play at being tramps in the streets.' He explains to the other child that he has been shopping in the town centre with his mum and saw two tramps living in a cardboard box.

The two children set about arranging the cardboard boxes in different ways. One of them says, 'Let's make a window so the tramps can see outside.' They set about making a window, but find it really hard to cut through the card with the scissors they have available. They ask a playworker if they can have a sharp knife to cut their window. The playworker asks whether the children have used a penknife before, and if so in what way. The eldest child explains that he often helps his granddad in his shed, and is allowed to use a knife. The playworker suggests they draw their window and then come back and get the knife. As they do this, the playworker watches from a discreet distance while the older child uses the penknife to cut out the window.

At this point a couple more children, who have been standing by watching, ask to play. The two children have a discussion and agree that the newcomers can join in, but cannot share their boxes, as they are going to be tramps who are about to go to sleep. As a group, the children set about making more dens and introduce some material they have found to put over the dens to keep them warm.

Then another playworker joins the group and asks the children what they are making. The younger child explains what they are doing but says the playworker cannot play as she has a funny hand and cannot be allowed in their dens. The playworker explains how upset she is by this comment and that she was born with a funny hand, but can still do lots of things with her other hand. After much discussion the children say she can join in, but to ask if she needs help.

Once the dens have been made the children put on some of the dressing-up clothes, as they think this makes them look poor. Then they lay in their dens with blankets on. As the other children come near, they start begging for money, which the other children find very funny.

If we study this brief story closely we are immediately able to identify a number of classic play and child development theories. For example: play as paradox (Bateson 1955); 'scaffolding' (Bruner 1978); the 'zone of proximal development' (Vygotsky 1978); 'looking on, joining in, and cooperative' forms of social play (Parten 1933); the Portchmouth Principle (Brown 2008). My focus here is upon the story as an example of the theory of loose parts in practice. However, as Taylor (2008) reminds us, the theory is not just about our use of materials, but also refers to:

- physical phenomena such as magnetism and gravity
- media such as gases and fluids
- sounds, music and motion
- chemical interactions
- cooking and fire
- other people and animals
- plants
- words, concepts and ideas.

The children in the following story are not only playing with the loose parts of the old furniture to create a pretend living room, but also with the loose parts of relationships to create their own make-believe stories.

Moving furniture

Ben Tawil – playworker

As the children arrived for the evening session they took immediate interest in the furniture. A group of about seven children, aged 8 to 12, both boys and girls, started to sift through it. At first their search seemed indiscriminate, almost chaotic, with very little communication between them . . . the children seemed to have concurrent ideas that stemmed from one person's initial placing down of a piece of furniture. Two leaders emerged – the eldest girl of about 12, and one of the younger boys of about 8. They seemed to be taking on the role of interior designers – telling the rest of the group where to position the furniture. These instructions were followed to the letter with great seriousness. Together they created a home environment . . .

Straight away a boy of about 11 sat down at the bureau and exclaimed, 'Can you keep the noise down? I'm trying to write a letter to the council', and without question or hesitation the oldest girl (until this point the chief interior designer) addressed the other children in a sharp authoritarian voice, 'Your dad's told you to keep the noise down. Now go and play quietly.' Immediately the rest of the group took on roles as brothers and sisters, grandparents, daughter and visiting boyfriend . . .

This play . . . continued for <u>two weeks</u> – every evening and for full eight-hour days at the weekend. Different groups of children used the materials and altered the environment and the narrative to suit their needs . . . Eventually the children's interest waned: perhaps they had played out their need for this type of play for the time being, they had certainly worn out the already dilapidated furniture. The play began to morph once more as the children found uses for panels from the furniture in construction play, and the remnants were put to good use fuelling our nightly campfire.

At its most obvious level these children are engaged in socio-dramatic play, which at its simplest is described as role play with more than one person participating (Smith 2010). In socio-dramatic play children engage in a number of play types all at the same time. Indeed Smilansky and Shefatya (1990: 27) say socio-dramatic play 'involves not only representation and pretence, but also reality, organizational skills, reasoning and argumentation, social skills, etc.' It is suggested by Frost, Wortham and Reifel (2011) that socio-dramatic play is the vehicle whereby young children use all of their developmental attributes.

It may seem a statement of the obvious to say that Nicholson's (1971) Theory of Loose Parts applies to all children, but in my experience there is a tendency in UK society to assume that disabled children will not be able to manage the apparent chaos of an adventure playground. Ward (1961) described adventure playgrounds as a parable of anarchy, and Battram suggests that good quality playwork takes place on 'the edge of chaos: where order makes the transition to complexity' (2008: 90). Both these statements carry the ring of truth, but that is just part of the story. My own view is that playwork should be characterized by 'fun, freedom and flexibility' (see Chapter 1), and there is no reason to think the vast majority of disabled children cannot enjoy the experience in the same way as any child. After all, Pellis and Pellis (2009) have shown that play is a basic human drive, so it stands to reason that most disabled children will have that drive as well.

Boxing training

Keith Ramtahal – inspector for early years

When I was an Early Years Centre Senior Manager in Hackney, East London, I worked one-on-one with a Turkish boy aged 4 who had been recently diagnosed with Asperger's syndrome, which is sometimes likened to high-functioning autism. This boy lived in a high-rise tower block with only a balcony to play on. He had no direct access to open areas, and was often found sitting on the window ledge of his open bedroom window so that he could see what was going on in the world 100 feet below him.

He was a fascinating child to observe as he had underdeveloped gross motor skills, repeated the same phrases to himself incessantly, never interacted with any of the other staff or children at the centre and delighted in walking around the centre in his underwear. His passion was playing outdoors with a wooden train set and reading books about 'transport' to himself over and over again. At the centre he was continually outside as he loved it.

One day we had a large delivery and the boy was telling the boxes not to go away as he needed them. 'Be good and stay here for me,' he told them. We had to decant the boxes' contents early the next morning and we placed the six large boxes outside in the garden area for the boy, when he arrived at 9.00 a.m. Immediately on arriving, he dashed to the boxes and kissed them all individually and said to them, 'good boxes, stay here and I'll tell you story about Thomas the Tank Engine'. He proceeded to read the boxes the tale in the book and asked the boxes if they liked the story. By his reactions, apparently they did.

He disappeared inside the main building and returned with pots of paint and numeral stencils. After hand-painting the boxes, and attempting to stick the numeral stencils on the side of each box with white paint, he returned indoors and emerged with paper, felt tips, scissors and a glue stick. He then made tickets and drew '5p' on each one. Next he went back inside and came out wearing a cap, and holding a large rod of balsa wood, to which he attached a piece of paper saying: 'WAIT HERE'.

By now he had attracted a large crowd of fascinated 3–5 year olds and staff who wondered what the paint-splattered boy in a hat, who was clapping his hands and laughing to himself, was going to do next. He roughly pushed everyone watching into a line behind the 'WAIT HERE' sign, and shouted while looking up at the sky, 'you need to buy a ticket to go on Thomas'. Everyone watching bought a ticket with an imaginary five-penny piece, and then the first five passengers were allowed on the still very wet Thomas the Tank Engine.

He then climbed into the first carriage and shouted, 'No hand out of window please and no eating the food.' The remaining watchful passengers waiting to get on next, all shouted, 'Woo, Woo!', and started waving goodbye. Then they broke into the sound of a chugging steam train and performed matching hand and arm motions. The driver's face lit up. He started laughing to himself and shouted, 'Good Thomas, Lovely Thomas!' All the passengers loved it too, as did Thomas.

Question: 'When is an ordinary box not just a box?'

Answer: 'When a very special child gets his magical hands on it.'

It is often suggested that autistic children cannot play, because the 'triad of impairments'[1] (Wing 2003) that typifies the condition is actually a combination of essential play skills. However, that constitutes a misunderstanding of the condition. The Autism Treatment Center of America suggests that autistic children have the potential for these skills to develop through play of a highly focused nature. They theorize that autistic children want to communicate, but their mechanisms for doing so are not understood by the non-autistic world. They recommend 'joining' the child in their world. This concept will be explored in Chapter 8, and there are examples of it being used in practice in Chapter 11 (Days 17, 18 and 29).

The following story provides more evidence of the impact of introducing loose parts into the play environment, and in particular cardboard boxes, but it also offers an insight into the value that children place on their creations.

Cardboard City

Mick Conway – Play England development officer

In Hackney during the 1980s and 1990s a local furniture import/export firm gave us a free supply of thousands of large boxes to run a project we called Cardboard City – most children instantly got the concept that you could make anything in a city out of cardboard.

Carton-sealing tape machines made it easy for even little children to tape large boxes up. Giant markers encouraged them to draw the shapes of doors and windows etc. at the right scale before cutting them – with smaller pens they tended to draw tiny doors the size of a cat flap (though many of the cardboard house doors featured a cat flap and indeed cardboard cats). We discovered that blunt-edged serrated letter openers were brilliant cutting tools that children could use safely.

We learned not to chuck out hundreds of boxes in one go – a more controlled supply created an interesting supply-and-demand dynamic, which produced an example of what we eventually came to know as the edge of chaos.

The dynamic swayed between competition and cooperation, between negotiation and fights over resources, between helping to make and deliberately wrecking other children's makings. It also meant that left-over bits were used in much more interesting and creative ways, like making the cats for the cat flaps.

---

[1] Impairments to creative imagination, social interaction skills and communication skills.

Over the years Cardboard City became a sort of culture, with old hands making a beeline for the boxes and tools, with new children circling round the edge and gradually being drawn in.

We saw some amazing things, in the early days: the 10-metre tunnel that older boys made and successfully charged 1p a head to get into at a Playday on a hot day in August – until it was stuffed with kids who refused to come out the other end and we had to cut holes so they could breathe; the bulldozer that a girl made as 'a present for my dad cos he's lost his job driving it'; the neighbourly terraced streets of houses that groups of girls cooperatively created in contrast to the more isolated camps that typically one or two boys tended to make. The girls spent a lot more time inhabiting and decorating their constructions, while the boys tended to make and break them quickly, and sometimes try to raid and destroy what the girls had made.

Most constructions only lasted a day, but others on adventure playgrounds lasted weeks or more and children sometimes took them home. I was told by parents that a boy had set his cardboard house up in the front room by the telly and refused to sleep anywhere else for weeks. A girl had set hers up at the top of her bed, put her pillow in it and carefully positioned her bedside light on the windowsill to shine through her cardboard cut-out window so she could read her books. Another boy put his cardboard tepee out on the balcony of his block of flats and insisted on eating and sleeping in it all summer.

This story contains so many lessons about children's play:
- with very basic materials you can make a whole city
- children can be both cooperative and competitive, constructive and destructive
- some children will use play to put one over on their friends
- children will use their play artefacts to confirm their feelings for loved ones
- some children are especially inventive in their ingenuity
- for some children the finished product is important
- children often form strong attachments to their own creations.

These last two observations are interesting because the children clearly place a high value on their creation, but it is often said that play is more about process than product (Bruner 1972). As a result Hughes (1996) suggests a good-quality playwork setting will be characterized by an absence of regular organized, goal orientated or competitive activities. Perhaps the key word here is 'regular'. If we are really to serve all the different tastes of the children with whom we work, then we should sometimes be offering opportunities for goal-orientated and competitive activity. After all, children who like that sort of thing are just as likely to be in need of the compensatory potential of playwork as any other child. However, we ought not to be doing that to the detriment of other activities.

In an additional communication Conway observed:

What the children made was precious to them at the time of making and for some of them over much longer times, for reasons we can never really know. But the children who insisted on keeping and bringing their constructions home were telling us something about what was important to them. The playworkers in play-grounds that left their constructions in place and respected them by doing so gave the children the message that anything was possible and that their play was important.

This last observation supports Hughes (1996), who suggests playworkers should only clear up children's creations to conserve materials and to satisfy the requirements of health and safety. This is all about showing respect for the children with whom you are working. By protecting their creations the playworker is sending out a message to everyone that these children are important. That is not just about the playworker's role as children's advocate, it is also about helping to build the child's self-esteem.

One of the most significant elements in creativity is the flexibility of the creator. It is worth noting that children's creativity doesn't only come from their interaction with the environment. When Tim Gill shared the following story with me, he said that what interested him was how, in such an impoverished environment, the children intuitively sensed that the only way to make things fun was to play with the rules themselves.

Swimming pool tag

Tim Gill – writer, independent researcher and consultant

I was waiting for my daughter to come out of a local swimming pool changing room. A boy and a girl (brother and sister, I would say), aged around 8 and 9, started playing hide-and-seek in the swimming pool reception area, while they were waiting to meet up with the rest of their family.

The reception area was not a large room – perhaps 7 metres long by 5 metres wide. There were precisely four viable hiding places: behind two display stands and a waste bin, and to the side of a vending machine (and the waste bin was so small that it did not properly obscure either child).

The first sessions or two were played by the book: the seeker closed her eyes and counted to 20, and then did a proper search for the hider. But, unsurprisingly, sessions did not last very long, so the game quickly evolved. First the counting got quicker, then the eyes weren't closed, and finally the seeker simply followed the hider around with no counting. This then evolved in turn into a chase game, with a large weighing machine designated as 'homey'. The transformation of the rules happened without protest, in fact with barely any discussion at all.

7

Emotional equilibrium: the therapeutic value of play

> The opposite of play – if redefined in terms which stress its reinforcing optimism and excitement – is not work, it is depression. Players come out of their ludic paradoxes . . . with renewed belief in the worthwhileness of merely living.
>
> (Sutton-Smith 1999: 254)

Psychoanalysts see play as supporting the child's emotional growth. Freud (1900) identified three reasons why children play:

1   reconciliation – coming to terms with traumatic events
2   gratification – satisfying libidinous desires
3   aspiration – enabling the achievement of wish fulfilment.

All this is done by altering the circumstances in play to how we might wish them to be in real life. When children 'play out' painful experiences in their fantasy play they come to terms with their own feelings, and those of other people. As a result they learn to manage their feelings more effectively (Dwivedi 1993). If play is inhibited, Sturrock and Else (1998) suggest an individual is likely to become neurotic. This is confirmed in the animal studies of Suomi and Harlow, who found that 'no play makes for a very socially disturbed monkey' (1971: 492). It is further confirmed in the study of abused and abandoned children in Romania, by Sophie Webb's description of the children at the beginning of the study:

> When I observed the children in the playroom, they were unaware of each other, fixed on their own activities – barely communicating. Some just sat and seemed bewildered and vacant.
>
> (Brown and Webb 2005: 144)

Some psychoanalysts suggest play provides 'a means of gaining access to the unconscious modes of thought' (Klein 1955). In some instances, this may facilitate diagnosis of their psychological problems. Some play therapists, the most prominent being Axline (1969), believe the process to be even more fundamental – such a natural thing that children who are given unrestricted opportunity to play in a richly equipped play room (with a non-threatening adult) are capable of solving their own emotional problems. Axline was envisaging this form of therapeutic healing in relation to individual children. The Romanian research study mentioned previously provides evidence of a slightly different therapeutic form, namely the healing power of the group play process (Brown and Webb 2005). All of these concepts will be addressed later in this chapter.

The National Scientific Council on the Developing Child (2005) has identified three forms of stress: positive, tolerable and toxic. Positive stress is essentially beneficial. This is where the child may be up against a deadline, or taking part in a competition, or simply engaged in play-fighting. In all such cases there will be a brief exhilarating release of adrenalin, lots of excitement, and in general a positive outcome. For most children the process is more important than the product when they are playing, and so they will not be greatly disturbed by losing a competition.

Tolerable stress occurs where the child experiences acute moments of anxiety or distress, but the event takes place within a supportive atmosphere. An obvious example would be a death in a child's family and the subsequent grieving process. The child is likely to be deeply disturbed and upset in the short term, but in the long run will probably manage the stress effectively as a result of the strong emotional support of family and friends. If that support is absent the child may seek help elsewhere, as in the next story.

Toxic stress occurs where a child has no control over his or her own destiny. The irony of our school system is that teachers are far more likely to intervene in the case of positive stress than in the case of toxic stress. In fact they may well be the cause of toxic stress, because most children feel entirely powerless in school. This is relevant to children's play, because teachers are very likely to intervene where they see normal boisterous play behaviour, which is actually doing no one any harm, and as we shall see in Chapter 8 may well be doing the players a lot of good. Sadly playfulness is too often seen as a negative by teachers, who are at best over-protective and at worst excessively focused on keeping order. In truth, children's apparently dangerous activity is often not dangerous at all, just mildly risky. A lot of the pushing and shoving that children do is highly choreographed, and carries hardly any risk at all. It actually primes our stress response systems, and makes us better able to cope when the risks are genuine.

Charlie's mum

Sophie Webb – behaviour specialist

6 August – Charlie's mother died two days ago. Today was his birthday. He is 3 years old.

Charlie has always enjoyed pushing things and transporting objects. He'll push other children's wheelchairs and buggies if he can. Today he decided to use his own buggy – but this was different. He wanted to push a baby doll around in it. We chose a doll together and Charlie even wanted to dress her appropriately for the hot weather.

I asked Charlie what his baby was called. He replied 'mum'.

At this point I realized that this meant more to him than a normal 'home corner' activity. This was his way of attaching an object to his loss. That afternoon the doll called 'mum' went out with us to the park and had to sit on his lap in the taxi. When we came back he needed the toilet (a big thing for him at the moment as we're potty training), but he wouldn't do anything until 'mum' was watching him. He sat the doll on the bath opposite him.

I then suggested we give the doll a bath. I did this because I wanted to give Charlie the opportunity to use the doll as a symbol for his mum if he wanted to, or he could simply play at dressing and bathing dollies. Charlie was really pleased with this idea and helped to run the bath. 'Lots of soap,' he told me, and dunked the doll in the water. He also wanted to wash her hair. While doing this Charlie was calm, thoughtful and gentle.

This was an activity that I hadn't played with Charlie before and he really enjoyed caring for the doll, all the while calling her 'mum'. This day has highlighted a number of vital messages to me, the most obvious being he still needs his mum around.

I learned the next day that, about an hour after I left, Charlie displayed extremely aggressive behaviour and was very difficult to manage. This little boy is still grieving and we need to find structured and unstructured ways of helping him. He is trying to speak to us through his play and I am concerned that there is no continuity in the way we are helping him.

This is an example of a child trying to use his play to come to terms with the traumatic event in his life (the loss of his mother). His use of the doll as a replacement for his mother is an example of symbolic therapeutic representation. The following stories also contain examples of symbolic therapeutic representation, but rather different forms – one is very personal, the other is an observation by an experienced playworker.

A dolly called boy

Ben Greenaway – father

When my partner was pregnant with our second child our eldest daughter was very keen to have a little brother. When our baby was born she was a girl. From that moment on her dolly who was previously called 'dolly' became 'boy'. Two and a half years later her doll is still called 'boy'. It has been breast-fed, potty-trained, and spent most of Ella's first year in school with her.

Thus, as Bettleheim says:

Play permits the child to resolve in symbolic form unsolved problems of the past and to cope directly or symbolically with present concerns. It is also his most significant tool for preparing himself for the future and its tasks.

(1987: 170)

The following story is considerably more dramatic, but nonetheless involves a form of symbolic therapeutic representation. As Penny Wilson says, the child in this story, 'doesn't know the signs for the feelings he has ... so he paints it all over his body'.

The painted boy

Penny Wilson – community play development worker

He's profoundly deaf and a fluent signer. He has been removed from the family home without signed counselling or explanation.

He knows that the playground is a safe place to explore his feelings but our sign-language skills are basic.

This visit feels significant.

He stands trembling in the cold and pours a bucket of dry powder paint over his head, then goes back for another colour to take outside and tip again.

We watch as layer after layer of colour covers him.

He stands alone knowing he is observed.

He trusts that he will not be interrupted by playworkers.

He is matted with layers of colour, pure and mixed. He has shown himself to be a mess. Layered in confusion; not knowing how to communicate this to himself, let alone anyone else. He doesn't know the signs for the feelings he has, as hearing kids do not have the words for these concepts.

So he paints it all over his body.

When he is ready we shower, clothe and comfort him as he needs.

For children, trauma comes in many shapes and forms. Sometimes it is deeply personal, as in the previous three stories. Sometimes it results from a shared catastrophe, as in the case of the tens of thousands of children orphaned by the boxing day tsunami of 2004, which took over a quarter of a million lives and left more than one and a half million homeless. How can children swept up in this tragedy ever be expected to come to terms with what has happened to them? In the words of the developmental psychologist, Jim Johnson (2012), 'Play keeps us sane in an insane world.'

Tsunami stories

Jo Nelson – community play development worker

In 2006 I began my student placement in an orphanage in a small village on the west coast of Sri Lanka, near Colombo. The east coast of Sri Lanka was badly affected by the devastating tsunami on boxing day 2004. Hardly anyone was left untouched – people lost family, friends, homes and belongings. More than 35,000 people lost their lives, and over half a million people were left homeless. All the

11 boys in the orphanage were from the east and had lost their families in the tsunami, so had to start again.

The orphanage itself was limiting for the children, not only due to space, but also the lack of freedom within the boundaries of their culture and belief system. There was a severe lack of play and play opportunities, mainly due to the rules imposed by the two carers, who felt religion and study were the only things of importance. Play was not a high priority.

The children were eager to talk about their experience of the tsunami, some more so than others. The first boy to tell his story asked the carer to help translate words he was unsure of so that he could tell us every detail. Once the children had talked about their loss and experience of the tsunami, the carers told the boys not to talk of it again as dwelling on the past or mourning their loss was not acceptable, and they should be thankful for being given this opportunity.

One of the boys not only talked about the event most days he also drew it at every opportunity. He said, 'This is my life so I want to draw for people to see.' He also suffered nightmares where he would scratch himself, and became emotionally upset when reminded of what he had experienced. He also on occasions wet the bed, whereupon the mattress was placed outside for everyone to see, and he was ridiculed by the carers.

One of the boys would only play on weekends as he had been told that weekdays are for studying and focusing on prayers. Through this, his interaction with the other boys had suffered as he blocked people from engaging with him. However, during a water fight one day it seemed he forgot about his strict rules not to play on weekdays, as he was one of the main culprits of us coming away wetter than anyone else. He totally let go of any inhibitions and really began to enjoy himself; he was laughing uncontrollably and didn't want it to end; he most definitely showed his mischievous side that day. As we were drying off he thanked us for such a fun day and asked when we would do it again. Sadly this was not to be, as the carers told the children they would get ill if they played with water again.

Perhaps the carers thought their tough regime would help the children to 'move on'. Clearly that was not working, and despite the carers' approach, these boys use their play to come to terms with the traumatic event. It seems the drive to use play as a therapeutic tool is deep seated, and available to anyone who has need of it.

Another therapeutic process that is strongly associated with play is the use of artefacts that Winnicott (1971) calls 'transitional objects' – the best-known example being Linus's security blanket in Charles M. Schulz's *Peanuts* comic strips. Entering into a world of insecurity, children commonly use a favourite plaything as a symbol of a secure past in order to help them feel more secure in the present day. This is a process that is not confined to childhood. For example, students moving away from home for the first time commonly take their favourite cuddly toy with them.

I was told a story by my nephew's daughter about an incident involving her younger brother, which illustrates the power of transitional objects.

Bunny

Alishia Hawkins – sister

When my brother Josh was born, mum and dad bought him a special cuddly toy, a furry rabbit. He really and truly loved it. Even when he was quite small he wouldn't go to sleep unless he was holding the rabbit. As he got older Bunny went everywhere with him, and every night Josh cuddled him in bed. Josh often got sick over Bunny, but mum would wash him, so he always looked as good as new.

When Josh was 2 years old he lost Bunny while we were out in the town. Mum said he probably lost his grip when he was asleep, and Bunny fell out of the buggy. Josh was really upset, so we went back round the route we had walked that morning, but we couldn't find Bunny.

About three years later I was looking through some family photographs on the computer. Josh was standing next to me. One of the photos showed him holding Bunny. When Josh saw Bunny he got really upset, and started crying. I thought I was going to get into trouble for upsetting him, but I told mum and dad anyway.

This story shows the symbolic power of such playthings. It is fascinating that Bunny was lost when Josh was 2, and this incident happened three years later. At the age of 5 it was certainly not possible for Josh to articulate why he got so upset, and yet the emotional attachment to this object was so strong it overwhelmed him. This story reminds us of the significance of transitional objects:

- they are familiar
- they are associated with security
- they are often used in strange surroundings
- their presence gives comfort in situations of uncertainty
- they offer reassurance when separated from a loved one
- they are usually, but not always, soft and cuddly.

Sadly, some children don't even have the reassurance of a transitional object to comfort them in their distress, but as the next story shows, sometimes even small playful actions can be a big event in a child's life.

The boy in the bed

Rachel Lacey – playworker

During my second student placement I worked in a hospital in Sri Lanka. Within the hospital the children experienced a general lack of stimulation; the walls were bare and the rooms were clinical and felt depressing. Stuffed bears took a place on a table in the corner of the room, but remained there during every visit and were not played with, seemingly only there for decoration.

I came upon a boy, around the age of 5 years, who was tied to the bed by his nurses. Their idea was to prevent him moving and scratching his infected skin, and to restrict the further spread of scabies within the site. His lower half was red raw, and at first glance looked as if boiling water had been poured over him. His face had a vacant expression and he made no sound. He just lay there while flies crawled all over his body. Some attention was given to his physical state, but none to his emotional state. There appeared to be no understanding that the resulting lack of stimulation could have a detrimental impact on his potential for recovery and his long-term mental state. Looking into his eyes, it felt as if he was empty, and that he was in a world of his own because reality was offering him nothing.

First interaction began with touching his hand and placing a toy soldier in it. He gripped the toy firmly. Following this, we tried blowing soapy bubbles around him, which led to a striking change. His face lit up, and it appeared for the first time as if someone was there. He began looking for the bubbles, and appeared to respond to their coldness when they landed on his body. When the bubble blower was placed in front of him, he moved his head to come closer and be able to blow it. The physical exertion appeared to tire him out. Although he had difficulty using the blower himself, the fact that other children were making bubbles nearby appeared still to give him enjoyment. Throughout all this the boy kept a firm grasp on the parachute man, gripping it as tight as he possibly could.

The lack of stimulation in the hospital appeared to be at its worst in relation to the boy tied to the bed. He manifested worrying symptoms and responses to interaction. When greeted by either adults or fellow children, the boy was non-verbal, and the only expression appeared to be when he wept. No one responded to his tears.

The contrast between the gentleness of the bubbles and the boy's 'firm grasp on the parachute man' is striking. Yet at the same time it is not really surprising. The excitement brought about by the fact that someone is playing with him is probably represented symbolically by the 'firm grasp'. It's almost as if he is trying to give the bubble-blowers a play cue, i.e. please keep doing this. Stimulation through play is just as important to children who are disabled or disadvantaged in some way as it is to their more fortunate counterparts. This is demonstrated in the following story about the play response of an autistic child.

Tegan's leap

Aimee-Beth Jones – playworker

Tegan and Rhys are my younger brother and sister. Tegan, aged 5, has been diag-nosed as being on the autistic spectrum, and has problems interacting with others.

A few months ago I introduced Mike to the family. Rhys, aged 3, was thrilled at having someone new to play with. Tegan spent her time ignoring him as she does with most people, including me.

One day Rhys invented a game during which Mike had to sit on the sofa while he ran from the other end of the room and launched himself at Mike. I noticed that Tegan was watching from the other side of the room. Every so often she moved a little closer. This went on for about 15 minutes, when I heard a voice shout 'and me', before Tegan ran and launched herself at Mike. The game went on for the next hour with both myself and my dad looking on in amazement.

Sutton-Smith (2008) suggests that one of the main benefits of play is the development of sophisticated life skills that enable the child, and subsequently the adult, to survive the trials and tribulations of everyday life. We are born with the potential to develop some of these skills, but without play no such development will happen. Among the most important of these life skills are:

- our sense of rhythm
- the ability to sympathize
- the ability to empathize
- the facility for mimetic representation
- affective attunement.[1]

Davy (2008) suggests that 'babies are "pre-designed" for perceiving rhythmic patterns that provide a structure for organizing experiences in human interactive events.' Babies in the womb develop auditory structures that enable them to respond to sound at around seven months' gestation (Sladen 2012). During the final two months in the womb they become aware of rhythmical sounds, such as the mother's heartbeat, respiratory rate, walking pace and voice pattern. We know also that babies are aware of sounds outside the womb, so they are likely to be aware of the rhythmical voice patterns of people who are regularly in the orbit of the mother during the latter stages of pregnancy – for example, the father, siblings, grandparents, etc. Consequently newborns come into the world with an understanding of the concept of rhythm. The rhythms that are heard regularly are likely to be firmly embedded in the baby's memory at birth. This means they are ready to relate to the mother and others, so long as their familiar rhythms are heard soon after birth. This may be one of the motivating factors in an infant's acceptance of primary and secondary attachment figures. Indeed, Trevarthen (1996) suggests rhythm is one of the most fundamental developmental building blocks. He says babies use their understanding of rhythm to interpret social relationships.

Rhythm, sympathy, empathy, mimesis, affective attunement – all of these are present in the following story. In the case of Liliana, by using the simple device of a rhythmical song to help her feel secure, I was able to form a relationship very quickly.

---

[1] See Chapter 3 for a discussion of sympathy, empathy, mimesis and affective attunement.

Liliana

Author's observation

In the summer of 2005, I was training a group of Romanian playworkers who were working in a paediatric hospital with a group of abandoned children. On my final day I came upon a very agitated 4-year-old girl who had been left in a ward totally alone. She stood at the bars of her cot rocking back and forth, making strange hooting noises. Every so often she walked rapidly round the cot, before settling back into her rocking.

Her doctors said she was 'blind and mentally retarded'. I felt uncomfortable with this diagnosis, as she was clearly aware of my presence, and appeared to be reacting to my movements (albeit not in a very positive fashion). There was obviously something wrong with her eyesight, but a quick experiment with moving lights showed she had some level of residual vision – seeing shadows, at the very least. An added complication was her fear of men's voices. This was confirmed when I called her name, 'Liliana'. Straight away she retreated to the back of the cot.

The playworkers were wondering how they could work with her. How could they get beyond the obstacle of her poor sight?

I started singing to Liliana quietly: 'Twinkle, twinkle, little star'. She calmed down immediately, moving her head to locate the sound. At the end of the song she made a noise in the back of her throat, which I interpreted as a request to sing again – a kind of play cue. I did this three times, and each time she moved closer to the sound.

Then I started to clap gently in time to the rhythm of the song. When I stopped, she reached for my hands and put them together – another cue for me to sing. I repeated the song three more times, and each time she gave the same cue. On the last occasion she not only took my hands, but also started clapping them together in time to the song. Finally she picked up the rhythm of the song in her own hand movements, and clapped in time to my singing.

This whole sequence took no more than five minutes. In that short space of time I was able to show the Romanian playworkers how to start making a relationship with Liliana by using rhythm and music.

Later that afternoon I went back into her ward, to find her rocking and hooting again. I called her name, 'Liliana'. She came across the cot and felt for my hands. Clasping them together in hers, she started to clap our hands together in a rhythm that I recognized – 'Twinkle, twinkle, little star'. This was truly a magic moment.

It is a basic playwork tenet that all children have similar play needs (Hughes 2001). The content of play may vary according to a child's culture, but the fundamental nature of play holds firm across all cultures. Children everywhere need to socialize, run about, investigate their environment, create new worlds, etc. This holds true for *all* children, including those with disabilities, so we should not allow ourselves to be unduly distracted by a particular child's disability. Thus, it was important to view Liliana as a little girl with the potential to learn and develop through her play, rather than as a child with a visual impairment. Having overcome that initial prejudice it then became possible to start from scratch. That non-prejudicial, non-judgmental frame of mind, which Fisher (2008) calls 'negative capability', is an essential part of the playworker's make-up. In this frame of mind it becomes second nature for the playworker to interpret the children's play cues accurately. Sturrock and Else (1998) highlight the importance of appropriate interpretation of play cues. In fact they suggest that continuous misinterpretation of play cues may lead to childhood neuroses. In this particular case it was important to understand Liliana's little noises, and her clasping of my hands, and interpret those cues accurately as an invitation to repeat the song.

It is striking that I was able to go back later that afternoon, and pick up the playful activity where we had left it. This demonstrates the strength of the playful connection. The fact that I was able to interpret and respond to Liliana's play cues carried a strong message for the child, i.e. this is someone who respects me; this is someone to be trusted. The peculiar strength of relationships forged during play is discussed in the next chapter.

Liliana had been dismissed as 'blind and retarded' by the doctors and nurses because of her visual problems and attendant strange behaviour. This story is a reminder that we should not be too quick to judge. The following story reinforces this message, but in a more amusing context.

Where's grandma gone?

Author's observation

I was visiting a student on placement at a special school for autistic children. During the morning session a young boy who was on the communicative end of the autistic spectrum took a liking to me, and wanted to hold my hand all the time. When it came to playtime, he suggested we go into the playground to look for his grandma. I said that sounded like an excellent idea, and he took me to a corner of the playground where he said we would find grandma. When we got there, he said she'd just left to do her shopping, and we'd find her in a different corner of the playground. On arriving there, he said grandma had gone to hospital, and we should look for her somewhere else in the playground.

While we walked round the playground he talked non-stop about grandma. He told me the sort of food she liked, the clothes she wore, her favourite TV programmes, the colour of her hair, and so on. After ten minutes of playtime I knew grandma pretty well. The longer the game went on the more I developed the thought that he was displaying a sort of autistic obsession about grandma. When we reached the final corner of the playground he announced that grandma was here, and had climbed into his hands. He held out his cupped hands and very gently passed grandma into mine. I promised to take good care of her. 'That's good,' he said 'cos she's just wet her knickers.'

As we proceeded round the playground I had wrongly begun to pigeon-hole this child into an autistic box of my own academic design. I really should have known better, especially given that autism is a spectrum disorder, which means the abilities of any particular autistic child can vary considerably from any other such child. The truth was he didn't actually fit my stereotype at all. In fact his ability to construct an elaborate joke over an extended period of time was well in advance of most children of his age. It is not clear whether his joke was simply a joke, or whether it may have been more complex, i.e. a joke at my expense. Had he perhaps become aware that adults tended to make erroneous assumptions about him, and had he therefore constructed his own sophisticated response?

When working in Romania with abandoned and abused children (see Chapter 11), I became increasingly convinced that all children are capable of utilizing play to make progress, no matter what their disability or disadvantage. Consequently, we should never make assumptions about any child's inability to make progress, especially if they are able to interact with an appropriate play environment. Children can make progress in their own way. The following story illustrates this.

Joey

Tony Chilton – playwork consultant

As the manager of an adventure playground and employed by the local education authority, I was attempting to develop a strategy aimed at attracting more children with disabilities to the playground. With the cooperation of the education department, and in particular the Chief Education Officer and the Educational Psychologist, I visited the families of those listed as having 'handicapped' children (1960s terminology) with the intention of trying to encourage greater use of the adventure playground.

It required considerable effort and sensitive planning to persuade parents to allow their 'special' children to play among 'ordinary' children. My efforts proved to be reasonably successful to the extent that the adventure playground was seen as one of the first to develop an integrated approach to play provision, attracting a considerable number of children who, for a variety of needs, attended 'special schools' throughout the area and who had rarely, if ever, been allowed to play out in the neighbourhood.

There were many instances where we had to design individual introductory sessions to the adventure playground. One in particular involved a young boy of 8 (Joey) who had multiple disabilities, some of which were self-determined as a consequence of perceived or actual reactions from other people. For instance, Joey would not open his eyes or communicate verbally when in the presence of others. He was particularly withdrawn and solitary; never expressing a desire to leave the house other than to attend school on a limited basis, much of his education was carried out by a home tutor.

I made numerous visits to the house in an attempt to introduce him to play opportunities, and with his parents' consent I introduced what would later be described by others as 'play therapy' sessions. I did not essentially set out to establish such a process. From play sessions in the sitting room of the house I gradually and progressively encouraged Joey to play in the small back garden and eventually into the front garden.

To the amazement of his parents, and indeed me, Joey began to mumble words rather than communicating through grunts, sighs and other non-verbal and more physical signs. He began opening his eyes when in the garden, though often rushed inside if he saw other children playing in the street.

After a little while I was able to introduce Joey to the adventure playground, which was only a few hundred yards from where he lived. He came to the playground during school times when I knew no other children would be present. He played very tentatively within the site; I allowed him the time to discover various spaces and items on the site. His favourite 'space' was that within the inside of a huge vehicle tyre I had acquired. He obviously felt very secure inside this 'protective' space. I introduced sand at first, then water, and Joey was quite content playing alone with such elements, but eventually – to everyone's delight and surprise – he 'allowed' other children to be gradually introduced into his space. Joey then began to extend his 'private' range by moving from the tyre into the sandpit, where he developed sufficient confidence and competence to play alongside other children of his own age. He became distressed if older and more boisterous children came into his zone, so we had to sensitively and carefully help protect his space until he developed an ability to accommodate and manage the involvement of others.

Joey made staggering progress in a short period of time being able to venture further afield, within the confines of the adventure playground, experiencing different play opportunities. Ultimately he was confident enough to be 'allowed' to come along the road on his own to the adventure playground following telephone calls from his mother informing us he was on his way. Eventually, through play, Joey became a fully integrated member of the adventure playground. His inhibitions slowly eroded and were replaced by confidence and the ability to move freely around. He smiled and laughed a lot, he communicated in his own way with the other children, none of whom displayed any anti-social behaviour towards him, perhaps because the adventure playground staff worked so well in creating a fully integrated play environment as though it were a simple and natural process.

Sometimes children reveal things in and around their play – a concept that is at the heart of play therapy (Klein 1955).

Georgie's digging

Sally Maguire – graduate playworker

Georgie is 4 years old. She is technically under-age to be on our adventure playground, but has declared to members of staff, including myself, that she is 'pretending to be 5 years old, so I can get my free dinner around the fire'. Georgie has several bruises upon her face and arms, some of which are noticeably severe. I work with her for half an hour until her mother arrives. Georgie asks me if she can play in the sensory garden with the sand and rocks. She asks me for a trowel to dig up the sand. I find a trowel, pass it to her and she begins to dig, targeting the layer of sand underneath the rocks. The rocks are larger in height than Georgie. She then gives me a 'play cue' by asking if I would like a trowel. She asks if I'd like to help her dig up the rock so that she can make a wish. I fetch a trowel and dig with her, mimicking her movements slowly.

She tells me she will have three wishes. I ask what her first wish would be, and she responds with, 'My first wish would be daddy not killing mummy's baby.' Georgie continues to dig, chucking the sand vigorously into the air. 'I've found the shiny part of the rock, we must give it a potion to keep it shiny and then make my next wish.' Georgie searches around the rocks and finds a green leaf. She places the green leaf into the sand, using it to mould the shape and structure of the sand into circles and lines. She runs to the fountain at the other side of the sensory garden, and appears with wet hands. As she smears her hands on to the rock, she whispers, 'It's shiny again.' She repeats this movement several times, washing the same part of the rock using her hands. She then makes her second wish: 'I wish that daddy wouldn't scream at mummy because it makes her feel sad.' I ask if she feels sad, and she shrugs her shoulders.

Georgie spends a few minutes with great concentration, balancing her leaf delicately on top of her mounded hill of sand, next to the 'shiny rock'. I find a leaf nearby and build a mound of my own. My leaf falls off my pile of sand, and Georgie quickly responds by chasing my leaf and holding it in her hand. She looks at me. I ask her how she will find her next wish, and she replies, 'I already know where to find it.' She points at the leaf and smiles, 'I wish for a baby brother.'

As Georgie plants the leaf deep within her mould of sand, her mother appears at the entrance of the adventure playground to take her home. The mother, while looking at me, says to Georgie, 'You fell down them stairs again didn't you in Blackpool, you clumsy girl, but you had a lovely time on the rides didn't you?' Georgie nods, still focusing on burying her leaf.

As they leave the playground, Georgie looks back at me and says, 'Keep my rock shiny for me.'

This story shows a playworker responding to a child in an appropriately sensitive way. She is not being intrusive, but rather she is there for the child, very much in the way recommended by Fisher (see Chapter 3). By adopting this position the play-worker is not closing anything off. She is not taking control of the situation, and this allows the child–playworker relationship to develop naturally. In such circumstances the relationship often develops rapidly into one of deep trust. This has to do with the locus of power. When playing, and only when playing, the child is in control. She has the power, and although this is not unusual in terms of play, it is certainly unusual for a child to be in the presence of an adult who is *not* taking control. As a result, the child will quickly come to trust the adult. Coupled with this, most children see adults as the solution to their problems. Therefore, in circumstances where a child has a problem, and finds herself in the presence of an adult who she trusts, she is likely to share her problem with that adult. Sometimes this occurs when we least expect it, and playworkers have to be prepared for that eventuality.

Sometimes children will simply share their problems with the playworker in a straightforward conversation. On other occasions they will express their thoughts and feelings via the medium of play, often using symbolism and/or role play. This can be quite dramatized and needs to be handled with great sensitivity. For example:

The leather belt

Ali Wood – playwork author and trainer

Periodically I used to go to a local authority open-access play centre, where I knew the playworkers well, to observe and reflect on playing, and be a spare pair of hands when needed.

I had not met Ben before. He was 6, in foster care and had started coming regularly to the centre. He had little speech and an awkward gait, a big happy smile, and on this occasion was full of enthusiasm. He came over to me soon after his arrival, took my hand and urged me to go outside. With me following his lead we trotted and skipped about the playground, waving our arms and making all kinds of noises and laughing at our antics.

After several traversals of the playground Ben urged me to follow him into the playhouse – a garden shed with windows, curtains and a big dressing-up box. We went in and started rifling through the clothes and props. Ben suddenly stood up, shut the curtains, and firmly shut the door. He then turned round and his face had totally changed. I can only describe it as menacing. I watched him carefully, wondering where we were going next.

He started to laugh in this menacing way, while clearly looking through the box for something. He found it – a leather belt – and then started to shout excitedly at me. I began to wonder what he might be playing out, so I played along, pretending to cower for a while, but he then got even more agitated and came over to me putting the belt around my neck.

It was one of those moments when you call on your instinct and hope it's an appropriate response. As he started to pull the belt tighter I changed tack and said firmly, 'No, I don't want to play this game anymore', and freed myself from the belt. Ben's face immediately broke into an expression of relief and he threw his arms around me. I hugged him back, thinking I had no idea what had just happened, but feeling sure it was quite significant to Ben. He then took my hand again, opened the door, and we proceeded to run round the playground again as before, but this time we sang made-up songs at the tops of our voices and he seemed full of happiness. He then stopped and moved away from me to play something else. I went to tidy up some ropes, I think. He ignored me for the rest of the session, but when his foster mum came to collect him, he ran over to me and gave me a brief hug and a sunny smile before going home.

I spoke later to the senior playworkers, relaying what had happened. They told me that his foster mum had told them that Ben had been discovered at 2 years old tied to his cot by a belt around his neck. It was thought he had never left the cot as he was unable to walk. He was immediately taken into care and, four years later, was still 'catching up' on his lost early development.

I was more than a little shaken. We reflected for a while on what had happened and discussed a number of possible future considerations and strategies (he had not behaved like this before). I hoped and hoped that my instinctive response was an empowering one for him as he played out the aggressor, and re-enacted his experience, but this time with the victim taking control. What had sparked that playing that day, and why me? I'll never know, but I remain in awe at the power and potential of play.

Here we have an example of Freud's (1900) concept of 'reconciliation' writ large. Play offers children the opportunity to explore and experiment in comparative safety. All manner of negative emotions and experiences can be 'played out' in detail, in order to understand or accommodate them – sometimes both at the same time. Children often replay traumatic events many times, and from several different perspectives, in order to gain a thorough understanding of something that was outside their normal daily life. At the same time they are also taking control of the event, and thereby making it less frightening. In these circumstances Russ (2004) suggests children create a safe play frame around their imaginative play in order to reduce anxiety, alleviate negative feelings and distance themselves from the problem. For example, my own daughter came close to death when she was 7 years old, and spent several weeks in hospital as a result. When she came home to convalesce she spent weeks playing hospitals. She did this from a range of different perspectives – doctor, nurse, patient, small child, dying child, etc. Sometimes she played a version where she had been left alone in the hospital ward and another child was dying. Sometimes the nurses were being unpleasant; on one occasion the hospital had run out of medicine. Eventually she 'played out' the event, and got back to reading and playing with her doll's house.

8

Self-realization, power and control

For most children, playing is the only experience they ever have of being in control of their own small world; on all other occasions an adult is in charge. Therefore, when working with children in a playwork setting it is crucial for the adult to resist the temptation to take control. Otherwise it ceases to be a high-quality play experience for the child. For children to find themselves in a largely equal relationship with an adult is rare and powerful, and has all manner of implications for the quality of the relationship between child and playworker.

Holme and Massie (1970) argue that play and socialization are interdependent. Through play, 'the child gradually comes to terms with the external world', while at the same time developing 'a controllable and secure world of its own'. Many of the processes described previously enable human beings to discover their true selves. Erikson (1963) suggests that play has an ego-building function, which leads to the development of physical and social skills that enhance a child's self-esteem. This in turn encourages children to discover and explore their social world, including their culture and social roles.

During play there are a number of clearly identifiable indicators to suggest that the gradual development of self is occurring. Children may shift easily between roles and true identity, which has led many writers to identify the 'paradox of play' (Bateson 1955). They may be stepping up the pace and range of their exploratory activity, and learning about cause-and-effect relationships (Tinbergen 1975). They may begin to exercise autonomy (Maslow 1973), and recapitulate the roots of their social and cultural history (Hall 1904). We may even see signs of the development of a personal *weltanschauung* (world-view) (Kant 1790), or at least a settled value orientation, as envisaged by Weber (Aron 1970).

Sometimes even the children wonder about this gradual development of self-awareness.

How do you know yourself?

Susan Caruso – Sunflower creative arts director and teacher

Jason, 5, loves smearing his whole body and face with paint, clay and leaves. He layers the dress-up clothes until the other children have no idea who or what is under there. They run away screaming as he chases them with green foam paint dripping from his fingertips. Sometimes toilet paper or silk scarves become his second skin, tightly wrapped over eyes and head, every inch covered except for a tiny nose hole. One day he spent most of the morning submerged like an alligator in a bin of water, mud and mulch until a water beetle crawled in his ear. We rarely see his face.

One morning I was all alone inside working in a corner when in runs Jason. He stops and stares at himself in the mirror. No paint, no costumes, no toilet paper or mulchy mask hide his body or face. Just Jason completely uncovered. I didn't think he noticed that I was in the room until, gazing deep into his own eyes, he asks, 'How do you know yourself Susan?'

Part of the process of self-realization is starting to take control of your own little microcosm of the world (Sutton-Smith 1992). Some would argue that children are trying to do this from the moment they are born. Certainly, there is evidence that the process starts quite young, as in the following example.

The tree

Martha Janos – pilgrim and explorer

I grew up in Peru, and outside our house were many trees. When I was about 5 years old I used to climb right to the top of the biggest tree, and sit there. I loved that because the branches and the leaves seemed to enclose me and make me feel safe. Sitting on top of the tree I could see the whole world – a world that the adults couldn't see.

Of course this is not just about being in control, but also about having ownership of a private space, and being removed from adults.

The slide

Mark Gladwin – play researcher

The playground has a popular aerial runway (which everyone calls the slide) and the playworkers try to enforce all sorts of rules about its safe use . . . but the children know better. Here are some typical 'modifications'.

Bradley goes down the slide standing up and bouncing . . . eventually Angela (playworker) notices what he is doing and calls out of the window that standing's not allowed.

Towards the end of the session, Grace and Cootie begin putting obstacles in the way of the slide, e.g. an upended plastic bread tray, for the slider to knock down in passing.

Micky and Julian race down the slope at the same time as the slider, to see who can touch base first. Then Julian runs down pulling Micky on the slider, to make him crash faster into the bottom buffer.

Angus, Damian and Baz deliberately 'misuse' the slide: going down in pairs, wrestling on it, holding one another in front of the buffer as someone comes down, bouncing on the slider, standing, spinning . . . later, Angus and Baz deliberately run on a collision course across the line of the slide as other kids come down. Then Damian and Angus lie prone under the lowest point, to stage another kind of collision with the descending slider.

JC, Jarod, Morris and Micky are all on the slide at once – unsurprisingly, it sags so much that they touch the ground. Jarod tightens the ringbolt at the bottom to raise the cable a bit.

Barry and Corin run across as Mark comes down the slide: 'I nearly killed you,' he says.

Some children take a run before they launch off, thereby increasing the speed of the slide and crashing into the end stop. Wesley announces 'I'm trying to whack into that black thing' (he means the tyre that acts as the end stop). He tries a few times, then mistimes his run and falls off the slider seat – turns it into a joke by lying spread-eagled on the ground as if injured. He enjoys this so much that he does it again, on purpose. Later he manages to get his 'whacking', but he also goes on doing the comedy act.

It is to the playworkers' credit that all this takes place on a supervised site, and yet the children clearly feel they are in control of this immediate environment; different children apparently having their own personal perception of what this piece of equipment means to them. This is very reminiscent of my own research on unsupervised fixed equipment playgrounds, where children who did not expect adults to be around played in a relaxed, carefree manner. As soon as adults appeared, the nature of play changed, from a chaotic form of free flow play (Bruce 1991) to an extremely rigid form of play, which lacked creativity, and gave little outward sign of the sort of fun and enjoyment described by Huizinga (1949). When adults were present the children played with the equipment in exactly the way the designer presumably expected – for example, making far greater use of the exercise equipment and generally conforming to 'age appropriate' physical and social activities. In the absence of adults, that changed to a relaxed atmosphere of exploration and experimentation (Brown 2003c).

Another way in which children begin to find out who they are and who they can be, is when they manage to identify a role with which they are comfortable in a social group.

JD finds his strength

Vejoya Viren – Associate Professor of Early Childhood Education

JD seldom had the right technique of entering a play situation. He often was uninterested in what his peers had to say to him. His fantastic ideas during play baffled his playmates. In short, JD was a lonely child, frequently rejected by his classmates.

JD had other problems that weighed greatly on him. His mother liked his long blonde hair and persistently talked him out of getting it cut, and she liked him to wear leather sandals instead of sneakers (the more popular footwear among the boys). This led to repeated confusion regarding his gender. To top it all, he and his mother had recently been abandoned by his father.

During one group time, the children were discussing their pet dogs. JD, who has no pet dogs, raised his hand to indicate he had something to say. However, he caught my eyes and winked before he spoke. I took it as an implicit appeal to play along with what he had to say. JD went on to tell a fabulous tale of how he had been to the pet shop to pick out two puppies, and how he had chosen names for them and even indicated what breeds they were. He described in great detail to the group that one had blue eyes and the other brown; and that the puppies wiggled when he tickled their pink bellies. The children listened riveted as he gave them interesting details of his new pet. They asked for more details and were impressed with his story. JD looked very proud. For once he was the centre of doting attention. A few minutes later as the class prepared to go outside, JD asked me, very uncharacteristically, if he could hold my hand. Then he gave it a tight squeeze, looked up at me and smiled.

As a teacher, one soon learns there are benefits to being an accomplice; that aiding a fantasy (and a white lie in this case) did not give birth to a compulsive liar, but wrought instead a, much in demand, teller of stories.

Each child needs to find themselves. It is the playworker's job to provide environments that enable that to happen.

When daddy's away she comes out to play

Keith Ramtahal – inspector for early years

I was seconded by a London borough to start up a playscheme for 50 children because the local parents felt their children needed a more community-based setting, as their nearest playscheme was on the other side of a very busy road. We were given a community centre hall, rent free, and a lock-up shed for storing our resources. I recruited a diverse team of workers as the area was made up of predominantly white Europeans. Only one child enrolled on the playscheme was of mixed parentage/heritage. All the other children were white European, and all of them lived in the most expensive houses for that part of north London. To give you an idea of the monetary wealth in the area, George Michael, Annie Lennox and Sting lived only three bus stops away!

One of the playscheme children was a young boy who was fascinated by our dressing-up box. As soon as he arrived he would head for the box and that would be his sole activity for the whole of the day, he even ate his lunch and went out on trips in his favourite outfit: a blonde nylon wig, a sequined black dress with accompanying silver shoes and a matching clutch bag. His mother a principal make-up artist for the BBC was happy with this and always encouraged it, as she believed in the boy exploring his world, dressed in whatever he felt comfortable in at the time.

However, the boy's father, a jazz musician, was totally against his son dressing in 'ladies' clothes', and the boy was severely verbally reprimanded when his dad unexpectedly picked him up from the playscheme early one day, as he had caught an earlier flight to Heathrow Airport from Los Angeles to attend and perform at the boy's 6th birthday party that evening. The boy's mum told us the next day how upset both dad and boy were when they returned home that afternoon, and that the boy's birthday party was a total disaster.

As dad was flying back to Los Angeles the next week we decided that the boy could continue his dressing-up, but mum asked if he could change back into his everyday clothes each day by 3.00 p.m. just in case dad did come to pick him up. Luckily for the boy, dad never came to pick him up from the playscheme that summer, so the next four weeks were spent with the boy preparing for a fashion show, with some of the other children performing the duties of make-up artist, hair stylist, dresser, disc jockey, photographers and audience. The show on the last day was fantastic, and the boy revelled in his admiration and approval from others, which included his mum and some of her BBC friends. He even gave them all autographs!

So, this boy's initial chosen sole play had moved from exploring his own identity in a safe environment to being creative with others, to help him fulfil his dream of being a model on the catwalk. It is a shame that his dad was not there to show and share in his approval and star turn, too, but as one mum said to me after the catwalk show: 'It's as if when his daddy's away, *She* comes out to play!'

Sometimes children use the boundaries of power and control to create hierarchies, to give themselves status, etc. Some children use their understanding of the boundaries to create their own excitement at the expense of others, as in the following story.

Ben

Mark Gladwin – play researcher

Baz (aged 11) and another boy around the same age occupied the pool table, but Ben (9) persistently disrupted the game by grabbing the balls and running off. Baz seemed amused, but his partner got seriously annoyed and, each time, chased Ben to wrestle the balls off him. In the end, this got quite violent. Ben was clearly loving it; grinning even when being thumped. The violence stayed within limits – no throwing pool balls, hitting with cues or full-strength punches. At length staff intervened. Angela (playworker) gave a judgement about the order of turns on the pool table that evidently wasn't to Ben's liking: he stormed off, kicking furniture and overturning dustbins, and went outside to sulk.

This is about trust, and whether Ben understands the limits, etc. He can be fairly confident that Baz and his friend will stay within those limits, and therefore he will not get badly hurt. Of course, the story might also be about the limits of violence and how little adults understand about that. Garvey (1991) suggests that one of the key characteristics of play is 'non-literality', i.e. it is not always what it seems – a fight is literally a fight, whereas play-fighting is not literally a fight. In fact Panksepp (2004) has shown that play-fighting may well be the most positive form of play in purely developmental terms, because it engages the child in four of the brain's eight genetically ingrained emotional systems: caring, social bonding, playfulness and explorative urges.

This is a complex matter, and one that needs exploring in greater depth, because the use and understanding of boundaries is something that children utilize in order to create hierarchies within their social groups. This is not always a pleasant process. It is often the case that bullies are able to control groups of children purely because of their willingness to blur the boundaries of non-literal and literal behaviour; of acceptable and unacceptable behaviour. Ironically, such children are not always unpopular (contrary to what most adults think). In some cases the other children in the group are fellow travellers who rather admire the bully's ability to blur the lines.

On the other hand, there are some children who simply don't understand where the boundaries are. In most cases those children will find it hard to make friends, because the other children are wary of them. After all, if they don't understand where the boundaries are, they might do something wrong without realizing it. Thus, they come to be regarded with suspicion and caution. When I was a child there was a boy in my neighbourhood who no one played with. I remember asking my father why he thought that might be. He said, 'It's because when you're all pushing each other around on the railway platform, he's likely to push someone under a train!'

In order to create and subsequently preserve their personal microcosm of the world, children will resist any adult control/influence that they think is intrusive. In the case that follows the adult is a well-meaning grandmother.

Imaginary horse

Anne Brown – carer

Our grandson was never very interested in eating when he was a toddler, which caused great anguish to all those who cared for him. I think playing was just so much more interesting. Anyway he used to have an imaginary horse, which he rode everywhere, so I began to use the device of encouraging him to eat by talking about the horse being hungry, and suggesting we could all eat together.

For a while this was successful, until one day we were in a cafe expecting to eat lunch. The conversation went something like this:

'What would you like to eat?'
'Nothing.'
'Do you think we should get something for your horse? I expect he's hungry.'
'I don't know. I tied him up outside.'

The next story reveals a similar sophisticated tactic on the part of the child, again in relation to food, but this time imaginary food. He is clearly not willing to play along with the teacher, despite the fact that she is trying to be engaging. He seems determined to stay in control.

Pizza

Laura Emsley – classroom assistant

It was September and the children had only been in school a couple of weeks. The reception class was set up with activities to enjoy and help settle the children into school. The teacher had explained the different areas to the children, and suggested ideas of what they might like to do. The children were then given free choice of the activity they preferred. Once everyone was settled, the teacher wandered around the classroom observing the children and encouraging them to play.

Katie, Lucy and Jack were busy in the home corner. The teacher bent down to join in the play and conversation. The girls offered the teacher a plate with a sandwich on and said, 'We are making tea.'

'That's lovely,' replied the teacher, tasting the sandwich, 'I really like ham salad sandwiches. Would you like a drink of juice?'

'Yes please,' the girls replied.

The teacher then asked Jack (who was sitting in the home corner on a chair) if he was going to make some tea. He put his arms behind his head, leant back on his chair and said 'I've just rung the pizza takeaway and I'm waiting for them to deliver it.'

'Oh right,' said the teacher.

'Are you going to get a plate out ready?'

"No, I'll eat it out of the box.'

In a variation on the well-known biblical doctrine, George Bernard Shaw said 'Do not do unto others as you would that they should do unto you. Their tastes may not be the same' (Shaw 2012: 5). It is one of the commonest mistakes of people who work with children that they believe all children will be excited by the same things that excited them when they were young. Not all boys want to play football; not all girls want to play with dolls; not all children like arts and crafts; etc. It is crucial for playworkers to identify each child's agenda, and make sure that their basic needs are being catered for. This basic principle applies regardless of the child's gender, race, religion, disability, etc. It is perhaps when working with children who have a disability or a learning difficulty that it is easiest to forget this. However, if anyone is in any doubt that even seriously damaged children nevertheless have a play agenda that is all theirs, just take time to read the extracts from a therapeutic diary in Chapter 11.

The next four stories focus on the play of disabled children, demonstrating that their play has the same characteristics as any child's play. One of those common characteristics is that it is unique to the individual child; another is the way in which children use play to establish their personal identity.

Pirates and treasure

Susan Waltham – childhood studies lecturer

I was meeting with a colleague this afternoon at her house, where her 10-year-old son was present. He is on the autistic spectrum. After persuading him not to play games on the TV by pure bribery, he spent over an hour making a den in the corner of the living room, using sofa cushions, books and a chair. He invited a large Labrador dog into his den, but soon ejected her after her tail dismantled part of the den. He had 'treasure', which he was sorting through – a jam jar with small found objects such as buttons and broken jewellery. All the while he was talking to himself (he actually does this a lot as he voices his thoughts rather like toddlers do), which seemed to be a narrative monologue about pirates and treasure. He took part this summer in a public production of Gilbert and Sullivan's *Pirates of Penzance* as he is a member of a youth choir, so he has a strong sense of story around this subject.

He was due to go to choir practice later that afternoon; his den play stopped when he asked his mother if it was time to go to choir. As it was, his mother and I packed up our paperwork and set a few action points. While we did this, he went and got a hat from his bedroom that was a plastic top hat. He came down and I commented that it was a great hat. He replied that he was going to wear it to choir. His sister (7 years older) came into the room and told him not to wear it as it was too embarrassing and he was too old to dress up in public. He completely ignored her and went to the front door, waiting to be let out to get in the car.

As part of its Son-Rise Program, the Option Institute of America has developed a technique called 'joining', which is very similar to the playwork approach of working to every child's agenda. This approach assumes that autistic children want to form relationships. Their problem is they don't know how to communicate in a way that non-autistic people can understand. Unlike many approaches to the treatment of autism, there is a total acceptance in the Son-Rise Program that the child wants to play. Unfortunately their play sometimes looks a bit unusual (Kaufman 2014).

> The idea is that children with autism are performing their behaviors for reasons that are important to them (and, as an increasing body of research shows, these behaviors often serve a physiological purpose, as well). When parents show interest in what their children are doing, they establish a powerful bond. In response, children begin to display a genuine interest. Once a child is willingly engaged, the door is open to help that child to learn and grow.
>
> (Kaufman 2014)

Examples of this approach in a therapeutic playwork setting may be seen in the Reflective Diary in Chapter 11 (Days 17, 18 and 29).

The following story illustrates how children use play as a communication tool.

David's trolley

Laura Chapman – inclusive play services development officer

I arrive at the playscheme and look for David to make sure he has settled okay as the children are outside and David is used to going in the lift, which he loves. I notice David in the trolley that is used to store equipment. He is being pushed in the trolley by a playworker. As I get closer I notice he has different-colour foam hands – red, yellow and green. He is using the foam hands to direct the trolley: red – stop, yellow – wait, then green to go.

David has only limited communication and does not always respond to questions. I ask him, 'What's going on here then, mister?' He smiles and holds up the green hand, shouting 'Go!' It is great to see him enjoying himself and communicating through his play. He doesn't stop to chat as he is clearly busy in his trolley.

Here is an example of a child imposing himself on the environment, while interacting with it.

Running through the daisies

Tim Doe – children's play services worker

I was an energetic child, always doing things, climbing, swinging and running. Then at the age of 13 I had a severe stroke, which left me unable to do the things I wanted to do. My family had a long garden, and my grandma planted big daisies with strong stems. I wanted to run; then I thought I would attempt to run through the daisies. I knew I would fall down, but it didn't matter, as those stems would cushion me. After weeks of charging down these daisies I still found this game hugely enjoyable, even though I fell down many, many times. My grandma was very pleased and my mother, too, but I wanted to capture this concept of movement fast, and was very happy to run and find a new game.

And here is an example of a child creating a whole new environment for himself (and others):

A change in the weather

Gill Evans – Play Wales communications manager (1967–2011)

Last year there was snow in the summer in south Wales, and one boy and a group of well-trained playworkers made it happen.

Don't tell this story to any junior school headteacher – just in case you pick the wrong one . . .

There is an inclusive playscheme that takes place every summer in a junior school in a semi-rural village in south Wales. The playworkers (most of whom came to the playscheme as children) are all *Playwork: Principles into Practice* (P³) practitioners and the playscheme runs brilliantly 'on the edge of chaos'. Children return summer after summer. Disabled children have been very much part of the mix from the very start; where needed, they are supported by playworkers. Most of the playing happens outside on the field and in the trees, but good use is also made of the school building. For the community the playscheme is a well-established local institution.

One boy, who needs the playworkers' additional support, has been a part of the playscheme since he was 5 – he has limited language skills but is a wizard with the school photocopier . . . don't tell the headteacher.

Last summer he discovered the school's heavy-duty paper shredder – one that cross-cuts the paper to produce tiny flakes.

For the first week of the playscheme he happily shredded all the paper he could find. All the recycling was recycled. This was *his* thing that only *he* did. Flurries of paper flakes flew out of the shredder. Drifts filled the room until they were two or three inches deep. He called the room where he shredded *The Snow Room*. It was his room.

The playworkers' role was simply to source paper and to ensure that he didn't shred essential documents or school children's work.

Other children and the playworkers started to call his room *The Snow Room*.

Once he had made plenty of snow, he played with it. He filled his clothes with it. He filled his underpants with it. He piled it on to desks and belly-skidded through the snow. Other children joined in. They could be heard discussing what they were going to do as they arrived on the site in the morning and *The Snow Room* began to feature as a popular option. Drifts of snow billowed out of the door into the school corridor.

The Snow Room was an important play opportunity for the whole playscheme – something that the playworkers hadn't planned or made provision for, but that the environment and atmosphere of the playscheme had made possible.

> At the end of the playscheme the playworkers swept up and dusted away every snowflake from the room. No evidence remained of the temporary change in the weather.
>
> And just in case . . . shhhhhh . . . don't tell the head.

The Snow Room story is a good example of Arthur Battram's suggestion that the best sort of playwork takes place at 'the "edge of chaos": where "order" makes the transition to complexity' (2008: 90). In this case it is hard to imagine any other children's workforce professional who would have allowed the story to develop, and yet it is clear from the end result that providing this child with the freedom to explore his environment has had massive benefits for everyone.

The following story is another illustration of the unique nature of playwork – not just in the type of behaviour that playworkers often have to deal with, but also in the fact that the playworker does not expect to discipline the child for her bad language. In most non-playwork settings this child would be banned within minutes of arriving. It is interesting also to note that the bad language reduces over time – presumably a reaction to the fact that the playworkers make no attempt to impose their agenda on the child. This allows the child to develop a social self (of sorts).

Fat bastard's first days at work

Louie Chrysanthou – playworker

After working for 12 years running my indoor adventure centre I was thrown into the world of playwork. My first placement was in the summer holidays of 2010 at Roughfields School. I had requested this placement, due to the fact that 50% were special needs. I had run a club for special needs children at the Fun House, so I had some knowledge of most of the local children.

The first day I sat back and observed what was going on – then I could do what I thought was most needed. On this day I noticed that one girl, we will call her R, was always in time out. I already knew her from the Fun House. The team leader who knew all the children was absent through illness, and her replacement, although very good, had little experience with children with behavioural problems.

After a few enquiries I was informed that R had been swearing at the playworkers a lot, and hitting out. This could have caused more problems because part of R's problem is that she has very bad joints and restraining her can cause more problems. On the second day I asked if I could shadow her for the morning and keep an eye on her. When she came in that day I approached her. She seemed very grumpy. I said, 'Good morning stinker, do you want to go and play?' Her reply was 'F*** off.' I replied, 'Thank you very much.' She then called me a 'wanker'. 'Thank you' was my reply. This carried on most of the morning, but by now she was much more relaxed. By lunchtime she had nearly stopped swearing and was very cheerful.

After lunch some of the other children were baking cakes, so I asked R if she would like to join the other children in the kitchen, as she seemed to have mellowed down a lot. As we approached the kitchen she asked me what cakes we would be cooking. I replied, 'Cup cakes. Can you make one for me?' She took my hand, and as we got to the door she looked at me and said, 'I'll make you two cakes you fat bastard.' I thanked her!

In the next five weeks, she spent a lot more time playing and not in time out. She did not stop swearing, but it was a lot less. And she enjoyed herself. This confirmed to me that when working with children with needs, you have to bend the rules sometimes to fit the child. When a parent drops a child at the play-scheme, our job is to make sure that each child, whatever their needs, has a good time; we must adapt to them.

As for R, she still swears at the playworkers, but now she enjoys herself.

Private space, where it is possible to do whatever you want, is important to children. However, it doesn't often exist. Children rarely have any space they can genuinely call their own, so when they come to the playwork setting they often colonize small pieces of the space for themselves. It is not unusual for more than one child to regard the same space as theirs. Sometimes a child will describe the whole setting as their 'personal space', because it is effectively a 'home from home' – oftentimes a sanctuary from the big bad world outside. The child at the heart of the story that follows is constantly creating his own small world within an area that he regards as his. It would be dangerous to read too much into the changing characteristics of his creation. Whatever its significance, the playworkers show an awareness that it is important to this child, and so they leave well alone.

Pod camps

Mick Conway – Play England development officer

This adventure playground has a series of 'pod camps' set among trees – free standing on paving slabs to avoid disturbing the tree roots, and to make it easier to dismantle and move them as needed. The camp entrances are deliberately aligned away from the play building and main area of the playground to give a sense of privacy. In the growing season they are mostly hidden in foliage.

One of the playworkers said she thought the children were under far too much surveillance already. Most have no private space at home because there's a lot of overcrowding in the local estates, and the pods give them a bit of personal space – what she called 'a bit of play privacy'.

There is one pod camp that has become a very special place. It is the most secluded as the entrance faces due south away from the main playground area, and is almost completely hidden in the foliage in spring and summer.

A little boy who shares a bedroom at home with four siblings has colonized it and uses it nearly all of the time he is in the playground.

The tapes between the tree trunks are a 'Keep out, private' signal. He has elaborate rituals of undoing them to signal that others are invited in.

The playworkers used to tidy away and bring inside the playground toys and other bits and pieces each evening but no longer do so. This is the reason why.

This particular evening his pod camp table is a landscape featuring a crashed ambulance and police car, upside-down and fallen-over animals and other bits and pieces overlooked by a tiger. All on a piece of shiny wrapping paper that represents . . . who apart from him knows what? On other days there are more cars and lorries, sand and a toy JCB. Or the whole interior might well be hidden under the rolled-up sheet on the floor.

The playworkers know this is a very important place for this child, and though they were worried about leaving it untouched overnight when the playground is closed (what if it got wrecked or everything was stolen?) they have decided to leave it as it is so he can pick up his play exactly from where he left it off.

Mick Conway suggested to me that this (circular!) pod camp perfectly illustrates the Manchester Circles concept (Hughes 2012). The playing child is at the centre. The play environment holds and protects his play, away from overt surveillance, though he can look out and see most areas of the playground and who is doing what in them. The playground organizational framework is such that it understands that this bit of the play environment has special meanings for this child. The playworkers are aware of the wider context in which he lives, and as a result understand and give affordance to his preference for mainly solitary play.

The locus of power is one of the most important concepts for the playworker to get right. In the playwork setting, unlike probably any other setting, the locus of power is substantially with the child. On the adventure playground that is described in Chapter 10, we had just one rule: that the children could do whatever they liked so long as it didn't interfere with the enjoyment of another child. Of course, there was another unspoken rule: that the playworker would intervene if a child was in danger. Other than that, the children pretty much did whatever they wanted.

This approach is not without its problems. First, it tends to mean the play environment is in a constant state of flux, which to the casual observer usually looks like a chaotic mess. This is especially difficult when working for an employer who wants everything to be neat and tidy, and have an end product. Second, there are always children who are so used to the fixed rules and regulations of school life that they don't know how to handle this sort of freedom. As a result they 'rebel' (ironically) by constantly pushing at the boundaries, and deliberately testing the patience of the play-workers. Maureen Palmer has been kind enough to share one such story:

The library

Maureen Palmer – playworker

Most of my working life I have kept some type of log book when working on the playgrounds. This wasn't something we had to do, or had been asked to at this time, and I don't think we particularly perceived it as reflective practice – we knew it helped us to remember, write reports and keep staff informed of what had been happening on the days they weren't on the rota, or were off on holiday or sick. There was no format, no particular information we thought should always be recorded. This habit was formed long before the Children Act or the publication of any meaningful playwork textbooks (e.g. Hughes 2001; Brown 2003a).

One winter some of the girls set up a library. This led to there being little left in the office, as all the stationery was removed by them for their library! We had only a small indoor space and the library took up a fair bit of the area. It was a long play narrative, and all this contributed to the tension surrounding the library play frame!

Here are some notes from one of the log books during this period. I have picked out the bits from each day's recordings that relate to the library

Friday 30 January – Frank writes, 'Two libraries now, which is causing problems'

Monday 2 February – Frank writes, 'Libraries to be disbanded, too much hassle'

(Note: the children now write in the log book, which they didn't generally do)

'Samantha and Ann-Marie have a very good reason not to talk to Frank'

Wednesday 11 February – Frank writes, 'Library goes on and on and on . . .'

Thursday 12 February – I write, 'Library game is still dominating the whole place, good and bad things from the game. Don't know how much longer the workers can take the rowing'

Friday 13 February – the children intervene again; they write, 'Library continuing!'

Saturday 14 February – I write, 'Library continues but on a more limited basis'

(Note: some negotiations must have taken place!)

Wednesday 18 February – I write-, 'Library finally closed due to arguments'

(Note: sounds like the final row and breakdown in the group of players!)

I don't remember all the details, but do recall the children complaining to me about Frank! They saw him as the enemy after closing them down and me as an appeals process. Attempts were made to close it when I wasn't on site – hence I think them resorting to writing in the log book. I think I was after its natural demise, but knew it was driving the workers mad!

Here is another example of the struggle for power and control.

Sand wars

Mark Gladwin – play researcher

The playground's sandpit is another arena of contest between playworkers' rules and children's play freedom. Throwing sand is strictly forbidden, for obvious reasons, but everyone does it. One day, Terry starts experimentally throwing sand ballista-style, using a plastic spade. Others imitate him. Gradually this becomes a team game with one team throwing, one team dodging, in turn. 'Bombs away!' is the cry. This takes place in full view of the playground office window. The senior playworker comes out and shouts at the children to stop . . . as soon as he returns inside, the game resumes – both sides digging bunkers in preparation for battle. One side chivalrously offers their opponents another spade to dig with. But then little Nobby snitches on the game by shouting very loudly 'Stop throwing sand!' This brings a second playworker outside; she repeats the ban and stays to enforce it, thus stopping the planned sand battle. Typically, Barry is the only one who gets punished, because he carries on throwing sand right under her nose – he lacks diplomatic skills and is often getting wound up by the other children.

Children at play are in control of their own world. When confronted with adults who are claiming to offer a playspace where children can 'do their own thing', they don't entirely believe it, and so they will constantly test the playworkers' resolve. It takes a while, but as the playworker gradually gets to know the children, and vice versa, most conflicts can be resolved to everyone's satisfaction.

9

The child's agenda: intervention and adulteration

As we have already seen, in a child's daily life, play is his/her only experience of being in control of events. If playworkers are not to 'adulterate' that experience, they have to ensure that wherever possible they are following the child's agenda (Sturrock and Else 1998). Too often adults intervene with a view either to stop children hurting themselves, or sometimes in order to help them sort out their disputes. We really need to have faith in children's ability to work out their own disputes and reach agreement about an agenda for a way forward. We also need to bear in mind Lady Allen's (1965: 71) well-known words 'It is better to risk a broken bone than a broken spirit.'

Here are two examples of children benefiting from being left to their own devices.

Den building

Author's observation

Many years ago I was employed on an adventure playground. It was the sort of facility where children used scrap materials to create their own play environment. To begin with, although their efforts were enthusiastic, they usually contained fundamental flaws. Six-inch nails were used where one-inch would do, with the result that the wood split; uprights were not buried deep enough in the ground, so their structures fell down; the roofs of dens were not protected, so everyone got soaked when it rained; etc. The children did not appear to be bothered by any of these things. In fact, once construction was finished they generally moved on to something else.

As I saw it (wrongly) I had a responsibility to help the children improve their building abilities. I was not especially skilled in construction techniques, so could only offer rudimentary advice. Students from the engineering course at the local college spent a day on the site, but wanted to do everything to a plan, which meant the children got bored. A couple of local dads who worked on building sites were quite knowledgeable, but really didn't have the patience to engage fully with the children.

Eventually, I realized the children were not unduly bothered by their failures. So long as the materials were available to try again, that is just what they did. Often they knocked down their own creations so the materials could be reused in a new project. Over the years they became highly skilled in their work. They constructed dens, built climbing frames, rope swings, seesaws and the like. However, I noticed that the pattern of involvement remained the same as in those early days. In other words, the children were enthusiastic about the activity of construction, but relatively uninterested in the end result. More often than not, the den would be handed over to a group of toddlers, while the children who had constructed the den moved on to build again elsewhere.

The children were more comfortable with my limited abilities than with the expertise of the engineering students. I suppose my approach was more along the lines of 'let's have a go, and see what happens'. That sort of playful experimental approach was more to their liking than the methodical approach of the students. The students would undoubtedly have achieved a higher-quality product, but that is really not the point of playing. In play, the process is generally more important than the product, albeit we have seen in Chapter 1 that it is wrong to suggest there is no product from playing. There clearly is, but that was not the main motivating factor behind why these children engaged in any particular activity. Nevertheless, it is interesting to note that the product of the older children often became the environment for the younger children to explore their own play processes.

In many homes this second story could not even happen, because playing with toy guns would be banned (even symbolic guns made of twigs). However, there is little evidence that playing with toy guns leads humans to become violent later in life. On the contrary, there is substantial evidence that being restricted in our play is likely to lead to psychotic tendencies in adulthood (Brown, 2009).

Rethinking gun play

Pat Broadhead – Professor Emeritus of Playful Learning

My sons are both in their early 30s now. This play episode happened about 25 years ago but had a big impact on me and contributed to setting me on the path of questioning whose view of play was important – the adult's or the child's – and leading me towards an eventual conclusion that it was the child's view that was important.

The boys were about 7 and 8, close together in age and so they had many friends in common. At this time, they were really 'into' playing with guns. I was taking the moral high ground and had said that I wouldn't buy them guns but wouldn't stop other people buying them and neither would I stop them playing with them, so they got their gran to do their shopping for them.

On this occasion there must have been 12 or 13 children playing together around our house. There were children of all ages, the youngest about 3 years and the oldest, a boy of about 14. They were chasing around the outside of our detached house, everyone carrying a gun of some kind – bought or made or a stick – both boys and girls.

Their commitment to the play and to keeping everyone involved in the play was total and very complex. The rules were shared in ways that everyone, even the 3 year old, could understand. Being dead was explained and, when the younger children did not comply, no one was angry with them or stopped them from playing; their idiosyncrasies were accommodated seamlessly. The turn-taking was impressive, with different children being in charge at different times. Disputes happened but never delayed the play for long. Someone would suggest a solution and everything would start up again with the play scenarios continuing or a new element taking off. The children showed care for one another even while they enjoyed the excitement, tension and fun. At no time did anyone cry. So many emotions were being expressed and responded to, and so much rich language was being used.

When Pat Broadhead told me this story, she said it had taught her a powerful lesson. The guns were waved around, held to heads, held against someone's back, twirled, pushed into belts, loaded and people were shot dead. However, the guns were not weapons of destruction, it seemed, even though dying was a theme within the play; they were tools that brought the play together, gave it purpose and focus, and a shared understanding of what was possible in the play.

Here is some more gun play, with playworkers enriching the child's play environment by being responsive but not interventionist.

Boy with gun

Chris Taylor – consultant and trainer, play and playwork

Suddenly he is on the grass, as if from nowhere.
He is pointing a gun at a child, and shooting him.
The trigger clicks, but nothing leaves the muzzle.
The other child doesn't know that he has been shot.
Another child comes into the gunner's sights,
This time the other child sees him and smiles,
He is shot, and carries on running, to join his friends on the swing.
Another child is targeted, this time, closer,
The boy with the gun walks up to him, points the gun at him,
The other boy smiles shyly and sheepishly and moves on with his friends.
The boy with the gun walks round the site, shooting randomly,
Always with an endearing grin on his face and sparklingly live engaging eyes.
In this way he makes contact with many of the boys in the play area.
Then his eyes fix on the playworker.
He is approached and shot at point blank range in the torso.
The playworker dies dramatically aaaaaaaaarrrrrrrrrrh! staggers back, grasps his wound, and collapses to the floor with a final groan.

The boy smiles.
The playworker starts to rise up off the ground,
He is shot again, an even bigger grin lights up the boy's face.
And again, and again.
The playworker dies next to me,
Now it is my turn, I am shot . . .
I die like a playworker.
I too, am shot, and shot again, dying three times.
Then the boy moves on.
Some time later, an older boy produces some plastic handcuffs from his pocket.
The gunner smiles, he is arrested, handcuffed and marched away by the older boy and his friend.
The boy returns without his gun, he is standing next to me.
Do you come here often? I ask.
He replies at length, I am hard pressed to understand a word he says . . .
When I talk to the playworker, he laughs, yes; it's very difficult to understand what he says.
Play, the magic that speaks volumes.

It is clear from this observation that the gun play contains all manner of subtexts regarding role play, friendship groups, who plays with whom, age-based relationships, etc. It also demonstrates that play may be used as a communication tool, because certain types of play are universal in their nature and characteristics.

Turn-taking

Chris Taylor – consultant and trainer, play and playwork

Observed on an adventure playground in Tower Hamlets . . .

Boy in a stripy jumper (Stripe) is sitting in the basket swing; he works it vigorously, furiously, faster and faster, higher and higher, then slumps into the basin of the swing; relaxed, passive. His knees straddle the sides, his feet dangle loosely. The swing pendulums back and forth, slowing down gradually. He stands and works the swing again, vigorously, furiously, faster and faster, higher and higher. The process is repeated, again and again.

A 5 year old, white T-shirt, grey trackies and trainers, grabs hold of the rounded edge of the swing, and pushes: on the return, it lifts and raises him off the ground . . . he grins, his feet reconnect with the floor as the swing shimmies back towards the sky. Both boys are flying high. The process is repeated again and again.

The young boy runs off. Stripe leaves the swing and wanders away.

Shula runs up, and dives and slithers into the basin of the swing. Asham joins her. The swing lilts gently from side to side. Asham jumps out to push and the momentum increases. A girl and her mother come on to the playground. 'Stop!

Come!' the mother shouts. Shula and Asham dismount and run to join them, the family walk home together.

Stripe is back in the swing. His legs dangling over the sides, it sways gently back and forth. He stares up at the sky, and at the flats in front of him, he sits up, turns and watches the kids making go-karts on the table behind him . . .

A boy in a blue shirt approaches; Blue pushes the swing from behind, higher and higher. He jumps on, and starts to work it, holding on to the ropes on one side; it goes higher and higher. Tyler (13 and female) shouts 'Let me have a go.' Stripe slopes off and climbs up a tree trunk, part of a nearby platform structure. He sits there and watches and waits.

Blue works one side of the swing, Tyler the other. Faster, higher and faster they go. The pace is wild. Ginger joins them and sits in the basin of the swing. He jumps out, returning minutes later. He throws a juice box into the swing. He hands the other drinks to Mike and Tyler as they swing back and forth. Tricky, but well accomplished.

A young mother and her daughter come on to the playground, approach the swing and grab hold of it. Tyler and her brothers get off. The two new swingers sit with knees akimbo over the side of the swing. Relaxed and chilled the pace is slow, they chat.

This is another demonstration that children are okay when left to their own devices. They all undoubtedly have their own agendas, but these become subordinate to the complex rules of their own particular subculture. They know these rules well, and that is what determines when to use the swing and when to give way to someone else. They are well aware of hierarchies and the relative status of different people in the community. All this has been learned while playing in and around the neighbourhood.

The following story introduces the subject of the way most adults fail to relate to the children in their care – even children they love. Adults tend to give children partial attention. The child in this story appears to have been taken to the beach because that will 'amuse' him, but he clearly wants the adult to engage with his play. Unfortunately, she has more pressing things to deal with, like chatting on the phone. Children get year after year of this. The subconscious message is 'your play is not important to me'. A growing awareness of this was at the heart of Rachel Pinney's (1990) development of the idea of children's hours. In Pinney's non-directive approach, children are guaranteed one hour of undivided attention from a sympathetic adult. This is something children never get from an adult, and it is hugely beneficial for their self-esteem.

Beach versus phone

Dr Sylwyn Guilbaud – playworker

Plink, the sound of a small pebble landing on others; a few moments later I see him. He picks up another pebble and throws it into the shallow breaking waves.

Then he turns, exclaiming something and throws another up into the sky, and again and again. He looks about 3 or 4 years old, and the movement of the upward underarm throws take a lot of him up with it. A woman has followed him down the beach; she has her phone in her hand and is looking at it. He says something to her; I hear the words 'up like the bird'. He throws again, his pebble lands two inches away from me. I laugh. She holds her phone to the sky. He persuades her to throw a pebble; she throws it about as high as he is managing but with no discernible effort. He seems dismayed. I hear the words again 'high', 'bird'. She walks a little way back up the beach.

He comes back to the breaking water and throws in a big stone, followed by a handful of tiny ones, then another big one. Next, while the sea has momentarily withdrawn, he picks up a clump of wet seaweed and throws that. He looks at his hands and walks up the beach towards the woman. She seems to be objecting. 'It's seaweed,' he tells her, picks up another clump and holds it towards her, 'just seaweed!' He goes back to the sea carrying a big stone held high with one hand; in it goes with some effort. I hear the woman say the word 'go', and he says 'NO'. He throws in more stones for a while before they leave.

In this story, the adult is merely uninterested in the child's play. Sometimes adults actively intervene in the child's play to its detriment. The playwork profession calls this 'adulteration'. Hughes (2001: 163) describes adulteration as 'the hijacking of the child's play agenda by adults with the intention of substituting it with their own'. Sturrock and Else describe adulteration as meaning:

> the contamination of the play aims and objects of the children by either the wishes of the adult in an urge to 'teach' or 'educate', simply to dominate, or by the worker's own unplayed out material.
>
> (1998: 25)

Thus, there are many ways in which adults adulterate.

Two examples illustrate these points. The first I have used elsewhere (Brown 2003a: 61–62), but it bears repeating, as it offers an excellent example of the shortcomings of a didactic approach to playwork. It concerns an incident I once witnessed where a 'playworker' had organized a game of football for about 20 children.

The footballing dog

Author's observation

During the game, a dog chased a second ball on to the pitch. Quite spontaneously the children incorporated that ball into their play, and a very complex, almost three-dimensional, game resulted. The adult blew his whistle forcefully, and stopped the game. The children moaned loudly, while he carried the spare ball to the touchline. Their body language should have sent a message to the whistle-blower, but he seemed completely unaware of their very obvious 'play cues' (Sturrock and Else 1998). Not surprisingly, during the next ten minutes the players became more aggressive, even to the extent of a fight breaking out. After a while, four of the children simply walked away, and the game broke up in disarray.

In this example the sports coach's didactic approach was ill-suited to the play-scheme environment. Having tasted the thrill of creative play, the inflexibility of organized sport was too much for the children to bear. A simple understanding of the compound flexibility process (see Chapter 12), and the importance of working to the child's agenda, could have saved the playworker a great deal of stress, and made the experience that much more enjoyable for everyone.

Sometimes adults adulterate without meaning to.

The threaded tray

Author's observation

The following observation occurred when I was conducting research in the Loose Parts Experimental Room at the Eureka! Children's Museum in Halifax. A boy sat threading tape through the ends of a cardboard tray. He did this intently for about four minutes. Eventually his dad asked him why he was doing that. He obviously had no specific reason, or at least none that he could bring to mind, and therefore the question made him feel foolish. Consequently he stopped what he was doing, and suggested they leave the room and move to the Me and My Body area. His dad said, 'I wish you'd make your mind up, we've only just come from there.'

The question 'why?' is a difficult one to deal with, because it is so open-ended. Questions such as 'when?', 'where?', 'how many?', etc., are straightforward, and children will happily engage in conversations that begin with those questions. 'Why?', on the other hand, invites any number of possible responses, including social, intellectual, emotional, philosophical, etc. In my experience most children struggle to respond, but instead either say 'I don't know' (not unreasonably) or else they don't respond at all. The child in this story chose a diversionary tactic.

In 2010 I completed a research study in two schools in Yorkshire, where I had been evaluating the introduction of Sutcliffe Play's 'Snug and Outdoor' play equipment into the playgrounds. Snug is unusual – instead of fixed equipment it consists of modular shapes that children can join together in numerous different and unpredictable ways. The nine tactile shapes include so-called walls, pads, cones and noodles (see the Snug and Outdoor Website at www.snugplay.co.uk/index.html). In light of the fairly critical remarks that follow, I should state clearly that both these schools appeared to be well managed and generally pleasant places to be, and I had good reason to think that children in both schools were receiving an excellent classroom education.

The following critique was purely related to the way in which the two schools managed their playgrounds. As such, the contrast between the schools was quite striking. In one school the teachers and supervisors were routinely intrusive, and their influence on the children's play was largely negative. In the other school the practice of the teachers and supervisors was to stand back and let the children explore their own ideas without interference. I make no apology for the majority of this section focusing on the negative influence of the teachers at the first school, because this is so representative of the sort of adulterated playtimes that are so common in the UK. For example, prior to the introduction of Snug, I witnessed the following.

- When skipping ropes and wobblers were combined, the children were told 'Use the skipping ropes properly, not like that' – in general, combinatorial activity appeared to be frowned upon.
- When a child tried to climb on top of the caterpillar, he was told forcefully, 'That's for crawling through, not for climbing on' – I couldn't see why.
- Girls were not allowed to sit on the floor, but it seemed to be okay for the boys.
- 'There are two ways to play with that equipment, and you're doing it the wrong way!' – I could not see why either way was right or wrong.
- Children were regularly told to 'play properly' – I'm never quite sure what that means.
- The playground has something the children call the 'naughty wall' (I'm not sure if the adults call it that) – one of the children who was told to go and stand against the wall said, 'I wasn't naughty, just excited.'
- Towards the end of playtime a bell was rung (time to put the toys away). Then the children have to line up. On one occasion a teacher was giving loud instructions, and marching around like a soldier. She then singled out a little boy who was still touching one of the toys, and made him walk all the way across the playground to stand in front of her while she told him off. He appeared to shrink in size while all this was happening. For some reason, she didn't do the same to a little girl who was caught doing exactly the same thing.

I witnessed nothing like this at School B, which was ironic because this was a school that had previously been in 'special measures'. In such a school, where children might be expected to exhibit 'challenging behaviour', a bit of forceful playground discipline would not have been so surprising, but it really wasn't necessary.

After the introduction of Snug, some interesting developments took place at School A. They decided to set the top end of the playground apart for Snug. The children were not allowed to move any Snug items to the lower end of the playground. However, all the other loose materials found their way to the Snug area. Clearly this was not a coincidence, and shows the way in which the equipment lends itself naturally to the sort of combinatorial activity described by Bruner (1972). The adults seemed not to notice this was happening, despite being quite protective of the two areas. Also, after Snug had been in place for a couple of months, there was a noticeable reduction in 'you can't do that' from the lunchtime supervisors, probably because the equipment does not come with an instruction manual. In fact the whole point of Snug is that it's really not clear what you can and can't do, which means an increase in the children's freedom to explore the possibilities. For example, it was interesting to note that no one stopped the children climbing on top of the tunnel-shaped element (the 'walls'), unlike the previous experience with the caterpillar.

Nevertheless, the overprotective, tightly controlled regime of School A generally continued. For example, at the end of a wonderfully creative playtime session, when the children must have been feeling great, a teacher told the children, 'no class stickers are going to be awarded' due to poor lining up at the end of playtime. I very much doubt whether this sort of thing helps children learn anything, but it certainly reminds them that playtime is at an end and the adults are back in control. On another occasion the children had all the 'noodles' piled in a corner and were playing a swimming game, which involved diving into the pile and 'swimming' your way out. The teacher put a swift stop to this 'rowdy' behaviour. She said, 'You need to use them properly, that's how you fall over', to which one of the children replied 'But that's why we're doing it.' Even the teacher laughed at this. Although 'good behaviour' was constantly praised, there were far more things 'we don't do', most of which were just natural play behaviour. For example, the game of 'how many children can we squeeze inside the mushroom house' was stopped by one of the lunchtime supervisors, with the words, 'Some children are sensible in this playground, and then there's you.'

The contrast with a conversation I overheard at School B was striking:

Child: 'Miss, how do you play with this?'

Teacher: 'Well, how would you like to play with it?'

Playground rules

Author's observation

Two weeks after the introduction of Snug a set of rules was posted up on the 'naughty wall' at School A, apparently developed by the School Council (frankly, I wondered how much adult prompting had been involved in this). After about two months, the rules were formalized into a properly printed notice. The teachers decided Snug couldn't cope with all the children at once, so the classes had to take it in turns to use the equipment. As a consequence of this, on one occasion the equipment did not get used at all (despite large numbers of children in the playground) because the relevant class had gone swimming. However, this arrangement had a positive side as well, i.e. because of the intensely focused activity in and around Snug, there was more space for children in the rest of the playground.

By way of contrast, School B agreed some rules with the children when the Snug equipment arrived, but in the words of the teacher responsible, 'After a few weeks nobody seemed to take any notice, and it all seemed to be operating well, so we abandoned the idea of rules.'

The teachers at School A had a tendency to turn play into behavioural guidance. To be fair to them, this may be a by-product of the government's EYFS scheme, which claims to be about learning through play. I watched a lesson in the playground, which the teacher said was 'learning through play'. He said the children would not be using the Snug equipment, but then spent much of his time trying to keep the children away from it, despite the fact that it obviously provided plenty of learning opportunities. At one point I heard him saying to a small boy, 'There's not enough room through there for that bike, so take a different way please.' Ignoring this, the boy got off and widened the gap (having presumably learned through his play). By the end of the 'lesson', despite the teacher's best efforts, the children had used Snug to create a beach and two dens, including a mushroom house from two 'walls' and a 'pad'.

There was some evidence that the supervisors at School A became more relaxed as the year went on – maybe it's the sun, maybe the people, maybe the Snug. For example, there was certainly more unchecked rough-and-tumble play than pre-Snug, and the rule about staying off Snug when it's wet was not enforced with much conviction. Also, teachers seemed fairly relaxed about children leaping to the top of the 'cone', despite the tarmac surface – a change in practice and attitude? I would like to think that this demonstrated the beginning of a recognition that children need to take risks in their play (see Chapter 4 for a discussion of this issue).

At School B, the Snug was tidied into a locked cage at the end of the lunch period, which was beneficial as it resulted in the equipment being taken out and spread around afresh each day. At no time were the children told there's a right way or a wrong way to use this equipment. At School A, the Snug equipment was left out at the end of playtime, and only superficially tidied away at the end of the day. This generally worked well because it meant children could easily follow their play stories from one day to the next. However, it carried the slight risk that play experiences would rigidify. For example, there was one occasion when a teacher laid out four of the 'walls' as a tunnel – presumably trying to be helpful and engage with his pupils. The children predictably took the cue, and started crawling through, largely because the teacher had set this up, and children do like to please their teachers. No child moved those items for the rest of the day, and they were still arranged like that when I next visited a week later.

At School B the teachers and supervisors were definitely available to the children, and more than willing to join in when asked, but they made a real effort to give the children as much space and time as they needed. They seemed to be aware that the presence of an adult in close proximity means children play differently. It also means the children don't try to sort out problems for themselves, and therefore don't learn as much as they might. Also, if the teachers get too closely involved it is likely to limit the child's adventurousness. Children are very keen to please their teachers, which may mean they tend to wait for clues regarding what the teachers want them to do. Clearly that is not what this particular equipment is intended for.

Sometimes adult intervention is nothing short of disastrous for children's play.

Play!

Author's observation

During the lunch period at School A, children have to take it in turns to have their lunch. Several times during the period, an adult appears and rings a bell. Those whose turn it is have to line up, and wait to go in. While this happens, all the other children in the playground are expected to stand still, not touching any equipment. Once everyone is quiet and standing still, and the relevant children are lined up ready to go in for their lunch, the adult yells 'Play!', and the children are free again. This process can take up to 5 minutes. Thus, the children's play is brought to a grinding halt several times during the lunch period. I witnessed this on every visit. The frustration was clear, and the negative impact on children's creativity was obvious. Just as a group of children were beginning to get into creating something with pieces of Snug, their play was brought to a grinding halt. By the time the word 'Play!' was shouted the child were so full of tension all they could do was race around the playground yelling.

It is fair to ask whether all this regimented lining-up was really necessary. The method used at School B was simply to blow a whistle. The children seemed to know whose turn it was to go for lunch, and off they went. No one else took much notice, just getting on with their play. At the end of the lunch period, a whistle was blown just after 1.30 p.m., Snug was put back in the cage, and all children were back in their classes by 1.40 p.m.

I have stated elsewhere that

> Playwork empowers its users by offering freedom of choice in a stimulating and empathetic setting, with the result that children constantly create and recreate their own play environment.
>
> (Brown 2003b: 59)

Thus, without knowing it, the teachers and playground staff at School B generally adopted a playwork approach during playtimes. In other words, they stood back and let the children explore their own ideas in their own time and space, while at the same time ensuring the children's safety by keeping a watchful eye from a respectful distance. Hughes (1996) suggests playworkers need good peripheral vision, and this was much in evidence among the staff of School B.

The playworker's relationship with the child is often vaunted in the profession as unique. I doubt whether that assertion holds water. However, the playwork approach is certainly unique. It is built on a respect for the child's agenda, and in particular it regards play as having value in its own right, not just as a tool for children to achieve adult goals. The following story shows the dilemma faced by a playworker working in a traditional school environment.

Super heroes

Leonie Green – playworker

When I was a student on placement I experienced a very interesting conversation with a 5-year-old girl, who I will call Cheryl. Cheryl approached me as I sat by a table, on which were some toy figures. She pulled two figures out of the box of her choice. She then observed them closely, taking a very good look at them. She kept her eye contact very close to the toys, building up a connection with the characters that she developed throughout playing. She then gave me eye contact and told me about the two characters she had created. She held two figures that were both male, dressed as superheroes – she also chose a green toy van that was placed within her reach.

Cheryl began playing while interacting with me verbally; she informed me that the two superheroes were on an adventure. She placed one of the superheroes on the table and picked up the van. She then stuffed the other figure into the back of the little green van; this amused both of us. She drove the van around the table to get the attention of the other superhero. Pulling the figure out of the back of the vehicle, she then told me that one of the superheroes was going to wee and cover the other character in their pooh. As she said this she took care to observe my reaction. I reacted by saying 'Oh really, and what happened next?' I made sure my reaction showed my acceptance of her, and that I was happy and comfortable with whatever she wanted to play. Curiosity is something in children I really appreciate and consider. As a playworker I believe curiosity is the key to working with children. Appreciating children's ability to be expressive through play is something I cherish.

She continued this process, taking turns with each figure to carry out the same behaviour on each character. I could see she was enjoying playing, because she smiled throughout and laughed for the majority of the time. The beauty of this interaction between me and this particular child was the child's undoubted faith that she knew she was able to talk to me and express whatever she wished.

Unfortunately a member of staff overheard our conversation and stopped the child's play process, in a very abrupt manner. She said very loudly 'Excuse me; Leonie doesn't want to hear you talking about that sort of stuff. Go and play with something else!' This made the child feel very inadequate and she looked at me for a reaction. I smiled allowing her to know that I was not upset with her. The child didn't seem particularly upset, but more disheartened that she had to stop a game she was enjoying playing.

Through my observations I noticed a recurring theme at the club. Every time one of the children said something verbally 'unacceptable' and the staff overheard, the children were given a negative response. For example, one of the children let out a belch while sitting around the table drawing. After her action the after-school club worker told the child, 'Father Christmas will not be bringing you any presents if he hears you. Father Christmas is listening. He hears everything.' With this in mind the child started to get upset and said, 'I don't want him to not bring me presents, can you tell him I won't do it again.'

Some adults might feel this is a perfectly acceptable way of teaching children good manners, but it is certainly not the playwork way.

Sometimes a teacher can adulterate without even speaking:

The water fountain

Mahmuda Khatun – playwork student

This observation was taken by the water fountain in the communal area of the Eureka! Children's Museum in Halifax. It is an open space visible to everyone, based in the pathway to other exhibits at Eureka! – due to this, the space is used in order to walk from the 'shop' to the 'bank' at the other side. Children and parents alike stopped and looked at the fountain in amazement. The fountain is a round structure that has metal chime-like tubes coming out of the water; attached to the tubes are round metal cylinders. The water fountain is at ground level and poses no real danger, although there is a wall around it. There is another barrier around and a sign to let adults and children know the children are not allowed to climb the barrier.

A group of children came with their teacher. The children arrived at the fountain ahead of their teacher. They all looked at the fountain and stared intently into the small pool that surrounds the fountain. Some of the children tried to climb into the pool. One boy kept slipping but persisted until the teacher arrived. The children were in conversation with their friends, and some were trying to climb the fountain while others looked around the other aspects of the area, the big tree and the bank. It was clear from their facial expressions the children were fully engaged with this environment – eyes wide open, concentration, tongues out trying to get into the water fountain, smiles and laughter at the ones who slipped. Baxter (2008) explains the need for children to engage with their environment. Through interaction with the environment children test and learn their boundaries. The children were actively participating within Eureka! All this time I was sitting nearby making notes. The children were not interested in me and carried on as normal.

Then the teacher approached, and saw the children around the fountain. The boys and one girl were trying to climb the frame at this point, but fast as lightning they stopped what they were doing. Guss (2005) explains play to be a mind–body connection that develops into imagination. If an adult halts their play when children are fully absorbed, it affirms for the child that their play is not as important to adults as it is to them. The teacher came in and stopped their play. She told them to stand in a line and take it in turns with their partner to view inside the water then move on to the bank. At this point the children lost interest, and became more interested in going to the bank.

As the children left the fountain, one little girl came back and tried to climb the water fountain, when it suddenly started to 'rain'. The little girl's eyes shot up in shock and amazement; she was puzzled where the rain came from. She stood silently with her head staring up at the ceiling until the adult at the top turned the wheel again. A child at the top stood staring in amazement while the child at the bottom stood staring in amazement at the top; both children had become engaged in a new experience just by a turn of a wheel.

There is so much in this story that illustrates the negative impact of the teacher, whether intentional or not. The average teacher's desire to keep control over the class has the unintended consequence that children quickly learn that teachers stop them doing exciting things. Eventually they come to assume that, if they are doing something exciting, it's probably not allowed. Hughes (2001) takes up this point, saying children will assume they cannot dig holes, climb trees, light fires, etc. It is therefore important for playworkers to understand the need to make it clear to children that it's okay to do exciting things in a playwork environment.

Sometimes the adulteration is rooted in our apparent contempt for children – not just for their rights, but for their abilities and understanding. The following story contains elements of pure joy and delight, and possibly a significant memory in a child's life. Sadly, it also contains an example of the ignorance and arrogance of adult power.

Small flames

Penny Wilson

A small natural playspace in the middle of an East End estate . . .

It is a deep, dark evening and the playworkers, mums and children have gathered tea-lights and nestled them on the buried tree crown that is a climbing space, a den, a gathering point. It is glowing with small warm shimmers of light, which is a new and exciting plaything. The children are tender with the tiny flames. Sometimes a birthday candle is more exciting than a huge bonfire. These flames transform our time together. Our cold, burning faces absorb their warmth. Our eyes cannot resist their flickering.

On the periphery of the playing, unknown adults are gathering – a local councillor, a project manager, an official from the RSL, an estate manager. They watch and talk amongst themselves as the children play with the small flames, supported by playworkers and mums.

One very little girl, absorbed and enchanted by the experience of the candles, picks a tea-light up and asks the playworker if she can take it to her mum. The playworker pauses, considers. She shows the girl how to shield the flame and hold it away from her nylon coat. They walk together over the dark uneven grass, up the stairs, along corridors. Will the family be horrified that the child is allowed to play with fire? This is a real possibility. How would the wonder of the experience and the confidence that the girl has acquired be crushed if the family is angry? However, the child is confident that this is what she has to do.

Trying not to show her nervousness, the playworker makes sure that the child negotiates her route safely and helps her to knock at the front door. She stands waiting for an answer with the child. The girl is expecting joy at her gift. The playworker is preparing an amelioration for the child in case of a negative response.

Door opens. Dad looks bemused. Girl explains in mother tongue what she is doing. Mum joins dad and they both beam at the girl and help her into the sitting room where the extended family is gathered. The flame takes pride of place. It lights the room.

The girl turns, beaming like a small flame to the playworker, and they scamper back to the playing square.

The next day we are told that the registered social landlord has forbidden naked flames in their open space.

Where does the greatest danger lie? Where is the greatest benefit?

We continue to use tea-lights despite the ban.

Sometimes the 'institutional' adulteration is just born out of disrespect for children. We make contracts with children and don't even realize that we have done so. For example, in the following story Maria doesn't use the word 'contract', but she is clearly annoyed that the stated opening times are being flaunted.

Against the fence

Maria Rowley – 9 years old

My family and me went to London for the weekend in May. When my dad and two brothers went to watch our friend play football, my sister Caitlin and me asked to go to the park. Regent's Park was nearby. I thought it was big and posh and royal with lots of pretty flowers. We liked it there. We explored the bushes and flowers, played leap frog, grabbed blossom and chased the pigeons. Then we found an exciting play area. It looked good because it had sand and bark and loads and loads of big play areas. The only problem was the gate was locked. My mum managed to convince us that maybe there was some work going on, and it was such a big park, maybe we could find another play area.

Caitlin and me played leap frog towards London Zoo. We did find another, even better park, but again it was locked. Mum looked at the opening hours. It was meant to close at 7.30 p.m., but it was still only 6.30 p.m. – there was no sign of work or repairs in this one either. I was disappointed, but surprised that I felt like I wanted to climb the fence to go and play. I started climbing and stopped and turned around to ask,

'Mum you will back me up if I get caught, won't you?'

'Yeah, go ahead if you want,' mum said, looking around, I think to make sure no one was watching us.

I don't think she was worried because the sign said it should be open. Maybe the caretaker or whoever was looking after it was on a break. But Caitlin didn't want to join me because she thought she would get caught. After a quick run around, a swing and a few slides, I started to feel a bit worried because some people were riding past on their bikes looking at me like they were going to tell someone so I climbed back out.

We left the park to start to walk back to the hostel.

'Is Play Wales gonna sort this?' I asked mum.

'This is England,' mum answered.

'Well I hope you're gonna tell Play England!' my sister said.

Mum said maybe we would write a letter. In the end it was pretty cool because I got to have the whole park to myself and I felt a bit like the queen's daughter in my garden.

I'm not sure why there is a fence there. It's like they are trying to stop something. It's not like anything is going to happen because it was in the middle of the park way away from the road. I don't know why there is an opening time on the play area anyway. It's not like a café or restaurant. The play area should close when the whole park closes. They shouldn't even have a play area there if they are going to lock it.

This story first appeared in the autumn 2008 edition of the Play for Wales *magazine.*

If the Parks Department says the playground will open and close at stated times, then that should be regarded as a contractual obligation. It is certain that they would open and close a golf club or a bowls club on time. The contracts we make with children are important because they are the start of a relationship. If we let the children down at the beginning, it is difficult to develop the sense of trust that underpins so much of the playworker's role.

It's not just adults who adulterate – power corrupts!

Organized skittles

Keith Ramtahal – inspector for early years

I have been fortunate to have taught not only in the English state sector, but also in the fee-paying sector in the capital of Egypt, Cairo.

During this time in Cairo I was asked to get the pupils in my international school to vote on what activities they wanted to take part in at playtime. They were to do this by using voting slips, which they placed in a ballot box by the end of the week following the Monday school assembly. To obtain any equipment that may be required I was allocated a budget of £500 per term. One of the most popular activities voted for was the game of skittles, which is a more basic version of 10-pin bowling. So I purchased two sets of skittles. And set them both out the next week, in the purpose-built games area of the playground, at the start of the children's first playtime.

The activity was very popular immediately. An unappointed leader/referee emerged almost at once; he was an 11-year-old boy from a very affluent Egyptian family. He sorted out the players into groups by age, told them the rules and regulations, and even kept a detailed record of all the scores, as well as reprimanding players for 'breaking the game's rules'. Each participating member played very competitively and would point out misdemeanours made by other players by shouting out to the referee, who would blow his whistle vigorously and call the 'offending' player over.

After three days the pupils became restless and agitated as the referee started to caution players for the slightest thing, such as accidentally dropping the ball before they played their shots. Soon the numbers participating in skittles matches dwindled from 50 pupils to about 5. The referee eventually started to kick the equipment over when a player broke *his* rules, throw the ball across the playground and even cautioned a player for having loose shoelaces. Eventually he hollered at one player, 'This is rubbish, my chauffeur takes me to play real skittles whenever I tell him to. Even at 11 o'clock at night!'

When undertaking research of any kind it is important to be sensitive to the situation that is being observed, otherwise we run the risk of creating the 'observer effect' – sometimes known as the Hawthorne effect because of the place where this was first noticed. Landsberger (1958) came to the conclusion that the improved productivity of workers at the Hawthorne Works, near Chicago, was caused by the fact that they were being studied, not because of any changes that were the subject of the experiment. In the case of children's play, the need for sensitive observation from a distance is paramount, because it is all too easy to adulterate their play without meaning to.

The woods

Lesley Creevy – photographer and playwork trainer

The woods echoed with the sounds of birds, running water, rustling leaves and children. Laughter, shouting and the hushed tones of children deeply involved in the serious business of play could be heard intermittently drifting through the trees. For the moment they could not be seen. Keeping low to the ground I checked the camera and made my way to the outcrop of rocks from where the shouting had come. As I approached I realized this group were still playing the game. This had started at the beginning of the holidays when those long relaxed sessions had enabled the children to embark in a play frame that expanded the summer. I had not heard of the play cycle, nor of Bob Hughes and evolutionary play, or in fact any of the play theory that I now know. I had worked part-time in this club for years totally unaware that what the children were experiencing at the club, although similar to my own childhood experiences, was quite unlike the play experiences of most other children of this generation.

I had permission from the children and their parents to take photographs. As part of a photography course, I had chosen to emulate the work of a famous photojournalist who had made her name photographing street children in American cities. My study was going to contrast this and depict children from a rural area playing in a natural environment.

The children had begun building dens before the end of term and had scoured the woods for suitable sites. As the holidays progressed so did the dens. The children turned these basic shelters into elaborate dens that had seating and storage, and sometimes sleeping arrangements. Some of the dens were maintained others destroyed. The surviving dens were protected and the children began making weapons. Initially they used sticks, shaping them into daggers with the tools in the club. The daggers developed into bow and arrows, and the children mastered the art of pulling and tying the string taut so that it would fire the bow. When one of the children found pieces of slate, they started making axes, learning first how to shape the slate into an axe head and then how to fix it to a stick.

Although both boys and girls were involved in den building it was mainly boys that became engrossed in making weapons. Both boys and girls began mixing potions from leaves and mud, but girls became adept at identifying the leaves and berries that could be foraged for food. Sometimes the children chose to eat these raw and sometimes they brought berries to the club to bake into muffins or blend into smoothies.

When the children discovered a piece of quartz in the dried-up riverbed their play moved into a new era. These white pieces of stone became sought after and the children would mine the riverbed in search of more. These were used like money to buy weapons and food and other interesting finds that were desirable to them at the time.

Over the course of the summer I had followed the children with my camera, careful not to interfere in their play. I had captured children behaving naturally in this environment and had hoped they had not found my presence intrusive. As I crept nearer to the outcrop of rocks from where the shouting had come, I witnessed a child fairly new to the setting being initiated into the 'tribe' by the leader. He was using language that most adults would have found unacceptable. The new child nodded in my direction then looked at the leader, 'She can hear you!' The leader replied without looking up, 'So, she won't say anything.' I can only say that I felt deeply honoured and privileged to have witnessed and captured all that I had, but more importantly throughout this process the children had not felt that my presence was a threat to their play.

As a general principle, playworkers should be very reluctant to intervene in children's play, because that would adulterate the experience for the child. However, for some children intervention is clearly necessary, as it aids the play process. Nevertheless, intervention should always be handled carefully, with the child's needs being paramount. It is also crucial that we keep the child's agenda right at the forefront of our choices.

David

Tricia Pedley – play development worker

David is a 6-year-old boy. He is an only child. He lives with his mum and dad in a middle-class area of Leeds. They live in a semi-detached house, and both mum and dad work full-time. David attends a mainstream school, and enjoys a range of activities, including: playing with water, rough-and-tumble play and running as fast he can. His best friend is James. He also loves washing machines. David has autism.

When Play Partners met with David and his family, David was already attending the Out of School Club. He had been a member for the past two years. David's parents had approached Play Partners to get some support for him while he attended the sessions at the Out of School Club. Concerns had emerged that David was spending the duration of the sessions playing independently and becoming lost among the other children. Play Partners were asked to encourage existing staff to work flexibly around David's needs, and help them develop play activities that would encourage him to play with other children.

We began by visiting the setting and met with the staff to discuss David and his needs while he attended the setting. We were also interested in the concerns of the staff and what they would like to accomplish with Play Partners' support. Here is my note on the third session:

Session 3

I entered the play room to find David and James watching a film, wriggling like worms on the sofa. You could sense the excitement. I approached the pair, and they both jumped up and launched themselves at me. David and James love rough-and-tumble play.

The first 40 minutes of the session was spent throwing cushions at each other, jumping on each other and using me as their play apparatus. This was watched by other staff members with no intervention. David benefited from having the support worker to play in this way, with somebody to enable their play, ensuring it does not escalate into an argument, which quite often happens with James and David. Playing like this is vital and avoids the prompt ending of a rough-and-tumble play session, which could signal that what they are doing is wrong – which of course it isn't!

David had had a bad day at school and the staff in the club had mentioned that this had flowed over into his play time. He had spent the duration of the session playing with James, but as James had left the session early this enabled him to play with others. David had chosen to build a tower with Michael. They spent the remaining time in the session doing this, building the towers up and knocking them down, over and over again.

I have observed David playing with a number of different children in this session, some fleetingly, others for quite a while. The time he spends interacting with the other staff seems to have lessened, but he still gives all staff a big hug goodbye. For this session the hugs were unusually the most time spent with other members of staff.

Play Partners spent seven weeks supporting the Out of School Club; we continue to support David in the school holidays and are currently working with the Out of School Club to secure funding for a permanent support worker for David. Play Partners is a Leeds Play Network project.

When to intervene, and when to hold back, is a difficult decision, but the essential thing that marks out the playwork approach is deliberate and calculated hesitancy. The playworker's response should always be that of reluctance to intervene, unless it is absolutely necessary in order to protect a child from harm.

10

The Colliery Adventure Playground: some personal reflections

The first extended reflection covers one year in the life of an adventure playground. The story dates back to the 1970s when adventure playgrounds were a more popular form of provision for children's play. Although the UK's Health & Safety at Work Act had been passed in 1974, we did not begin to feel its full impact until several years later, so Sorensen's (1931) idea of children using scrap materials to create, dismantle and re-create their own play environment in an ongoing process of change, was still alive and well. The adult world had a more relaxed attitude towards children, and insurers were more willing to cover play providers against the risk of injury to children in their care. Of course those attitudes have changed substantially in the last 35 years (Gill 2007), but that subject has already been addressed in earlier chapters, so there is no need to cover the same ground here.

I was appointed 'playleader' (as we were called at the time) in January of the year in question. The Colliery Adventure Playground (CAP) came about after two successful summer playschemes led to the formation of a community action group, which then lobbied their councillors for improved play provision on the Colliery Estate. The local authority responded positively, albeit with a hidden agenda. Its Social Services Department was having difficulty getting any sort of foothold into the Colliery Estate, an extremely disadvantaged area of public housing. They hoped that an adventure playground worker might be able to form effective relationships with the children of troubled families, and that might act as a catalyst for social workers to become more accepted in the area. It was not uncommon in those days for playwork to be regarded as predominantly a form of children's social work. In order to help me become more easily accepted they established an unusual management arrangement – namely, I was employed by the local authority, but responsible to a local community group, the Colliery Adventure Playground Association (CAPA). Although I did not see social work as my primary role, there is no doubt that the local authority made progress in that direction because of the presence of the playground.

The Colliery Adventure Playground was funded with a five-year grant from the Urban Aid Programme (Home Office 1968), and when I was appointed it still existed only as a plan on someone's desk. This would be a good model for any such project. Most providers would erect a fence and construct a play building in advance of appointing staff. Employing me in advance of any construction work enabled me to keep the local community well informed throughout that phase. This meant the children and the local community felt involved in the creation of the playground right from the beginning, which in turn created a strong sense of ownership.

The first few weeks of my employment were spent in preparatory work, which included spending every evening, and most weekends, sitting on the site of the playground with the children who would be its future users. Apart from playing games and chatting, our most regular activity was banging sticks into the ground to mark where the fence was going to be. These sticks often disappeared overnight, but that didn't seem to dishearten the children. They just found more sticks and banged them in all over again.

The stories that follow are included because they speak for themselves. They do not in any way constitute a history of the adventure playground. They are merely intended to give a flavour of life on an adventure playground around 35 years ago. As far as I remember they are true, but of course over the years it is possible that my memories of these events have become slightly romanticized. For that reason, names and places have been changed to protect the innocent.

Getting wet in the first den

During their half-term holiday the children had constructed the first den – basically a large hut made from scrap materials. Their only thought was of 'camping out', so that's what we did, on the final Saturday of the holiday. Unfortunately, it had not occurred to any of them (or me) that it might get cold during the night, nor that it might start raining. At first, most of the children were moaning and swearing (something they did a lot). A couple of them went home as soon as the water started dripping through the roof. However, as the night wore on, and things became steadily worse, it was as if the shared misery created a bond between us all – one of those experiences that live on for a while in everyone's memory. We ended the night freezing cold and soaking wet, having had a great time.

The story of our adventure spread around the estate, and three days later a lorry driver 'donated' a huge tarpaulin. 'That's for your next camp. It got damaged when it fell off the back of my lorry.' He actually used those words, and in my innocence I took the story at face value. The next time we camped out in the children's dens we were all well protected from the rain. Over the next few years the children constructed one den after another, and often subsequently demolished them in order to build yet another. The older children's dens were nearly always constructed with a view to 'camping out'. Younger children generally had a more immediate aim in mind. In all cases the time and effort employed in construction far outweighed the den's subsequent use. Strictly speaking it is not entirely true to suggest (as some have) that play is a non-goal-oriented activity. That is sometimes the case, but not always. More often than not children have a goal in mind when they are playing. However, that goal is often of secondary importance, and in most cases the actual process of playing is far more significant than the end result.

Protecting the slab

After I had been in post for around two months, work started on the construction of our play building. The first step was for the builders to lay a huge slab of concrete on which the building (actually a builder's site hut) would rest. We were told that the slab had to remain untouched for at least two weeks, while the concrete set hard. It was important that there were no ridges or holes where the walls would be located – otherwise the pre-fabricated sections would not sit squarely, and it would not be possible to complete the construction. The children took this very seriously. A small group of them camped out every night to protect their slab from intruders. These 'guardians' were children who I had been told were dangerous. Someone even suggested I ought to carry a weapon if I wanted to remain safe 'up there' on the Colliery Estate. Utter nonsense!

After laying the slab, the builders had a lot of concrete left over. I persuaded them to dump it in the middle of the playground to create an area where we could safely light fires. That night someone carved his initials in the wet concrete of the fireplace. The guardians were incensed, and subjected him to their own rough justice. In truth all the children could have carved their initials in the fireplace. It wouldn't have mattered, but for the guardians concrete was concrete and in need of protection. This was just the first of many demonstrations of how protective the children were towards 'their' playground.

The aerial runway (sometimes called a zip wire)

In order to use the aerial runway the children had to climb the grassy ridge at one end of the playground, and clamber up a net leading to a platform. This design meant that using the aerial runway was beyond the capacity of the smaller children. Once on the platform they had to grab hold of a rope, which was attached to a pulley wheel suspended from a long cable running down to a net about 50 metres along the playground, and launch themselves out into space. In retrospect the whole thing was highly dangerous. The drop from the launch platform was probably in the region of 10 metres, and the line of travel was straight through the middle of the playground.

The aerial runway was entirely built by adults – a rarity on CAP, where our core philosophy meant that almost everything was left to the imagination and creativity of the children. However, I felt an aerial runway was potentially dangerous, and so its safety had to be pretty much guaranteed. In retrospect that is ironic, for two reasons. First, as is clear from the above description, it was still extremely dangerous by today's standards. Enabling children to engage with risk is an important part of the core philosophy of playwork. Putting them in danger is quite another thing. However, it has to be said we only ever had one accident on the aerial runway in the time I was there – a broken arm when a boy ignored the instructions and tried to come down upside down and hanging on with one hand.

The second irony is far more significant. Having been built by adults, the structure took on a different quality in the eyes of the children. When building something for themselves they constantly tested and re-tested its safety. An engineer once said to me that the Victorians' approach to safety was to calculate what was needed and then double it. The children on CAP adopted that sort of philosophy in most of their construction techniques. However, their attitude to the aerial runway was entirely different – in fact it was bordering on reckless. This is illustrated by the following episode.

We finally completed the construction at about 1.30 p.m. on a school day. I was aware the aerial runway was easily the most risky structure on the playground, and had to be tested before the children used it. Since I was the only paid employee on this playground it was clearly my responsibility to test it out. I climbed on to the platform, and stood there for many minutes before finally plucking up the courage to leap into the unknown. Fortunately everything was okay. The scary thing was, when the children came out of school most of them climbed on to the platform and zipped straight down the wire, without a moment's hesitation. I am convinced their faith in the safety of this risky structure was rooted in the fact that they knew it had been built by adults.

The German volunteers

During the first summer holiday an international volunteering agency offered me two German students for two weeks, so long as we could feed and accommodate them. I readily agreed, but on the day before they arrived someone painted a large swastika on the side of the playground building. One of the local fathers, who had been helping out a lot during evenings and weekends, took extreme exception to this and made it his business to search out the culprit. Two hours later he appeared with a teenage boy in tow, and stood behind him while he scrubbed the offending item off. We then repainted the wall. In truth, I don't think the boy had any idea what he was doing.

When the German students arrived there was no sign of the offensive symbol, and that particular father took them under his wing for the whole fortnight – feeding them, teaching them how to play snooker, taking them to nightclubs, etc. I happen to know he is still in touch with one of the students today. During their stay, the students constructed a seesaw. I found it interesting that, apart from the aerial runway, that seesaw was the only item of equipment that remained in place despite the ever-changing nature of the playground.

Robbie

In my first few weeks I tried to get to know all the significant people in the children's lives: the local policeman, the vicar and, of course, their school teachers. The deputy head of the local secondary school was known as 'killer' by the children. I wasn't sure why, but when I met him for the first time I began to understand. He was a very large man, with a craggy face that took on a look of pure contempt when he started talking about the children.

'You'll have to deal with that little bastard Robbie Walker.'

'Pardon?'

'Yeh – little bastard! We manage to get him suspended every now and then. Little sod.'

My experience of Robbie over the next couple of years was the exact opposite. He had all manner of skills that the school was failing to recognize – not least he was an expert den builder. Perhaps more importantly, he was a pleasure to be with, always reasonable, always fair and hugely respected by everyone – children and adults. The smaller children often used his wisdom to sort out their disputes. If Robbie gave them a judgement they generally took notice and acted accordingly. He was not strong academically, but had an acute sense of right and wrong. Those two things don't go together very well in a school environment, so he regularly fell out with the teachers.

One Saturday I came upon Robbie talking to one of the dads, a collier called Geoff. Robbie had been suspended from school again.

Geoff: 'So what happened this time?'

Robbie: 'Well I couldn't do the maths, and the teacher called me a Crofter' (Croft House was the local mental hospital). 'So I said, don't you call me a Crofter, and he called it me again, so I hit him.'

To be honest, my first thought (as a not very professional playworker) was that the teacher deserved it, but Geoff and Robbie had other ideas.

Geoff: 'Well, that's no way to sort out your problems Robbie.'

Robbie: 'I know. I feel quite ashamed of myself.'

That sort of honest self-reflection was typical of Robbie. To this day I still don't understand how the school could get this child so completely wrong.

Jimmy Widge

Jimmy Widge was a rather sad little boy, around 7 years of age, who attended a special school and never played out with the other children, until the arrival of the adventure playground. On my first day his mother came and asked me whether he would be safe with us, and of course I said yes, not knowing what lay in store for him. Apparently, he had previously been looked after in his house by his grandmother, who for some reason kept him in a state of undress. Whenever the door was left open he would come running out into the street with his little 'widge' dangling before him. So, the children knew him as Jimmy Widge.

Whenever he came to the playground in the first few months someone would get him to take his clothes off. Obviously this was very distressing, albeit I don't think he was worried. The playground was nearly an acre of undulating scrubland, so it was difficult to police. His mother and I would often spend a period before closing time searching for his clothes. However, after a while the children began to adopt a different attitude to him. A couple of older girls became very protective, and put a stop to the abuse quite firmly. Gradually the children started to treat Jimmy as someone special. Newcomers would be taken and introduced to him. He even featured in the playground song that was written by a couple of children.

I used to be very proud of all that, but as time went on I realized it was only partial progress. Eventually all the fuss-making stopped, and the children started treating him not as someone special, but as just one of their number – a bit different maybe, but just another child on the playground. That is real integration. It cannot be forced, but takes time to develop naturally, so long as children are given the time and space to come to a realization that there is no need to be frightened of someone just because they are a bit different.

Donna's fighting

Girls came from far and wide to fight Donna. The first time it happened I was ill-prepared. A large group of children appeared in the playground building:

'Fight, fight – we want blood! Fight, fight – we want blood!'

Donna charged out of the playground with the chanting children in her wake. About half an hour later she returned triumphant, surrounded by her cheering supporters. She was a mess, but one of the children told me the other girl looked much worse. The second time it happened, I tried to reason with her, to no avail – and the third time, and the fourth.

But Donna grew up quickly on the playground. When she was about 15, another challenger arrived, and the children were there baying for blood. To everyone's surprise Donna refused to fight. The children called her a chicken and a coward, but the truth was quite different. I'm convinced Donna gained real strength from the playground. She didn't have to use her muscles to prove anything anymore, because she had become so comfortable with the person she really was.

Bonfire night

By the end of the first summer the children had created an amazing chaotic tapestry of dens and climbing frames, a boat swing, a sandpit, etc. The playground was in a state of constant change, but always developing into something more and more wonderful. Not everyone agreed. My father visited when the children had a craze for building 'tower' dens. He said 'It looks a bit like a concentration camp.' However, in my eyes the playground was a creative wonder. So, imagine my horror when I arrived on Saturday 4 November to find children and parents tearing the whole thing down to make the 'biggest bonfire there's ever been' (see the front cover). It seemed like reckless and wanton destruction of a year's work, and all for the sake of a couple of hours of excitement. In truth I have never seen a bonfire like it before or since. It lit up the night sky like a millennium beacon. Our plans of cooking potatoes on it came to nothing, because you couldn't get within 20 metres of it. It was still burning the next day, and for two days after that. We eventually had to get the fire brigade to come and put it out. All that was left were the charred embers of a once beautiful thing. But, that was my mistake.

We struggled our way through the cold nights of winter, but as soon as the days started to lengthen the children were out again rebuilding their playground. Of course this year's playground was completely different, and after another end-of-year bonfire so was the following year's. Drummond Abernethy (1977) suggested we should see the adventure in adventure playgrounds as being in the mind of the child. Too often playworkers feel protective of the adventurous structures, with the result that successive generations of children have less opportunity to impact on the play environment, and consequently feel less possessive about 'their' playground. This is fundamentally bad practice. Adventure playgrounds should be an ongoing blank slate on which children can explore their own ideas. If the structures stay the same over many years the playworkers are effectively adulterating the children's play (Delorme 2013). The annual bonfire made sure that could not happen at the Colliery Adventure Playground.

Burly's pantomime

At first I wasn't sure about 'Burly', as the children called him on account of his name being David Curle. In fact he was anything but burly. There was really nothing of him physically, and for some reason I couldn't quite take to him. That happens sometimes, and playworkers have to find a way of dealing with it. It's the same dilemma for teachers, and for anyone who works with children. They are not all loveable. Having said that, it is fortunate that in general children can rely on their mothers to love them (albeit, see the next chapter).

At the beginning of December, Burly and a couple of other young teenagers told me they wanted to put on a pantomime for the toddlers. I was thrilled. This seemed to me clear evidence of progress. These youngsters had been failed by society at every turn, and had previously adopted violence as a solution to all their problems, yet here they were planning to do the most charming thing you could imagine. Burly had seen *Rumpelstiltskin* performed somewhere, and wanted to do that.

'But you've got to write it, Fraser!'

It is not an easy task to write a pantomime for teenagers to perform, which toddlers will understand. Also, I was in two minds, because my philosophy of play-work was for the children to create the experience for themselves from the raw materials provided by me. On this occasion I reasoned that I would be providing the raw material of a script, and they could make of it whatever they wanted. This worked like a dream. They took my script and changed it beyond recognition, until it was entirely their own creation. For example, they introduced a character called Belch, who was the King's butler. This part was taken by an older teenager who had the ability to burp to order. So, whenever the king called for his butler, 'Belch!', that character would appear on stage and let out a great big belch! The toddlers thought that was hilarious.

On the night of the pantomime, Burly took centre stage. He came alive as Rumpelstiltskin. He used all the pantomime tricks, silly jokes, catchphrases. At one point he divided the audience into two groups for a competitive sing-song. He even manufactured a scene where a ghost appeared, and the toddlers were yelling 'Behind you!' In short, he was a revelation – yet another youngster with hidden talents that the education system had somehow missed.

Leaving

Before working at CAP I did not even know the town existed. When I eventually left, the only people I knew in the town were children and adults connected with the playground. I was the only employee, and thought it was my life's work. It was a sort of obsession, which I would not suggest is the best way to run an adventure playground, but nevertheless had positive benefits, as I hope I have illustrated. However, in what seemed like no time at all I was suffering from total emotional exhaustion, and knew I had to leave for the sake of my own health. On the evening when I handed in my notice we were having the annual Christmas party. It had not seemed appropriate to tell the children I was leaving until the next day. So there I was, enjoying the joyous occasion, but feeling slightly guilty, when a little girl took hold of my hand. Looking up at me with big brown eyes she said:

'You know you can never leave this place.'

'Why's that?' I asked.

'Cos we'd all drown in the tears.'

There was a clear downside to that sort of intertwining of the playworker with the whole life of the playground – not least in the way the playground struggled to survive my leaving. The children's attitude was simple: 'You said this was our playground – we didn't want you to leave – now the adults are giving us a playworker we don't want – so is it really our playground?' On one occasion when CAPA advertised for a new worker I received a petition from the children asking me to come back. The first person to replace me was unfortunately named William – a lovely man, but he didn't stand a chance. The children called him Big Willy, and it was all downhill from there. The next person was a married man, with children. Clearly he could not be expected to give the same sort of total commitment that the children had become used to. The playground struggled on for a few more years, with a constant turnover of staff, and finally folded, to be replaced by a traditional swing park.

My colleague and friend Tony Chilton did not make the same mistake as me. During his time working at Blacon Adventure Playground in Chester, he put huge efforts into expanding both the budget and the staff. As a result, when he left, the playground was able to survive the departure of its much-loved first playworker, because there were still a number of familiar faces around. Blacon has today morphed into a facility that incorporates a city farm, but it is still operating some 40 years after its inception.

Epilogue

The years spent at CAP had (and still have) a deep significance in my life. On the occasions when these experiences have been presented to an audience, it has often been suggested that I should write them down. Well, this book has given me the chance to do just that. However, I am also going to take this opportunity to make a more general point about spreading the message of playwork. This involves a slightly painful story.

Many years ago, when I worked for the National Playing Fields Association, I presented these reflective stories to my colleagues. One of them sat reading a newspaper throughout my retelling of experiences that meant a great deal to me. At the time that hurt me deeply, but in retrospect it was just the first of several such experiences. Some people 'get it', and some just never will, because their minds are closed. Perhaps, as Sutton-Smith (1997) might suggest, their brain cells have already rigidified. Presumably most readers of this book will already share my commitment to the cause of playwork and the child's right to play. I expect many will have tried to 'spread the word', only to be greeted with lack of interest and/or negativity. It's frustrating and emotionally draining, and so I want to share with you the wise words of the artist David Reeve Fowkes (1990), written when he was a gunner in Italy during the Second World War.

> In war it is difficult to stem one's ready affections, for in the discomfort and monotony one tends to welcome friendliness because it gives opportunity for

self-expression, a two-edged way to relief; two-edged because in my experience, invariably he to whom you told your ambition betrays it by his lack of understanding. The fault is not his, it is your own because you failed to perceive that he would not understand, and because you were too ready to talk. In effect, you have spread a priceless cloth on the ground and invited a man with muddy boots to trample on it. Then when you see the filth disfiguring something which is part of your mind, cool reason is lost in bitterness and you begin to despise. Learn never to be bitter, never to despise, learn understanding and compassion without priggishness – without priggishness, one of the most difficult things to learn.

(2 January 1944)

Too often we spread the priceless cloth of playwork on the ground only to have it trampled on with someone's muddy boots. I think the lesson from Fowkes is, when faced with a narrow-minded response, we must take care not to be self-righteous and narrow-minded ourselves. On the contrary, we need to be flexible in our thinking and our approach – living proof of the value of play – and that is a theme to be taken up in the final chapter, where I will be revisiting the concept of compound flexibility.

11

Therapeutic Playwork Project: extracts from a reflective diary

The second extended set of reflections concerns the impact of a playwork project on a group of abandoned children living in a ward of a Romanian paediatric hospital. This was also the subject of a research study that focused on the children's development (Brown and Webb 2005). The reflection draws on extracts from a research diary kept by Sophie Webb during the early months of the project.

The children, ranging in age from 1 to 10 years old, had suffered chronic neglect and abuse. They had spent most of their lives tied in a cot; they were poorly fed and their nappies were rarely changed. Although able to see and hear other children, they were unable to leave their cots, and so experienced little in the way of social interaction. The focus of our study was the children's play development, which we assessed using an instrument developed for a previous study (Brown 2003c). During a period when nothing changed in their lives, other than their introduction to the playwork project, the children themselves changed dramatically. Their social interaction became more complex; physical activity showed a distinct move from gross to fine motor skills; the children's understanding of the world around them was improved; and they began to play in highly creative ways. They no longer sat rocking, staring vacantly into space. Instead they became fully engaged, active human beings. Our conclusion was simple, but striking: the children's developmental progress was clearly identifiable, and apparently made possible through their experience of the playwork project (Webb and Brown 2003).

The therapeutic playwork project began in the summer of 1999 and continues today, albeit in a much reduced form. It started as a result of the concern of the newly appointed Director of the Sighisoara Hospitals, Dr Cornel Puscas. Although neither a paediatrician nor a psychologist, when confronted with a ward full of disturbed children sitting rocking in their own solitary worlds, he was reminded of one of the most powerful conclusions from the studies of Suomi and Harlow (1971: 493): 'play is of utmost importance for the subsequent social well-being of the individual and those around him'. In common with most Romanian institutions at that time, the hospital had no spare money. So, hoping to help the children recover, he set aside a room to be used as a 'playroom' and approached the UK charity White Rose

Initiative (WRI)[1] for funding to employ someone to play with the children. The WRI employed Edit Bus as the first Romanian playworker, and brought her to Leeds Beckett University for a specially designed training course run by myself. Upon her return to Romania, Edit worked with the children for four months by herself, before being joined by Sophie Webb (a Leeds Beckett playwork student) for an extended period, and later by me for briefer periods. Towards the end of the first year, WRI expanded the staff team to four Romanian playworkers.

In the early days of the project, Edit and Sophie had to untie the children in the morning, bathe them, change their nappies and feed them properly, before taking them to the playroom. The two playworkers worked with the children all day, bathing, changing and feeding them as and when necessary, and enabling them to begin the long road to recovery through play. At the end of each day, the children were returned to their hospital ward. As soon as the playworkers left the hospital, the nurses went into the ward and tied the children to their cots for the night. This daily pattern continued for at least the first year of the project. No amount of pleading or persuasion could change the nurses' behaviour. I have often been asked for an explanation of this inhumanity on the part of nurses. It is of course difficult to understand. Was it rooted in contempt for disabled children, or possibly discrimination towards Roma children? Both prejudices are widespread in Romanian society. Perhaps the nurses were busy and under-resourced, and found the children less troublesome when they were tied up. Possibly they did not see their role in terms of care, but rather more as wardens. Perhaps they were merely taking their lead from a particular doctor who was in charge of the ward at that time.

When children are deprived of play, the consequences are catastrophic. The emotions of this group of children were in turmoil. When the project started they just stared vacantly into space, rocking to and fro in that rolling motion so familiar to anyone who witnessed the television images emanating from Romania in the early 1990s. They generally looked several years younger than their actual age. We worked with a 10-year-old boy (complete with nappy) who could have passed for a toddler in any UK nursery. Their gross motor skills were poorly developed, and they possessed hardly any fine motor skills at all. They were incapable of meaningful social interaction, and showed few signs of cognitive functioning. In the first few months the slightest disturbance was deeply frightening, and resulted in a return to the rocking motion.

In those early days it was hard to assess which children had been born with a disability, and which were merely suffering from years of neglect and abuse. However, those distinctions quickly became apparent as the children began to develop. Although every child made progress, some forged ahead at such a rapid rate that it has forced me to question my own assumptions about attachment theory, the long-term impact of abuse, and the 'ages and stages' view of child development. The change in the children's demeanour and behaviour resulted in 13 of the original 16 being either adopted or fostered within Romania – something that would have been unlikely in the extreme at the beginning of the project.

[1] For further details, contact White Rose Initiative, The Flying Ferret, 96 Huddersfield Road, Shelley, Huddersfield HD8 8HF.

In less than a year, these chronically abused and neglected children made the sort of progress that many experts assumed would be impossible. During the period of the research study the only change in the children's life experience was the playwork project. Therefore, it is sensible to ask, what it is about playwork that has contributed to these changes?

Clearly the children's learning and development resulted substantially from the playworkers' ability to create an enriched play environment that was substantially supportive of the play process. The playworkers' non-judgmental approach, coupled with a determination to take each child's agenda as his/her own starting point, helped to create a good-quality playwork environment – in other words, an environment that offered adaptability to the children, and so encouraged the compound flexibility process (Brown 2003b). Through their empathy, and their ability to interpret the children's play cues effectively, the playworkers were able to create strong, trusting relationships, which we argue helps enhance the children's self-esteem (Brown and Webb 2012). If such approaches were applied in a typical playwork setting in the UK, we would take it for granted that children would learn and develop naturally. The remarkable thing about our experience in Romania was that this straightforward playwork approach appeared to work just as effectively with some of the most play-deprived children in the world.

Thankfully the hospital's approach to the children changed dramatically after about 18 months. Today all children are treated the same, no matter what their reason for being in hospital. They are bathed regularly, properly fed and their developmental needs are addressed. Staff turnover saw some of the worst offenders move on, but I am convinced the major causal factor was the example provided by the WRI playworkers, who were encouraged to treat the children with love and respect at all times.

The following extracts are taken from the research diary kept by Sophie Webb during her first months of working with these children. As is often the case with this sort of record, her reflections ran to many thousands of words, sometimes hundreds of words on just one day. Restrictions on space make it impossible to reproduce the whole diary. Instead, what follows is intended to give a flavour of the experience, and also to illustrate the value of this approach. Palmer (2008) suggests being a reflective practitioner is a fundamental skill that playworkers need to develop.

Week 1

I decided not to write anything for this week, except for personal notes. There was just too much to take in to try and make sense of it all. I've watched a lot, and stood back a little. I need to be aware of giving wrong signals.

These were my first impressions of the conditions at the hospital and the way the children are treated:

The silence. Every room was full of children in cots, but it was so quiet. Even when we entered the room there was no sound from the children. They just looked at us. The smell of urine in every room was almost unbearable. *The emptiness.* Each room had just the cots with plastic mattresses. The children were dirty and wearing clothes that were too big for them. Some were wearing jumpers as trousers, and none of them were wearing shoes. There were rags around their waists, which I later found out were ripped up sheets tied, to keep the nappies in place. These rags were also used to tie the children to the cots. Most children were sitting rocking and others were standing up banging the sides of their cots against the walls. Giving the children a cuddle was strange as they either held on too tightly, or they remained stiff and unfeeling.

When I observed the children in the playroom, they were unaware of each other, fixed on their own activities – barely communicating. Some just sat and seemed bewildered and vacant.

Notes on the children I'll be focusing on – Virgil, Olympia, Nicolae, Ion, Elena, Alexandru.

All six children are abandoned, and are from Roma families. They appear to have been in the hospital all their lives, although no one is absolutely sure as there are no formal records about them. Edit has worked with these children since last August. Before that they could not walk, talk or communicate. They had little human contact and no stimulation, and seem to have spent every day tied to their cots. My aim is to work on what changes have already been made, and help with new ideas and encouragement.

Day 8

One day last week I was in our room and Edit came in wanting to show me something. She led me next door to the salon that Carol stayed in and what I saw shocked me so much I just stood there with my mouth open! The nurses had not changed him again, so his nappy had probably been on all night and day and it had leaked everywhere – all over the walls, in his cot, all over his little body, on the floor . . . everywhere. It was just awful. I've got to know Carol quite well in these last few days, and he is such a loving, happy child with so much potential, and here he is being treated worse than a dog. I knew it was important to keep any feelings I had about this to myself until I was away from the nurses – but in the playroom I had to let go and cried for ages.

I wonder what tomorrow will bring? Each day has a different challenge and a new problem to get over.

Day 9

Virgil appears to have made improvements – or maybe he could do these things anyway but just hasn't been encouraged. He sat with Edit for a few hours and learned some colours and numbers. He is one of the children that can concentrate for a long time, so he could really absorb what he was hearing. It just shows how much they enjoy any stimulation/interaction. The other children couldn't concentrate for this long at all. It's also excellent how extensive his vocabulary is, considering that just three months ago he couldn't say a word.

One of my aims for Virgil is really simple and more on the social side really. I want to encourage him to sit down at the table to eat his meals. Alexandru and Olympia are fine but Virgil really won't sit down! He is used to the routine of being fed standing up in his cot and must feel secure with it. I need to gradually give him opportunities to feel more comfortable sitting at the table.

Nicolae is walking a lot more and doesn't get so nervous about being on his own, before long he'll definitely be more confident. I make sure that every morning I walk around the room with him several times.

Carol came in with us this afternoon and I could see he really enjoyed the interaction with the other children. He cries so much when he has to go back to that room, and it's just horrible leaving him in solitude. I feel continually shocked by the way the nurses are with him. When he cries the door is closed and the latch put on like he's an annoying animal.

I think the hardest part of the day for me is having to put them back in their cots again. People would probably think I'm awful for doing it, but I've had to accept that this is part of the hospital's system, whether I like it or not. I know the nurses will tie them back in after we leave, but it will create even more aggravation if I argue about this and that could ruin everything. I remember Fraser saying how important it is to get our priorities right. We are here to improve the lives of the children, and if we annoy the doctors and nurses there is always the risk that we will be asked to leave, so we have to pick our battles very carefully, and hope that things will change over time.

Day 10

I can see why Edit gets disheartened sometimes. It is hard work, but while we can't take them to the playroom, we should at least get them on the floor to play. This does mean we have to put socks on them (a hospital rule), which creates another problem, as there are rarely enough socks to go round. That means the ones without socks get left in their cots, which is really frustrating! Aghhhhhh! I didn't say a word and tried not to show how annoyed I was and went to get the socks and put them on the children. I'm finding it so hard to do the right thing.

I have lots of questions about Elena and need to find out more about autism. I haven't worked with children like this before and would like to know what I'm dealing with. She is aware for a few seconds and then looks away. She also smiles a lot but never at the other children. She seldom cries or makes any loud noises. She stares at things endlessly. I helped her to push the walker today, which showed me she is capable of developing.

Day 11

We got the big cuddly toys down this afternoon and the children loved it. Nicolae especially enjoyed it and I've noticed touch is very important to him. He likes to feel things. I caught him scratching his armpit with a baby's fork today. It was so funny as he was completely focused and unaware of anything else. When the big fluffy duck is on the floor, he lies under it for ages – really happy for the others to climb all over him.

The children seem to be interacting with one another so much more already. Virgil and Olympia had a 'phone conversation' today and played together really well. They have learnt 'La' for the phone and these two particularly enjoy drawing, so I want to expand on this somehow.

I found some feathers in the cupboard today and went around tickling them, to observe their reactions. Virgil was really afraid at first and threw his arms up shouting, but when I tickled my own arm and showed him it was okay – he was more curious. The look on his face when he felt comfortable to feel the feather was absolutely beautiful . . . so fresh and innocent.

Day 16

Alexandru has a tendency to throw things and can only concentrate on something for a short while. Today Edit told him firmly to stop. She then held him tightly for a while and then let him go. He didn't throw anything for at least half an hour afterwards and instead put things into a big yellow box. The way he put them in the box was really interesting: fast, repetitive, angry and forceful. It was almost like he couldn't do it fast enough. When he started to throw things again, Edit held him.

Virgil was happy about playing with the crayons, he was laughing about taking them out of the box and putting them in again. He likes doing this more than colouring with them! He does it with other toys he plays with – always has to tidy! Is there some sort of theory behind this? Putting things away and moving things around?

When we arrived back after lunch, the nurses on duty had taken all of the toys out of their cots again, even the toys I had tied in. Virgil and Alexandru were crying and they hadn't been like that when we were with them. They were also tied to the cots already.

Day 17

I've been watching Nicolae today. He plays a lot on his own but when he does interact with one of the others he tends to tease them. It can be quite amusing and the others (such as Virgil, Olympia and Ion) are aware of it now. He knows what he's doing, because he laughs to himself afterwards. His obsession with socks and shoes is interesting – he's always taking them off the feet of the other children and putting them on his own hands!

Something else I've noticed today . . . the children are playing together more than they have done. I'm wondering if it's got something to do with them now eating together. We put the soft toys on the floor again and they just lay on them chilling out. It was lovely to watch.

Day 18

I made sure I spent some time with Nicolae today. I have played 'shoes' with him for the past two weeks and that appears to have led him to trust me. Today, after playing 'shoes' yet again, I stood him in the middle of the room, about four steps away from me. Usually he just sits down, but this time he walked towards me with his arms stretched out for a hug. I think these may have been his first independent steps (after ten years!).

He's improved so much this week and it's so encouraging. I think that even the aided walk to the playroom is really good practice although he does tend to get hurried along because the nurses won't wait with him. He's using the walker a lot more now and can push it on his own. It's so strange when I remember he's 10 years old and here I am helping him to walk like you would a baby.

It really upsets me when they start to rock; they even do it when they're outside their cots. Ion and Elena did it today when I was filming, and I had to stop and distract their attention.

Day 19

Ion got inside a big yellow box today, which really made us laugh. Virgil was very curious and wanted to get in with him and then he started some imaginary play, which was fascinating to watch.

While Ion was sitting in a big yellow box, Virgil started to play a game with him, involving an imaginary object. He pretended to receive something from Edit and then took it back to Ion in the box, who took it from him and put it in his lap. The spontaneous interaction between them both was fascinating to watch. Afterwards Virgil continued playing with the yellow plastic box, by putting it on his head and walking around the room, which made me laugh and laugh. He created a sort of obstacle course out of the cots and tables. They seem to like the sensation of being under it and are not afraid any more. They'll love the tent that the charity is bringing over.

The hardest thing on Fridays, is leaving them knowing they'll be tied into their cots all weekend and not changed at all. Now I know the system better and feel more confident about being there, I think I'll go there on Saturday for a bit – to change them at least. Even that is nice interaction for them.

Questions to ask on reflection:

- What have I observed about the children's play behaviours and social behaviours?
- What have I observed about their stages of development, and the whole concept of stages?
- What have I learned about playwork in Romania?
- What have I learned about the children generally?
- What have I learned about myself?
- How should I deal with these children objectively?
- What has been my contribution to the team (Edit, Simona and me).
- What is the best for Edit/children? (compromising).

Day 22

I played with Elena a lot today and can see little improvements in the way she interacts with other children. She sat in the car and started to move it along. She has only ever looked at this car while others play on it and hasn't approached it on her own. We played a run-and-jump game too and she remembered what to do each time. I didn't think she would remember, as she doesn't focus on one activity for very long.

We were going to bathe them this afternoon but there wasn't any hot water, so we just washed them. They enjoyed it just as much as a bath. While undressing Carol, I noticed the bruises on his back from him banging the cot. It was awful and covered his whole back. What must these poor kids be thinking when they are tied to the cots each night? Quite a lot of them punish themselves physically. Is this to get noticed, to get attention, or what? It's so sad. I put some cream on him and hopefully it should heal.

The way the children sit around the table has proved to be more than just eating together. Olympia started to feed Nicolae today, so they are really interacting with one another so much more. They seem to be enjoying the social event.

Day 23

This morning Edit brought some balloons into the salon! They all really loved them, and their facial expressions when they were watching the balloons float down were beautiful. This was especially good for Alexandru because of his need to throw things. It worked really well until he burst one, and then became angry and afraid.

I saw something today that made me really happy . . .

Virgil has started to carry around the car, he won't sit on it as he's too afraid but at least he is now touching it. Olympia came over to him and sat on the car while he had put it down for a while. I thought he might become angry and throw his arms up like he usually does, but he began to pull her around instead! They must have played like this for hours and hours and even when we left the room to go home, he was still pushing her around. They were laughing together and obviously really enjoying it . . . brilliant!

I have noticed that although as a group they are becoming more sociable, they still spend a lot of time in parallel play. Virgil and Olympia in particular, they seem to have a mutual understanding and don't feel threatened by each other. When Carol comes in to play with us, he is very sociable and I rarely see him playing on his own.

Elena is the one I have been observing very closely – she is always on her own and seems to prefer it that way. She is beginning to touch the other children (usually by pulling hair!) and she has also allowed Virgil to push her around on the car. She also enjoys adult company very much, and loves cuddles and an intense touching of faces.

I remember when I first met her; she sat on my knee and started touching my hair and putting the back of her hand up to it. She was so gentle and was aware of every sense – smelling and feeling my breath. It was actually a very moving experience for me and something I'll never forget. I've also noticed her hand gestures are a way of her getting to know something or interpreting a new object. Elena needs to watch the other children playing as a way of encouraging her to join in, and we need to allow her to become involved when playing with two or more children.

Day 24

Edit decided to take them outside this afternoon. She brought the children hats, huge coats and scarves. I found out later this evening that it was only the second time the children had been outside in their lives! Last summer they were put on a blanket and couldn't walk, but they hadn't been out since. This explained the children's strange behaviour. Olympia just stood there shouting and making growling noises. She didn't make any effort to walk. At the time I didn't understand, but now I realize she was probably scared. Edit took her in after a while, as she was too distressed.

Elena was total amazement; looking around and examining the walls with her hands in the same way she does your face. She was comfortable about walking around though, but didn't run around like she does inside the hospital. After a while I played the run-and-jump game with her where she laughed a lot. So lovely when she laughs.

Virgil and Alexandru were the same as they are inside, and really enjoyed it. They were very inquisitive and explored the area.

Day 25

I've had a really special time with the children today. They are still in the horrible room, so it's important to stimulate them as much as possible. Virgil took an old colouring book and held it up to me, so I sat down with him on my lap looking at the pictures and pointing to the colours, and saying the Romanian words.

It's at times like this where I do find the language barrier frustrating, although it didn't stop our enjoyment. Olympia was on one side of me looking at the pictures too – she was really interested in every detail and pointed at things. It just struck me again how these children appreciate any time or interaction given to them. We were there for at least two hours looking at the same pictures! Occasionally Olympia would wander off, look at me from the other side of the room and then walk back to me laughing and laughing. She knew she would get a tickle when she got to me! Her reaction and cheekiness made me laugh with her. She also does this little movement with arms that I did to her weeks ago when she was dancing. It means so much to me that she remembers and can differentiate between me and Edit. With Elena it's the run-and-jump game, and with Ion it's the blowing on faces.

All these things might sound so little and even insignificant to anyone else, but these individual characteristics of the children are the things that keep me going. Actually, it's the children that encourage me to continue with the whole thing, despite all the frustrations. I feel that I would not only be letting myself down if I left early – but most of all the children.

Day 29

This week has started off much better than I thought it would. There are some nurses at the hospital who are much nicer to me now. I notice them looking through the window while I'm playing with the children – it's as though they haven't seen this kind of behaviour before and I'm hoping it might stick in their minds.

Alexandru's mother came to take him today. I was only thinking this morning how much I can see an improvement in his behaviour and concentration since I've been here. I have a nice memory of Alexandru and me playing with the balloon . . . remembering him laughing when he watched it float down towards him and the excitement in his eyes when he pushed it away. It'll be quiet without Alexandru. I can't imagine how he'll cope with such a change or the mother with him. Before she took him we gave him lots of food and dressed him warmly – his mother had no clothes to take him home in.

Today I started to repeat the noises that Elena makes, 'waaaaoooo waaaaoooo', and her reaction was amazing! The look on her face was just like someone had spoken her language. It felt like a little breakthrough as you can rarely communicate with her. Touch is so important to her. I started to repeat this noise back to her and she responded by instigating the sequence when she saw me, exploring my face and trying to decide where the noise was coming from. By making myself the play environment Elena was comfortable to allow herself the freedom to communicate and investigate.

Day 31

I spent some time watching Virgil this afternoon and noticed again how different his play activities are compared to the other children. He plays well with other children and more than often is the instigator in made-up games – although, when he plays on his own, his play is more serious. He is always busy collecting objects and putting them in the yellow box, he'll move the box around and then empty whatever is in inside. This is repeated so many times and he never gets tired of it. He likes to be in control but is learning to share his 'work' with the others, and is definitely more confident. It struck me how much enjoyment he got from the building blocks and it was so lovely to watch him laughing and laughing to himself when he knocked them over. In one afternoon watching Virgil I saw at least ten types of play.

Day 32

I was greeted this morning with hugs from Nicolae, Ion and Elena – it's lovely to see their faces when you open the door at the beginning of the day. They are just so pleased to see you. Nicolae has started to run towards me with his arms open – like we used to when I was coaxing him to walk around a lot more.

Day 38

The cleaners came in and told us to hurry up when we were feeding the children again. I wish they would understand that this is a time of development for them. It's important that they get to explore the texture and taste of the food. Plus the interaction they receive from one another at the table is different from when they are playing. They all have different ways of eating, too, which is amusing to watch; it's a really big event for these children.

Day 39

It was snowing really heavily when I woke up this morning – I've never seen snowflakes so big. The last few days have been really warm and sunny and I thought maybe we wouldn't have snow for a while, but it changes so quickly. I don't mind walking to the hospital; it gives me a chance to think about what I'm doing and the snow is so beautiful.

Edit came in later today so I had the morning to myself. I put some music on really loudly and danced with Virgil, Olympia and Nicolae. They all held hands – it was great. It's hard work when you're on your own though, these children throw such temper tantrums. The noise is unbearable at times. What a change to when I first started – it was the absence of noise when they played that was strange and unsettling.

What do you do when children start to hit themselves really badly? I've tried different approaches with Olympia in particular. When she starts to hit herself I hold her tightly until she stops and calms down. I've tried ignoring it but I can't for long as she becomes very violent. I've also tried putting her in a cot but she then bangs her head against the bars. She doesn't seem to remember when I say stop and she just does it again and again, or if I say no she'll hit another child instead. Do children like this ever learn to stop punishing themselves for attention? Will she grow out of it?

Day 43

I wish I could capture the atmosphere sometimes so that people at home could really know what it's like here. I was thinking about how I've got used to so many things that shocked me when I first saw the children: the cots, the children being tied in, their clothes and nappies, what the children looked like, the condition of the hospital – so bare, basic and empty.

A little girl came in on Friday who has also been here before and she is so thin. When I first saw her I thought she had AIDS, but Edit said it's from lack of food and care. She arrived in hospital this time with a broken jaw and her leg had been broken but had mended itself so a bump sticks out. How that happened I really don't know as the poor little thing just lies there shaking her head. She's unbelievably tiny, and her arms and legs are so tiny. I can't begin to think what conditions she has lived in. When I see things like this I desperately want to do something, but there isn't anything except to make them smile or laugh maybe.

Day 45

Elena held hands with Olympia and Virgil today and walked around the room with them! I haven't seen her do this before as the only interaction she has with the others is maybe hitting their heads occasionally or taking another child's toy. She is quiet most of the time and never cries. She fascinates me and I would love to know why she puts her hands up to your mouth when you try to speak to her. I recorded her doing this with me on the video and also got me repeating the noises she makes. She remembers a lot, which I'm surprised about, and if I'm sitting down on her level she still moves my arms out to play our run-and-catch game.

The children do fight a lot and I only intervene if it gets too violent or if I can see they won't work it out themselves. I think they learn more from their own reactions than from adults at times and it's good for them to work out their own disagreements.

Day 46

Things are quite tough this week as I haven't got a lot of money left, which means I can't buy food or have any independence. It's worked out OK, though, as Edit was sent some money from her grandmother so she's offered to buy food for us for the next three days until the charity organizers arrive. Maybe it's good for me to experience the same feelings Edit does this week, as she has this worry all the time. Yesterday all I had was one of those 'moon' breads (as I call them) and then later in the evening we cooked some rice, sauce, onions and carrots. I'm feeling irritable because I'm hungry most of the day, which means it's difficult to give my all to the children. I came back early today because I was so tired – the children seem to be much harder work now they are becoming more confident. Definitely great progress though.

Day 47

They were all so pleased to see us this morning. When we came in they were all shouting and laughing. The difference in these children is unbelievable and they seem so normal now. I really want to continue with this fantastic improvement and development that I'm seeing, but I'm going home next week. Such mixed feelings about that.

Today I sat Elena on the car and she stayed there, so I showed Carol how to push her and then they were able to do it on their own! I think it was a real step for Elena, as she never 'plays' with the others. She just touches them every so often. (This IS her play? . . . a beginning that needed nurturing.)

Day 50

The group working for White Rose arrived on Saturday. I was so excited to see them and felt proud when I introduced them to everyone. It was interesting to see the different reactions to the children again – lots of staring.

Anne came in with me while Edit was away and it was good to have the company. It's hard working on your own. She suggested getting some Lego that we found yesterday when we were taking everything out from the playroom. The children were so into the Lego, it was wonderful to see their reactions – it kept them quiet for ages! I think I've got to the point now that I'm running out of ideas and I'm not sure what to do with them at times.

Virgil especially loved the bricks and we helped him build a house, which is 'casa'. He walked around the room saying 'casa – casa' in his little voice, and he was so proud of it.

I also found a tube of bubbles, which was great! When I arrived I was so disappointed that I hadn't brought any over and I've found some just in time. It was gorgeous and they all gathered around me, reaching up to burst them or letting them pop on their faces or hands. The noises they made were lovely and I couldn't blow the next one fast enough. Ion, Olympia and Virgil wanted to blow too. Elena loved them, she smiled all the time and even laughed a few times – out loud.

Today I started to doubt myself. I really wondered if I've been doing the right thing with these children. Maybe with Fraser and Anne there I was a bit more aware of things – but not in an awkward way, I'm just not used to having people there. I was also exhausted today and felt that I couldn't cope a day more. I've been tired each day that I've been here but not as much as this afternoon, maybe it's because I know I'm going home soon and my body is starting to unwind. The children were also a bit different and more hectic at times – not sure why as I've been on my own with them before.

Day 51

Olympia's reaction to another child crying almost made me cry today! I brought in Alex from the other room, as he had been crying for a long time and I couldn't stand listening to him any longer – no one seems to care. When I brought him into our room, I sat him down on the floor with me and I showed him the building blocks. Olympia came straight over to us and started to stroke his head saying 'ahhhhh'. Alex just looked up at her and immediately stopped sobbing. She shows such a different side to her at times and cares so much when anyone is upset.

I thought about why the children seem to be more difficult this week. They really have been disrupted, which has made it harder to play with them. They are definitely affected by different adults coming into the room. They have become upset and very noisy. I feel quite frustrated again for some reason and this tiredness is bringing me down. Since Sunday it's like something has hit me as I haven't felt like this since I've been here.

Day 52

When I was on the floor with the others today, I called Elena and she reacted straight away. It took me by surprise as she gave me a huge smile! She went to get up and then sat down again – it's almost like she desperately wants to get involved but is so afraid. Although I caught her almost bullying Ion soon after and she definitely knew what she was doing. She kept running up to him and hitting him on the head with a mirror and then running away again! Each time I said no to her she did it again and in the end I had to move Ion. It was just really strange as she really knew she wanted to hit him. Poor Ion, I often feel sorry for him as he's not big enough yet to retaliate.

Day 55 – last day

Before we left last night we had to go back to the hospital to collect a few things. I was able to sneak away and go and see the children. They were all sleeping . . . I just stood at the window watching them all and thinking about how much I'll miss them and how much I've learned from them. I wondered what they were dreaming about. Carol had climbed in with Robi and was all curled up against him. This was actually a perfect way to say goodbye.

I feel grateful that I have had the opportunity to work with Edit and to help these children grow and develop. Even in a short space of time I have seen so many changes in each child:

Elena . . . More of an interest in play materials. . . Instigating play activities and play cues . . . a greater social involvement . . . not so much solitary play.

Virgil . . . More confident . . . concept of sharing . . . speech and word development.

Nicolae . . . Physical development . . . walking by self confidently.

Olympia . . . Caring and loving side of her more frequent . . . not so many temper tantrums . . . grasped the concept of sharing (food) . . . hugging dolls . . . affection.

Ion . . . physical development.

Carol . . . Development of social skills . . . calmer acceptance of affection . . . not so many harsh and sudden movements . . . happier!

Alexandru . . . Calmer – the throwing aspect . . . more confident . . . speech development.

In the beginning things were very difficult and I started to question how I was going to make the play setting work. The salon was very small and hot, and the nurses were watching a lot of the time; I wasn't even allowed to bring in any extra materials such as paint and so on, and there wasn't any routine for the children to start with. However, through simple things like putting that blanket on the floor, I saw that play-work doesn't have to involve materials or toys; it's more to do with the interaction between the playworker and the children as a group.

The greatest aspect for me was to watch them all come together as a group . . . playing together, feeling comfortable with one another, touching, exploring, sharing, imagining, watching, becoming more confident and, most of all, laughing – I have loved hearing their laughter.

The thing I'm going to miss most of all is coming into the room in the morning. Sometimes Carol or Ion are still sleeping and it's lovely to be there when they open their eyes. When we open the door there are lots of shouts of happiness and excitement, jumping up and down in their cots. The noise only starts when we open the door or when they see us through the window – they are so quiet before that. The first thing I do is go around saying good morning to each one, and untie them from their cots and get them on the floor. There are lots of morning cuddles. Something I won't miss is having to put them in the cots again and leave them to the nurses.

12

Conclusions: revisiting the concept of compound flexibility

Part 1: The ideal world

In an ideal world children's play is beautiful, enchanting, often surprising and full of natural enrichment. It is deeply significant, often therapeutic, and full of psychological reference points. It gives us our own transitional objects and aids our emotional balance. It provides us with privacy and puts us in control of our own destiny. It helps us develop essential life skills and promotes our children's subcultures. It can be risky, exciting, exhilarating and challenging. It is sometimes physical and, more often than not, social.

In *Playwork: Theory and Practice* (Brown 2003b), I explored the concept of compound flexibility, and proposed it as a theory of play and playwork, which sits at the very heart of the developmental process. This is the idea that over time there is a direct link between the degree of flexibility in a child's play environment and the extent to which the child develops flexibility of thought and action. That has great significance for all of us, because the exponential rate of technological change means modern societies desperately need flexible thinkers. The reason this is a theory of playwork is because the process is showing signs of breaking down at its roots, i.e. our children's play environments are becoming increasingly inflexible, with potentially catastrophic results – but more of that later.

The theory of compound flexibility as a developmental process goes like this, with each proposition leading on to the next:

Proposition 1

The degree of flexibility in a child's social and physical play environment influences the child's opportunities for experimentation, control, etc. This is supported by the work of the respected psychologist Jerome Bruner (1972) and is shown best in Nicholson's (1971) Theory of Loose Parts (see Chapter 6).

Proposition 2

When children explore, experiment and exercise control over their world, they produce positive chemicals in the brain (opioids), which makes them feel good about

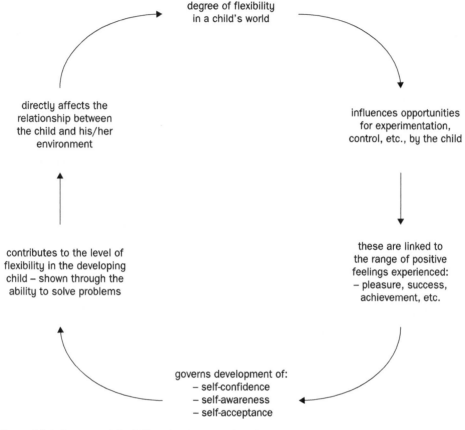

Figure 12.1 Compound flexibility: the theoretical cycle

themselves. This has been shown in a number of experiments by neuroscientists such as Panksepp (2004), and is very clearly explained by the child psychotherapist Margot Sunderland in her award winning book *What Every Parent Needs to Know* (2006).

Proposition 3

Feeling good about themselves helps children develop self-confidence, self-acceptance and even self-awareness. This is confirmed by Loizou (2005) and Salovey *et al.* (2000) (see Chapter 8, especially Maslow 1973).

Proposition 4

A more self-confident child is better able to cope with the problems of day-to-day life. This is reflected in the work of Pepler (1986), and Pressman and Cohen (2005) (see Chapter 6).

Proposition 5

Good problem-solvers are able to make better use of the opportunities that exist in their environment, i.e. flexible thinkers will make the most of a flexible environment. (see Sutton-Smith 1997; Frederickson 2006).

Thus we find ourselves back at Proposition 1, with flexible thinking children in need of a flexible environment if they are to reach their full potential. In such an ideal world playing might be thought of as a self-regulated developmental activity taking place within a free-flowing natural environment. Provided that children have that sort of flexible environment all will be well, and the 'compounding' process will work its developmental magic.

Compounding is a concept borrowed from the financial world, and in particular from the compound interest earned on investments, where it contrasts favourably with flat-rate interest. There are two types of bank interest: (1) flat rate and (2) compound.

1   Flat-rate interest means that an investor who deposits £10,000 at 10% per annum will earn £1,000 in interest at the end of every year, so long as the original deposit is not withdrawn. At the end of five years the yield will be 5 × £1,000 = £5,000. Together with the original investment, the investor now has £15,000.

2   Compound interest works more beneficially for the investor, by building on itself. Thus:
   • £10,000 is invested for a year, and earns interest at 10% per annum = interest of £1,000
   • that £1,000 is added to the original amount and reinvested
   • £11,000 is invested during a second year, earning interest at 10% p.a. = interest of £1,100
   • that £1,100 is reinvested, so the investor now has £12,100 in the bank, earning 10% p.a.

If this process continues for five years, the yield will be £6,105.10. Together with the original investment, the investor now has £16,105.10. In fact, if left untouched over 25 years, the original investment of £10,000 would yield over £100,000. The scientist and inventor Ben Franklin is reputed to have described compound interest as the eighth wonder of the world.

In the case of child development, compound flexibility describes the ability of children to generate their own developmental benefit, which then becomes reinvested in order to generate further benefit. In other words, the child is engaged in an ongoing process of generating developmental benefit from previous developmental benefit. At first it might seem logical to represent this with a cycle (see Figure 12.1), but in fact the ideal representation of the compound flexibility process is not a cycle, but a growth spiral[1] (see Figure 12.2).

Although compound flexibility was conceived as a longitudinal process, it is nevertheless possible to see it in some short-term events, as in the following story.

---

[1] In mathematical terms this is known as a logarithmic spiral.

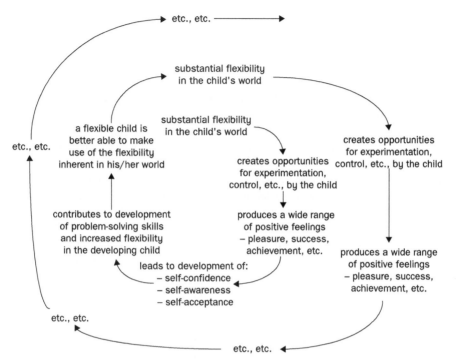

Figure 12.2 Compound flexibility: a positive spiral

Bubbles

Rachel Lacey – playworker

... activities with paint were used to help encourage the children to be messy and lose themselves in their play, and not be worried about the reaction of others. One such activity began with one young girl painting a stone from the yard. More children arrived, but as the growing group of children increased, the resources (such as brushes) ran short. It was then suggested the children drop the stone in the paint pot and retrieve it with their fingers. This led to a need to wash their hands. To do that we used a bucket with Fairy Liquid in it, which had bubbles at the top. This then led to the children *not* washing their hands, but lifting the bubbles off the water and placing them on the artificial flowers.

As happens with water, curiosity got the better of everyone. One splash led to another, and a full-blown water fight ensued, with all the children involved playing with each other and the playworkers. The children made it clear with their shrieks of delight and their body language that they wanted this to carry on. The play flowed from one thing to another seamlessly. The props we had introduced were not specifically to evoke this reaction, but the children took their play where they naturally wanted it to go.

When we discussed this sequence of events, Rachel Lacey told me the play environment had previously been relatively inflexible, but none of the playworkers felt precious about any of the activities they introduced. The activities were intended to provide a stimulus, and nothing more. They were not seen as a rigid programme. As a result, the children were able to interact in a free-flowing way with their play environment, and benefit accordingly. In the event, they became more flexible with their ideas and gestures.

The concept of compound flexibility has relevance to one of the best-known child development theories, namely Vygotsky's *Zone of Proximal Development* (ZPD). For Vygotsky (1978), at any moment in a child's development, s/he will have acquired a range of information, knowledge and skills. However, the child will also have developed the potential to acquire more. The only reason this has not happened is because the additional information, knowledge and skills have not crossed the child's path yet. This new, and as yet unacquired, material Vygotsky called the zone of proximal development. He suggests a child may be helped into the ZPD with guidance from a sympathetic adult, or perhaps by a more knowledgeable peer. This concept has often been used to justify didactic styles in teaching, and is regularly linked to Bruner's interventionist concept of *scaffolding* (Sawyer 2006).

However, Vygotsky was also keen to highlight the role of play in a child's development. For example, he states:

> Play creates a zone of proximal development of the child. In play a child always behaves beyond his average age, above his daily behaviour; in play it is as though he were a head taller than himself. As in the focus of a magnifying glass, play contains all developmental tendencies in a condensed form and is itself a major source of development.
>
> (1978: 102)

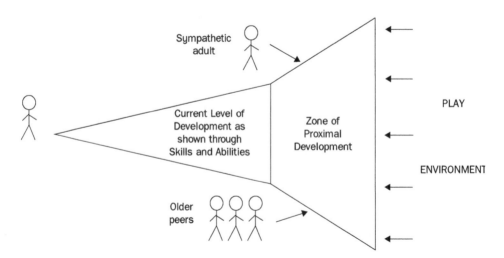

Figure 12.3 Development while playing – based on Vygotsky's Zone of Proximal Development

Relating this back to compound flexibility, the very act of playing brings the child into contact with the social and physical environment in a potentially flexible, interactive way. Playing inevitably means the child will have new experiences. Consequently, it is possible for them to enter their own *zone of proximal development* in a completely natural way, without the active guidance of anyone else. Thus, play enables children to learn for themselves (see Figure 12.3).

Part 2: The real world

Sadly, in the real world the child's play and the compound flexibility process are too often subject to adulteration (see Chapter 9), which Sturrock and Else describe as:

> the contamination of the play aims and objects of the children by either the wishes of the adult in an urge to 'teach' or 'educate', simply to dominate, or by the worker's own unplayed out material.
>
> (1998: 25)

Thus adulteration is sometimes intentional on the part of the adult, and sometimes unintentional. Whatever the intent, it is nevertheless real and potentially damaging. Most definitions of adulteration focus on personal interactions, but general social attitudes can also be significant. In fact, modern western societies are increasingly restricting children's freedom to play (Gill 2007) as a consequence of a confused combination of fear, mistrust and protectiveness – on the one hand, fear of what the little monsters might do if left to their own devices – on the other hand, over-protectiveness because of the perceived vulnerability of our little angels – i.e. Nietzsche's (1999) classic Apollonian vs Dionysian dialectic (broadly speaking, the rational vs the emotional).

In 2008 the United Nations Committee on the Rights of the Child (UNCRC) singled out the UK for its 'general climate of intolerance and negative public attitudes towards children' (UNCRC 2008). In 2011 the research organization ICM released the results of a poll commissioned by the children's charity Barnardo's confirming the UNCRC statement. The poll found nearly half the UK population (49%) agreed that children today are beginning to behave like animals. An amazing 44% agreed that children in the UK are becoming feral. Nearly half (47%) agreed that young people are angry, violent and abusive. One in four (25%) think children who behave badly or anti-socially are beyond help by the age of 10.

Barnardo's chief executive Anne Marie Carrie's response to these findings was bold, but slightly optimistic:

> We seem to have forgotten the fact that most children are well behaved and instead we are unquestioningly accepting a stereotype of young people as criminal and revolting. But it's never too late to believe in children and change their life story.

It is distressing that the British public holds such a negative view of children, despite the majority being well behaved and attending school (NAO 2005), and a significant number contributing to their communities by volunteering and taking part in out-of-school activities (Atkinson 2010). For example, the organization C4EO (2011) found 'around three quarters of all young people participate in some form of positive activities'. Nevertheless, the Victorian attitude that 'children should be seen and not heard' appears to be alive and well in modern Britain.

Gill (2007) details changes over the last 30 years that, when taken together, have had a substantial impact on children's freedom to play. He also lists the factors that have produced the 'risk averse society' referred to in the title of his book. These include:

- a general lack of understanding that risks can be intrinsically beneficial
- a fear of litigation on the part of those who should be providing play facilities
- the disproportionate sums of money spent on safety surfacing for children's playgrounds, at the expense of more and better play equipment
- stories about anti-social behaviour exaggerated in the media
- the redefining of bullying to include teasing
- excessive child protection measures that have the effect of reducing the number of volunteers prepared to run after-school activities for children
- parental fear of strangers, exacerbated by media stories about paedophiles
- fear of the internet, exacerbated because children are so much more competent at using modern technology than their parents.

When all this is added to the very real increase in traffic on our streets, it is clear that the opportunities for children to explore their neighbourhood in free-ranging play activity are becoming more and more restricted.

In *Rethinking Children's Play* (Brown and Patte 2013), we listed the damaging effects, as shown by research across multiple disciplines, linking negative responses to the play agenda to the following negative impacts on children:

- reduction in social competence (NAECS-SDE 2002)
- increasing incidence of attention deficit hyperactive disorder (ADHD) (Marano 2008)
- inability to create strategies for dealing with the uncertainties of life (Marano 2008)
- health concerns, especially obesity (Ogden *et al.* 2010)
- increasing incidence of anxiety and depression (Panksepp 2002)
- decrease in creativity and imagination (Marano 2008)
- inflexibility when faced with new environments and situations (Bekoff and Pierce 2009)
- aversion to risk (Marano 2008).

Thus, for numerous reasons, the compound flexibility process is being adulterated, and this is likely to have dangerous consequences for child development (see Figure 12.4). That is where playwork comes in.

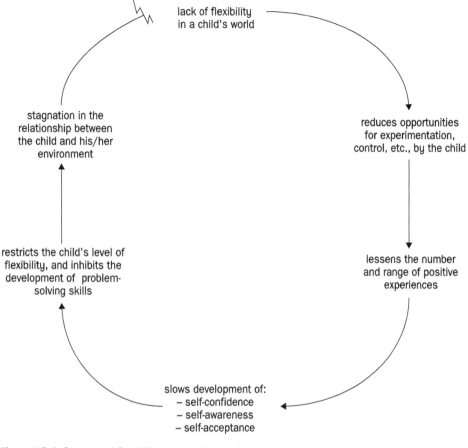

Figure 12.4 Compound flexibility: a negative cycle

Part 3: What does playwork have to offer?

The role of the playworker is to create compensatory environments that enable children to engage in all those aspects of play behaviour that are being stifled by society. In practice that means applying the Playwork Principles (PPSG 2005) (see Appendix 1), but the most significant factor is flexibility. Playworkers need to have flexibility at the heart of everything they do; not only in the way they create the physical play environment, but also in their personal interactions with the children.

What does this mean in practice? As far as possible the playspace should be the child's space, but for the playworker certain factors need to be remembered.

Removing barriers to the play process

Clearly, as caring adults, playworkers have a responsibility to make sure the children come to no harm either physically or emotionally, so their first task is to analyse the child's environment in order to identify and remove any barriers to the play process. This does not only mean checking the safety of any play equipment, but on occasion may involve taking on a wider social responsibility, such as making sure the children are not being neglected or abused in any way. After all children will not be able to benefit fully from their play if they are in a state of emotional turmoil.

Enriching the play environment

An enriched play environment holds greater potential for child development, but for the playworker this is not about imposing an adult agenda on the playspace – rather we seek to adopt a holistic approach to development, one that respects the idea that children develop while they are playing. Although playworkers are not seeking to take control of the development process, they should nevertheless keep in mind those aspects of child development that are covered in this book. However, the most important overlay on all this is the need to ensure that the play environment is a playful one, i.e. a place where children are able to engage in non-serious activities for enjoyment, satisfaction and fun (Starbuck and Webster 1991).

The Portchmouth Principle and Nicholson's Theory of Loose Parts

Taking on board Sutton-Smith's (1997: 231) assertion that the function of play is 'adaptive variability', it is reasonable to suggest that the role of the playworker is to create flexible environments that are substantially adaptable or controllable by the children. One way of doing this is to ensure there are lots of 'loose parts' in the play environment (see Chapter 6 for a full explanation of Nicholson's 1971 theory). Underpinning this idea is the Portchmouth Principle (Brown 2003: 63), which states: 'It helps if someone, no matter how lightly, puts in our way the means of making use of what we find.' In other words, the playworker's role is to provide the basic tools and materials to enable the children to play. There is no need to tell them what to do. The play environment contains its own play cues in such circumstances.

Negative capability

As previously stated, the play environment should be, as far as possible, under the control of the children who use it. In order to achieve this, playworkers need to suspend their prejudices and be non-judgmental in all their dealings with the children. They need to be prepared to go along with the flow of the children's needs and tastes, i.e. they need to adopt an attitude of 'negative capability' (Fisher 2008). Fisher's thinking is that adopting this approach to the child–adult relationship opens up the creative flow of the mind. That enables the playworker to be truly there for the child. This approach requires a great sensitivity to the learning potential of the playwork setting, and means the playworker has to be prepared to stand back when others might be inclined to rush in (see Chapter 3 for a fuller explanation of this concept).

A non-interventionist approach

Intervention is sometimes necessary, but the child's agenda has to be taken as the starting point for playworkers' interventions. In children's lives the only time when they are truly in control of events is when they are playing. If playworkers are to avoid 'adulterating' that experience, they have to ensure that, wherever possible, they are following the child's agenda. Therefore, in most circumstances the playworker should be adopting the approach recommended by Hughes of 'preparation followed by withdrawal' (1996: 23). For the playworker in a therapeutic setting it is especially important to take the child's agenda as the starting point for interactions. Even in the case of the therapeutic playwork project in Romania, where the children required a stronger presence over a more extended period, it nevertheless remained the case that most of our interventions were a response to the specific play behaviours of each child (see Chapter 11).

Using personal life skills

Our own experience of play enables us to develop the human attributes of sympathy, empathy, affective attunement and mimesis, and so make appropriate responses to children's play cues. Indeed, it is my view that these personal life skills, and many others, were easily absorbed and developed during play, so long as we had a reasonably well-balanced play experience as a child. It is extremely doubtful whether these fundamental life skills could be learned in a classroom. They are all skills that are essential to playworkers if they are not to misread the sort of situations that confront them every day (see Chapter 3 and also Brown (2008) for a fuller exploration of these concepts).

Playwork is about creating relationships and building the child's self-esteem

One of the most significant elements of the playwork role is the way in which relationships are made with the children. If the child–adult relationship is effective, there is a good chance of not only helping children with their problems, but also raising their self-esteem generally. As we have already seen, the playwork approach has unique elements; most especially there is no attempt to take control of the child's agenda. That is an unusual experience for most children, and one that encourages the formation of a strong bond of trust with the playworker. Examples of this process may be seen in numerous stories throughout this book. The non-interventionist, non-judgmental and non-controlling approach carries with it a powerful message of respect for the child's social, physical and emotional space. Not only does this help the formation of a strong relationship, but it also helps to build the child's self-esteem.

Cultural competence

Regardless of the setting in which they are working, playworkers need to develop their own cultural awareness – macro and micro. In other words, they need to understand both the culture of the local community and also the children's own subculture(s). Both will be characterized by their own unique *webs of significance* (Geertz 1993: 5), i.e. a complex intertwined mesh of social, political, economic, philo-sophical, spiritual and emotional principles that underpins everything that happens within any particular community. The playwork author Perry Else (2009: 137) suggests 'we exist in the world at the interface of the personal ecology (feelings, symbols, thoughts, concepts) and the physical ecology (environment and others)'. All these things serve to create the *webs of significance* referred to by Geertz, and with which playworkers must aim to feel comfortable.

Conclusion

Finally, I would like to make a plea for simplicity. There is no need to over-complicate something that is basically very straightforward. Children like to play. They get all sorts of benefits from playing. They get the most benefit from play when they are in control of what they are doing. There are lots of circumstances today that mean chil-dren are not able to control their own play. That's where playwork comes in. The role of the playworker is to create environments that enable children to take control of their playing. In playwork settings the children's development largely results from their playful interaction with other children. It is the playworker's role to create the sort of environment that enables that to happen – in other words, an environment that offers adaptability to the children, and so encourages the compound flexibility process. Through their empathy, and their ability to interpret the children's play cues effectively, playworkers are able to create strong trusting relationships, which in turn help to enhance the children's self-esteem. We can add lots of detail, but at its heart there is no need to make it much more complicated than that.

Appendix 1: The Playwork Principles

1. All children and young people need to play. The impulse to play is innate. Play is a biological, psychological and social necessity, and is fundamental to the healthy development and well-being of individuals and communities.

2. Play is a process that is freely chosen, personally directed and intrinsically motivated. That is, children and young people determine and control the content and intent of their play, by following their own instincts, ideas and interests, in their own way for their own reasons.

3. The prime focus and essence of playwork is to support and facilitate the play process and this should inform the development of play policy, strategy, training and education.

4. For playworkers, the play process takes precedence and playworkers act as advocates for play when engaging with adult-led agendas.

5. The role of the playworker is to support all children and young people in the creation of a space in which they can play.

6. The playworker's response to children and young people playing is based on a sound, up-to-date knowledge of the play process, and reflective practice.

7. Playworkers recognize their own impact on the play space, and also the impact of children and young people's play on the playworker.

8. Playworkers choose an intervention style that enables children and young people to extend their play. All playworker intervention must balance risk with the developmental benefit and well-being of children.

The Playwork Principles (PPSG 2005) were developed after a lengthy consultation exercise, and have been officially recognized by SkillsActive (the lead body for education and training in playwork). They are intended to replace the previous statement of assumptions and values, contained in SPRITO (1992) *National Occupational Standards in Playwork*. London: Sport and Recreation Industry Lead Body.

Useful internet resources

Academy of Play and Child Psychotherapy (APAC) – http://www.apac.org.uk/

Aid for Romanian Children – http://www.arccharity.org
American Journal of Play – http://www.journalofplay.org/
Association for the Study of Play – www.tasplay.org
Charter for Children's Play – http://www.playengland.org.uk/media/71062/charter-for-childrens-
    play.pdf
Fair Play for Children – http://www.fairplayforchildren.org/index.php
Fields in Trust (formerly National Playing Fields Association) – http://www.fieldsintrust.org
International Journal of Play – http://www.tandfonline.com/loi/rijp
iP-D!P magazine – http://ip-dip.com/
Journal of Playwork Practice – http://www.policypress.co.uk/journals_jpp.asp
Leeds Beckett University – http://leedsbeckett.ac.uk/
London Play – http://www.londonplay.org.uk
Ludemos – http://www.ludemos.co.uk
Play Board Northern Ireland – http://www.playboard.org/
Playeducation – http://www.xnd76.dial.pipex.com/
Play England – http://www.playengland.org.uk
Play Scotland – http://www.playscotland.org/
Play Therapy UK – http://www.playtherapy.org.uk/
Play Wales – http://www.playwales.org.uk
Rethinking Childhood (Tim Gill's website) – http://rethinkingchildhood.com
SkillsActive Playwork Section – http://www.skillsactive.com/sectors/playwork
The Strong: National Museum of Play – http://www.museumofplay.org/

References

Abernethy, D.W. (1977) *Notes and Papers: A General Survey on Children's Play Provision*. London: National Playing Fields Association.

Adams, J. (2001) *Risk*. London: Routledge.

Aldis, O. (1975) *Play Fighting*. New York: Academic Press.

Allen of Hurtwood, Lady (1965) Junkyard Playgrounds. New York: *Time*, 25 June 1965, p. 71.

Apter, M.J. (2007) *Danger: Our Quest for Excitement*. Oxford: One World.

Aron, R. (1970) *Main Currents in Sociological Thought 2* (trans. from French by Howard, R. and Weaver, H.). Harmondsworth: Pelican Books.

Atkinson, M. (2010) Young people contributing positively and creatively in their communities. Available online at: www.childrenscommissioner.gov.uk/content/blog/content_352 (accessed 15 June 2014).

Axline, V. (1969) *Play Therapy* (rev. edn). New York: Ballantine Books.

Ball, D.J. (2002) *Playgrounds – Risks, Benefits and Choices*. Contract Research Report No.426/2002. Sudbury: HSE Books.

Bateson, G. (1955) A theory of play and fantasy. *Psychiatric Research Reports*, 2: 39–51.

Battram, A. (2008) The edge of recalcitrance: playwork in the zone of complexity, in F. Brown and C. Taylor (eds) *Foundations of Playwork*. Maidenhead: Open University Press.

Baxter, N. (2008) Playwork and the environment, in F. Brown and C. Taylor (eds) *Foundations of Playwork*. Maidenhead: Open University Press.

Bekoff, M. and Pierce, J. (2009) *Wild Justice: The Moral Lives of Animals*. Chicago, IL: University of Chicago Press.

Bentham, J. (1802) *Theory of Legislation* (reprinted 2012). Hong Kong: Forgotten Books.

Berlyne, D.E. (1960) *Conflict, Arousal and Curiosity*. New York: McGraw-Hill.

Bettleheim, B. (1987) *A Good Enough Parent*. London: Thames & Hudson.

Brock, A., Dodds, S., Jarvis, P. and Olusoga, Y. (2008) *Perspectives on Play: Learning for Life*. London: Pearson.

Brown, F. (ed.) (2003a) *Playwork Theory and Practice*. Buckingham: Open University Press.

Brown, F. (2003b) Compound flexibility, the role of playwork in child development, in F. Brown (ed.) *Playwork – Theory and Practice*. Buckingham: Open University Press.

Brown, F. (2003c) An evaluation of the concept of play value and its application to children's fixed equipment playgrounds. Unpublished PhD thesis, Leeds Beckett University.

Brown, F. (2006) *Highlight No. 223: Play Theories and the Value of Play*. London: National Children's Bureau.

Brown, F. (2007) *The Venture: A Case Study of an Adventure Playground*. Cardiff: Play Wales.

Brown, F. (2008) The fundamentals of playwork, in F. Brown and C. Taylor (eds) *Foundations of Playwork*. Maidenhead: Open University Press.

Brown, F. (2012) The play behaviours of Roma children in Transylvania. *International Journal of Play*, 1(1): 64–74.

Brown, F. (2013) Joy and trauma in Romania. *The Prompt*, special edition, Winter.

Brown, F. and Patte, M. (2012) From the streets of Wellington to the Ivy League: reflecting on a lifetime of play – an interview with Brian Sutton-Smith. *International Journal of Play*, 1(1): 6–15.

Brown, F. and Patte, M. (2013) *Rethinking Children's Play*. London: Bloomsbury Publishing plc.

Brown, F. and Taylor, C. (eds) (2008) *Foundations of Playwork*. Maidenhead: Open University Press.

Brown, F. and Webb, S. (2005) Children without play. *Journal of Education*, 35: 139–158.

Brown, F. and Webb, S. (2012) Children without play, in R. Johnson and N. Maguire (eds) *Complex Trauma and its Effects: Perspectives on Creating an Environment for Recovery*. Brighton: Pavilion Publishing Ltd.

Brown, S. (2009) *Play, How it Shapes the Brain, Opens the Imagination and Invigorates the Soul*. London: Penguin.

Bruce, T. (1991) *Time to Play in Early Childhood Education*. London: Hodder & Stoughton.

Bruce, T. (2005) Play, the universe and everything!, in Moyles, J. (ed.) *The Excellence of Play* (2nd edn). Maidenhead: Open University Press.

Bruner, J. (1972) Nature and uses of immaturity, in J.S. Bruner, A. Jolly and K. Sylva (eds) *Play: Its Role in Development and Evolution*. New York: Basic Books.

Bruner, J. (1978) The role of dialogue in language acquisition, in A. Sinclair, R.J. Jarvelle and W.J.M. Levelt (eds) *The Child's Concept of Language*. New York: Springer-Verlag.

Bruner, J. (2006) *In Search of Pedagogy*. London: Routledge.

C4EO (2012) Increasing the engagement of young people in positive activities so as to achieve the ECM outcomes. Available online at: http://archive.c4eo.org.uk/themes/youth/positiveactivities/ (accessed 15 June 2014).

Caillois, R. (2001) *Man, Play and Games*. Chicago, IL: University of Illinois Press.

Csikszentmihalyi, M. (1980) The concept of flow in play, in B. Sutton-Smith (ed.) *Play and Learning*. Hoboken, NJ: John Wiley & Sons.

Davy, A. (2008) Exploring rhythm in playwork, in F. Brown and C. Taylor (eds) *Foundations of Playwork*. Maidenhead: Open University Press.

DCMS (Department for Culture, Media and Sport) (2004) *Getting Serious about Play – a Review of Children's Play*. The Report of the Review of Children's Play chaired by the Rt Hon Frank Dobson MP. London: DCMS.

Delorme, M. (2013) Play and playwork comparative study. Unpublished assignment for the BA (Hons) Playwork degree, Leeds Beckett University.

Donald, M. (1991) *Origins of the Modern Mind*. Cambridge, MA: Harvard University Press.

Donald, M. (2002) *A Mind So Rare: The Evolution of Human Consciousness*. New York, NY: W.W. Norton & Co.

Durkheim, E. (1893) *The Division of Labour in Society* (trans. W.D. Halls, 1984). London: Macmillan.

Dwivedi, K.N. (1993) *Group Work with Children and Adolescents*. London: Jessica Kingsley.

Else, P. (2009) *The Value of Play*. London: Continuum.

Erikson, E. (1963) *Childhood and Society* (2nd edn). New York: Norton.

Fagen, R. (1981) *Animal Play Behaviour*. Oxford: Oxford University Press.

Fein, G.G. (1981) Pretend play in childhood: an integrative review. *Child Development*, 52: 1095–1118.

Fisher, K. (2008) Playwork in the early years: working in a parallel profession, in F. Brown and C. Taylor (eds) *Foundations of Playwork*. Maidenhead: Open University Press.

Fowkes, D.R. (1990) *A Gunner's Journal, Italy 1943–1946*. Hull: University of Hull, Department of Italian.

Frederickson, B. (2006) Unpacking positive emotions: investigating the seeds of human flourishing. *Journal of Positive Psychology*, 1(2): 57–59.

Freud, S. (1900) The interpretation of dreams, in S. Freud *The Standard Edition of the Complete Psychological Works of Sigmund Freud* (1974 edn), 24 vols (trans. from German under the general editorship of James Strachey, in collaboration with Anna Freud; assisted by Alix Strachey and Alan Tyson). London: Hogarth Press, Institute of Psycho-Analysis.

Froebel, F. (1888) *The Education of Man*. New York: Appleton.

Frost, J., Wortham, S. and Reifel, S. (2011) *Play and Child Development* (4th edn). London: Pearson.

Gallahue, D.L., Ozmun, J.C. and Goodway, J.D. (2011) *Understanding Motor Development: Infants, Children Adolescents, Adults* (7th edn). New York, NY: McGraw-Hill.

Garvey, C. (1991) *Play* (2nd edn). London: Fontana.

Geertz, C. (1993) *The Interpretation of Cultures*. London: Fontana Press.

Gill, T. (2007) *No Fear: Growing Up in a Risk Averse Society*. London: Calouste Gulbenkian Foundation.

Gladwin, M. (2008) The concept of risk in play and playwork, in F. Brown and C. Taylor (eds) *Foundations of Playwork*. Maidenhead: Open University Press.

Goodall, J. (1989) *In the Shadow of Man*. London: Weidenfeld & Nicholson.

Griffiths, L.J., Cortina-Borja, M., Sera, F., *et al.* (2013) How active are your children? Findings from the Millennium Cohort Study. *BMJ Open*, 3:e00 2893 Available online at: www.bmjopen.bmj.com/content/3/8/e002893 (accessed 15 July 2014).

Groos, K. (1898) *The Play of Animals*. New York: Appleton.

Groos, K. (1901) *The Play of Nan*. London: Heinemann.

Guilbaud, S. (2011) A phenomenological inquiry into the possibility of played-with-ness in experiences with things. Unpublished PhD thesis. Leeds: Leeds Beckett University.

Guss, F. (2005) Reconceptualizing play: aesthetic self-definitions. *Contemporary Issues in Early Childhood*, 6: 233–243.

Haeckel, E. (1901) *The Riddle of the Universe at the Close of the Nineteenth Century* (trans. Joseph McCabe). London: Watts & Co.

Hall, G.S. (1904) *Adolescence: Its Psychology and its Relations to Physiology, Anthropology, Sociology, Sex, Crime, Religion and Education*, Vol. 1. New York: Appleton.

Hart, R. (1992) *Children's Participation: From Tokenism to Citizenship*. Florence: UNICEF International Child Development Centre.

Health and Safety at Work Act (1974) (c. 37). London: HMSO.

Henricks, T. (2013) Play as self-realization: toward a general theory of play. Paper presented at the 39th Annual Conference of the Association for the Study of Play (TASP), with the 26th Conference of the American Association for the Child's Right to Play (IPA/USA), 'Play as a Pathway', University of Delaware, Newark, DE, 6–9 March.

Holme, A. and Massie, P. (1970) *Children's Play: A Study of Needs and Opportunities*. London: Michael Joseph.

Home Office (1968) *The Urban Aid Programme*. London: HMSO.

Hughes, B. (1996) *Play Environments: A Question of Quality*. London: PLAYLINK.

Hughes, B. (2001) *Evolutionary Playwork and Reflective Analytic Practice*. London: Routledge.

Hughes, B. (2002) *A Playworker's Taxonomy of Play Types* (2nd edn). London: PLAYLINK.

Hughes, B. (2012) *Evolutionary Playwork*. London: Routledge.

Hughes, F.P. (2010) *Children, Play and Development* (4th edn). London: Sage Publications.

Huizinga, J. (1949) *Homo Ludens: A Study of the Play Element in Culture*. London: Routledge & Kegan Paul.

Hutt, S.J., Tyler, S., Hutt, C. and Christopherson, H. (1989) *Play Exploration and Learning: A Natural History of the Pre-school*. London, Routledge.

ICM (2011) *Life Story Survey*. London: Barnardo's.

Jennings, S. (2011) *Healthy Attachments and Neuro-dramatic Play*. London: Jessica Kingsley Publishers.

Johnson, J. (2012) Play help us. A poem by Jim Johnson (inspired by ICCP, Tallinn, Estonia).

Johnson, J.E., Christie, J.F. and Wardle, F. (2004) *Play, Development and Early Education*. London: Pearson.

Jung, C. (1956) *Two Essays in Analytical Psychology*. New York, NY: Meridian Books.

Kant, I. (1790) *Critique of Judgement* (trans. James Creed Meredith, 2008). Oxford: Oxford University Press.

Kaufman, R. (2014) The Son-Rise Program versus ABA. The Option Institute. Available online at: www.autismtreatmentcenter.org/contents/other_sections/aba-vs-son-rise-program.php (accessed 15 June 2014).

Kilvington, J. and Wood, A. (2010) *Reflective Playwork: For All Who Work With Children*. London: Continuum.

Klein, M. (1955) The psychoanalytical play technique: its history and significance, in J. Mitchell (ed.) (1986) *The Selected Melanie Klein*. Harmondsworth: Penguin: 35–54.

Landsberger, H. (1958) *Hawthorne Revisited – Management and the Worker, Its Critics and Developments in Human Relations in Industry*. Ithaca, NY: Cornell University Press.

Lazarus, M. (1883) *Uber die reize des spiels*. Berlin: Dummler.

Lean, V.S. (1902) *Lean's Collectanea*. Bristol: Arrowsmith.

Lester, S. and Russell, W. (2008) *Play for a Change: Summary Report*. London: Play England.

Locke, J. (1690) *An Essay Concerning Human Understanding*, edited with an introduction, critical apparatus and glossary by Peter H. Nidditch (1975). Oxford: Clarendon Press.

Loizou, E. (2005) Infant humour: the theory of the absurd and the empowerment theory. *International Journal of Early Years Education*, 13: 43–53.

Mackett, R. and Paskins, J. (2008) Children's physical activity: the contribution of playing and walking. *Childhood and Society*, 22: 345–357.

Marano, H. (2008) *A Nation of Wimps: The High Cost of Invasive Parenting*. New York: Broadway.

Maslow, A. (1973) *The Farther Reaches of Human Nature*. Harmondsworth: Pelican Books.

Meyer, P. (2010) *From Workplace to Playspace: Innovation, Learning and Changing through Dynamic Engagement*. San Francisco, CA: Jossey-Bass.

Millar, S. (1968) *The Psychology of Play*. Harmondsworth: Penguin Books.

Moyles, J.R. (ed.) (2010) *The Excellence of Play* (3rd edn). Maidenhead: Open University Press.

NAECS-SDE (2002) *Recess and the Importance of Play: A Position Statement on Young Children and Recess*. National Association of Early Childhood Specialists in State Departments of Education. Available online at: http://naecs-sde.org/policy/ (accessed 15 June 2014).

NAO (2005) *Improving School Attendance in Britain*. London: National Audit Office.

National Scientific Council on the Developing Child (2005) Excessive stress disrupts the architecture of the developing brain. Working Paper No. 3. Cambridge: The Council.

Neill, A.S. (1968) *Summerhill*. Harmondsworth: Pelican.

Nicholson, S. (1971) How not to cheat children. The theory of loose parts. *Landscape Architecture Quarterly*, 62(1), October: 30–34. Also in *Bulletin for Environmental Education*, 12, April 1972. London: Town & Country Planning Association.

Nielsen, G. (2011) Children's daily physical activity: patterns and the influence of socio-cultural factors. Unpublished PhD thesis. University of Copenhagen. Summary available online at: http://nexs.ku.dk/english/phd_thesis/prev_ifi_phd-thesis/2011/glenn_phd/ (accessed 15 June 2014).

Nietzsche, F. (1999) *The Birth of Tragedy and Other Writings* (eds Raymond Geuss and Ronald Speirs, trans. Ronald Speirs). Cambridge: Cambridge University Press.

Ogden, C., Carroll, M., Curtin, L., Lamb, M. and Flegal, K. (2010) Prevalence of high body mass index in US children and adolescents 2007–2008. *Journal of the American Medical Association*, 303(3): 242–249.

Palmer, S. (2003) Playwork as reflective practice, in F. Brown (ed.) *Playwork Theory and Practice*. Buckingham: Open University Press.

Palmer, S. (2008) Researching with children, in F. Brown and C. Taylor (eds) *Foundations of Playwork*. Maidenhead: Open University Press.

Panksepp, J. (2002) ADHD and the neural consequences of play and joy: a framing essay. *Consciousness & Emotion*, 3(1): 1–6.

Panksepp, J. (2004) *Affective Neuroscience: The Foundations of Human and Animal Emotions*. New York: Oxford University Press.

Parten, M.B. (1933) Social play among preschool children. *Journal of Abnormal and Social Psychology*, 28: 136–147.

Pellis, S. and Pellis, V. (2009) *The Playful Brain: Venturing to the Limits of Neuroscience*. London: Oneworld Publications.

Pepler, D. (1986) Play and creativity, in G. Fein and M. Rivkin (eds) *The Young Child at Play, Reviews of Research: 4*. Washington, DC: National Association for the Education of Young Children.

Piaget, J. (1951) *Play, Dreams and Imitation in Childhood*. London: Routledge & Kegan Paul.

Pinney, R. (1990) *Children's Hours*. London: The Children's Hours Trust.

Portchmouth, J. (1969) *Creative Crafts for Today*. London: Studio Vista.

PPSG (2005) *Playwork Principles*, held in trust as honest brokers for the profession by the Playwork Principles Scruting Group. Available online at: http://www.playwales.org.uk/eng/playworkprinciples/ (accessed 15 June 2014).

Pressman, S. and Cohen, S. (2005) Does positive affect influence health? *Psychological Bulletin*, 131(6): 925–971.

Robinson, K. (2006) How schools kill creativity. Presentation to the TED gathering, Monterey, CA. Available online at: www.ted.com/talks/ken_robinson_says_schools_kill_creativity. html (accessed 15 June 2014).

Roche, J. (2004) Children's rights: participation and dialogue, in Roche, *et al.* (eds) *Youth and Society: Contemporary Theory, Policy and Practice*. London: Sage Publications.

Russ, S. (2004) *Play in Child Development and Psychotherapy: Towards Empirically Supported Practice*. Mahwah, NJ: Lawrence Erlbaum Associates, Inc.

Salovey, P., Rothman, A. Detweiler, J. and Steward, W. (2000) Emotional states and physical health. *American Psychologist*, 55: 110–121.

Salter, M. (1980) Play in ritual: an ethnohistorical overview of nature in North America, in H.B. Schwartzman (ed.) *Play and Culture*. New York: Leisure Press.

Sandseter, E.B.H. (2007) Categorising risky play: how can we identify risk-taking behaviour in children's play. *European Early Childhood Education Research Journal*, 15(2): 237–252.

Sandseter, E.B.H. (2009) Children's expressions of exhilaration and fear in risky play. *Contemporary Issues in Early Childhood*, 10(2), Winter: 93.

Sawyer, R.K. (2006) *The Cambridge Handbook of the Learning Sciences*. New York: Cambridge University Press.

Schechner, R. (1988) Playing. *Play and Culture*, 1(1): 3–27.

Shaw, G.B. (2012) *Maxims for Revolutionists*. London: CreateSpace Independent Publishing.

Sheridan, M., Sharma, A. and Cockerill, H. (2007) *From Birth to Five Years: Children's Developmental Progress* (3rd edn). London: Routledge.

Singer, D.G. and Singer, J.L. (1979) The values of the imagination, in B. Sutton-Smith (ed.) *Play and Learning*. New York: Gardner Press.

Singer, D.G. and Singer, J.L. (1990) *The House of Make Believe*. London: Harvard University Press.

Sladen, D. (2012) Pediatric auditory assessment: using science to guide clinical practice. 22nd Annual Audiology Conference, 16 February, Rochester, Minnesota: Mayo Clinic.

Smilansky, S. and Shefatya, L. (1990) *Facilitating Play: A Medium for Promoting Cognitive, Socio-emotional and Academic Development in Young Children*. Gaithersburg, MD: Psychosocial and Educational Publications.

Smith, A. (1759) *The Theory of Moral Sentiments* (eds D.D. Raphael and A.L. Macfie, 1976). Oxford: Clarendon Press.

Smith, P. (2010) *Children and Play*. Chichester: Wiley-Blackwell.

Sorensen, C.Th. (1931) *Open Spaces for Town and Country*, cited in Allen of Hurtwood, Lady (1968) *Planning for Play*. London: Thames & Hudson.

Spariosu, M. (1989) *Dionysus Reborn*. Ithaca, NY: Cornell University Press.

Spencer, H. (1873) *Principles of Psychology*. New York, Appleton, cited in Hayes, N. (1994) *Foundations of Psychology*. London: Routledge.

SPRITO (1992) *National Occupational Standards in Playwork*. London: Sport & Recreation Industry Lead Body.

Starbuck, W.H. and Webster, J. (1991) When is play productive? *Accounting, Management & Information Technologies*, 1: 1–20.

Steiner, R. (1965) *The Education of the Child in the Light of Anthroposophy* (trans. George and Mary Adams). London: Rudolph Steiner Press.

Stern, D.N. (1985) *The Interpersonal World of the Infant: A View from Psychoanalysis and Developmental Psychology*. New York: Basic Books.

Sturrock, G. and Else, P. (1998) The playground as therapeutic space: playwork as healing. *Proceedings of the IPA/USA Triennial National Conference, Play in a Changing Society: Research, Design, Application*, June. Colorado, USA.

Sunderland, M. (2006) *What Every Parent Needs to Know*. London: Dorling Kindersley.

Suomi, S.J. and Harlow, H.F. (1971) Monkeys without play, in J.S. Bruner, A. Jolly and K. Sylva (eds) (1976) *Play: Its Role in Development and Evolution*. New York, NY: Basic Books.

Sutton-Smith, B. (1992) In Channel 4 documentary, *Toying with the Future*. London: Channel 4 Television.

Sutton-Smith, B. (1997) *The Ambiguity of Play*. Cambridge: Harvard University Press.

Sutton-Smith, B. (1999) Evolving a consilience of play definitions: playfully, in S. Reifel (ed.) *Play and Culture Studies, Play Contexts Revisited*, 2. Stamford: Ablex: 239–256.

Sutton-Smith, B. (2008) Beyond ambiguity, in F. Brown and C. Taylor (eds) *Foundations of Playwork*. Maidenhead: Open University Press.

Sutton-Smith, B. and Kelly-Byrne, D. (1984) The idealization of play, in P.K. Smith (ed.) *Play in Animals and Humans*. Oxford: Blackwell.

Sutton-Smith, B., Mechling, J., Johnson, T. and McMahon, F. (eds) (1999) *Children's Folklore: A Source Book*. Logan, Utah: Utah State University Press.

Sylva, K. (1977) Play and learning, in B. Tizard and D. Harvey (eds) *Biology of Play*. London: Heinemann: Ch. 6.

Sylva, K., Bruner, J.S. and Genova, P. (1976) The role of play in the problem-solving of children, in J.S. Bruner, A. Jolly and K. Sylva (eds) *Play: Its Role in Development and Evolution*. New York, NY: Basic Books.

Taylor, C. (2008) Playwork and the theory of loose parts, in F. Brown and C. Taylor (eds) *Foundations of Playwork*. Maidenhead: Open University Press.

Tinbergen, N. (1975) The importance of being playful. *Times Education Supplement*, January.

Trevarthen, C. (1996) How a young child investigates people and things: why play helps development. Keynote speech to TACTYC Conference: A Celebration of Play. London, November.

UNCRC (2008) United Nations. Committee on the Rights of the Child: Forty-ninth Session: Consideration of Reports Submitted by States Parties Under Article 44 of the Convention – Concluding Observations: United Kingdom of Great Britain and Northern Ireland. Geneva: United Nations.

UNICEF (1991) *United Nations Convention on the Rights of the Child*. Svenska: UNICEF Kommitten.

Vygotsky, L. (1966) Play and its role in the mental development of the child. *Voprosi Psikhologii*, 6. Originally published 1933, trans. Catherine Mullholland. Available online at: www.marxists.org/archive/vygotsky/works/1933/play.htm (accessed 15 June 2014).

Vygotsky, L. (1978) *Mind in Society*. Cambridge, MA: Harvard University Press.

Ward, C. (1961) Adventure playground; a parable in anarchy. *Anarchy*, 7: 193–201.

Ward, C. (1978) *The Child in the City*. London: Architectural Press.

Webb, S. and Brown, F. (2003) Playwork in adversity: working with abandoned children, in F. Brown (ed.) *Playwork: Theory and Practice*. Buckingham: Open University Press.

Weininger, O. and Fitzgerald, D. (1988) Symbolic play and interhemispheric integration: some thoughts on a neuropsychological model of play. *Journal of Research and Development in Education*, 21: 23–40.

Welsh Assembly Government (2006) *Welsh Assembly Government Play Policy Implementation Plan*. Cardiff: Welsh Assembly Government. Available online at: http://wales.gov.uk/topics/educationandskills/publications/guidance/playpolicy?lang=en# (accessed 15 June 2014).

Williams, H. (1984) Playing together. *Playwork* leaflet (proposed course). Milton Keynes: Open University.

Wilson, P. (2009) *The Playwork Primer*. College Park, MD: Alliance for Childhood.

Wing, L. (2003) *The Autistic Spectrum: A Guide for Parents and Professionals* (2nd rev. edn). London: Constable & Robinson.

Winnicott, D.W. (1971) *Playing and Reality*. London: Routledge.

Index

FOUNDATIONS OF PLAYWORK

Fraser Brown and Chris Taylor (Eds)

2008
9780335222919 – Paperback

eBook also available

Play impacts on all aspects of human behaviour and development, including the social, physical, cognitive, creative, emotional and spiritual worlds. The profession of playwork endeavours to provide enriched play environments with a view to enabling children achieve their full potential.

This book provides a holistic overview of contemporary play and playwork. Straightforward and accessible, it covers topics such as playwork identity; play environments; the role of the playworker; values and ethics; play and playwork theory; and at the heart of the book, a special chapter located at the cutting-edge of 21st century play theory.

The authors position play and playwork within the broader social context of the management and development of play settings, work within and between different sectors of the children's workforce, and the socio-legal framework of children's rights, and legislation. The book has international interest, considering playwork in the UK, US and Romania. It looks at diverse settings such as prisons, hospitals, parks, adventure playgrounds and play centres, schools, youth settings and nurseries.

Contributions from many of the leading names in playwork offer the most current theory and practice in the field. They present approaches to playwork using a range of techniques such as case studies and critiques, applied and emergent theorizing, story-telling and reflection. This encourages the reader to gain a breadth of perspective and develop their own contribution to the playwork tradition.

Foundations of Playwork is a vital resource for playwork students, practitioners, members of the children's workforce, carers and parents.

www.openup.co.uk

MAKING SENSE OF PLAY
SUPPORTING CHILDREN IN THEIR PLAY

Perry Else

2014
9780335247103 – Paperback

eBook also available

Making Sense of Play straightforwardly describes how self-chosen, engaging and satisfying play is best for children. It explores how adults can best support children's free play with an approach that is holistic, inclusive and practical and offers clear tools to highlight better ways of relating to and providing for playing children.

The book extends two key concepts developed by the author, the Integral Play Framework and the Play Cycle, showing how practitioners can implement these ideas on a day-to-day basis. The author makes clear how the Integral Play Framework works, how it helps makes sense of other models and how it can be used to help plan provision for playing children physically, socially, cognitively and culturally. Everyday practice with playing children is explored in line with introductory and extended understandings of the Play Cycle or 'play process'. Accessibly written with a rich range of examples showing the concepts in practice, these models are further used to explore creativity, the ways in which children play, how provision might be improved and how the approaches can be used to research practice.

With its distinctive blend of theory and practice together with reflective questions, this book is essential reading for all playwork students and practitioners and helps put these innovative ideas into practice with playing children.

www.openup.co.uk

PLAYWORK
THEORY AND PRACTICE

Fraser Brown (Ed)

2002
9780335209446 – Paperback

eBook also available

Children learn and develop through their play. In today's world the opportunities for that to happen are increasingly restricted. The profession of playwork seeks to reintroduce such opportunities, and so enable children to achieve their full potential.

This book brings together many leading names in the playwork field, to produce a text that has something for everyone. The in-depth exploration of a range of theoretical perspectives will appeal to both playwork students and practising playworkers. Experienced practitioners offer sound practical advice about ways of improving playwork practice. There are chapters on the role of adventure playgrounds (past, present and future); the challenge of starting a playwork section in a local authority; and the value of networking. Contributors explore the essence of play; the historical roots of playwork; and the role of play cues in human and animal behaviour. There is an exploration of the astounding impact of a therapeutic playwork project on the development of a group of abandoned children in Romania. The final chapter reinforces the need for playworkers to be reflective practitioners in all aspects of their work.

www.openup.co.uk

OPEN UNIVERSITY PRESS
McGraw - Hill Education